HEALTH POLICY
AND POLITICS
A NURSE'S GUIDE

FOURTH EDITION

Edited by

JERI A. MILSTEAD, PhD, RN, NEA-BC, FAAN

Senior Nurse Consultant
Professor and Dean Emerita
University of Toledo (Ohio) College of Nursing
Dublin, Ohio

JONES & BARTLETT
LEARNING

World Headquarters
Jones & Bartlett Learning
5 Wall Street
Burlington, MA 01803
978-443-5000
info@jblearning.com
www.jblearning.com

Jones & Bartlett Learning books and products are available through most bookstores and online booksellers. To contact Jones & Bartlett Learning directly, call 800-832-0034, fax 978-443-8000, or visit our website, www.jblearning.com.

Substantial discounts on bulk quantities of Jones & Bartlett Learning publications are available to corporations, professional associations, and other qualified organizations. For details and specific discount information, contact the special sales department at Jones & Bartlett Learning via the above contact information or send an email to specialsales@jblearning.com.

The author, editor, and publisher have made every effort to provide accurate information. However, they are not responsible for errors, omissions, or for any outcomes related to the use of the contents of this book and take no responsibility for the use of the products and procedures described. Treatments and side effects described in this book may not be applicable to all people; likewise, some people may require a dose or experience a side effect that is not described herein. Drugs and medical devices are discussed that may have limited availability controlled by the Food and Drug Administration (FDA) for use only in a research study or clinical trial. Research, clinical practice, and government regulations often change the accepted standard in this field. When consideration is being given to use of any drug in the clinical setting, the health care provider or reader is responsible for determining FDA status of the drug, reading the package insert, and reviewing prescribing information for the most up-to-date recommendations on dose, precautions, and contraindications, and determining the appropriate usage for the product. This is especially important in the case of drugs that are new or seldom used.

Production Credits
Publisher: Kevin Sullivan
Acquisitions Editor: Amanda Harvey
Editorial Assistant: Sara Bempkins
Production Manager: Carolyn F. Rogers
Marketing Manager: Elena McAnespie
V.P., Manufacturing and Inventory Control: Therese Connell
Composition: Laserwords Private Limited, Chennai, India
Cover Design: Scott Moden
Cover Image: © Condor 36/ShutterStock, Inc.
Printing and Binding: Malloy, Inc.
Cover Printing: Malloy, Inc.

To order this product, use ISBN: 978-1-4496-6509-8

Library of Congress Cataloging-in-Publication Data
Health policy and politics : a nurses guide / [edited by] Jeri A. Milstead. — 4th ed.
    p. ; cm.
  Includes bibliographical references and index.
  ISBN 978-0-7637-9776-8 (hardcover)
  I. Milstead, Jeri A.
  [DNLM: 1. Legislation, Nursing—United States. 2. Health Policy—United States. 3. Politics—United States. WY 33 AA1]
  362.17′30973—dc23

                                                                                              2011036257

6048
Printed in the United States of America
16 15 14 13 12   10 9 8 7 6 5 4

Contents

Preface

This book is a contributed text for advanced practice nurses (APNs) who are interested in expanding the depth of their knowledge about the process of making public policy and in becoming more sophisticated in their involvement. The chapters are written by contributors who have experience in real-world policymaking and political action. The scope of the content covers the whole process of making public policy. Components of the process are addressed within broad categories of agenda setting; government response; and program/policy design, implementation, and evaluation. The primary focus is at the federal and state levels, although the reader can adapt concepts to the global or local level.

WHY A FOURTH EDITION?

The first edition was well received and was used by nurses in at least five countries. When the original publisher changed its focus from health, education, and criminal justice to law and business, Jones & Bartlett Learning picked up the option for this book and encouraged us to write a second edition. The contributors were enthusiastic and agreed that it was time to update. The Information Age was upon us and everyone struggled to stay current.

The third edition found us in a different place. We live in a world of much uncertainty. The United States had lost its place as the benevolent, wise-for-our-age country where world leadership was a given. Other countries had lost confidence in our vision of economics, the environment, education, health care, and politics. We had been thrust into the world spotlight not because of our successes, but because of our failures. The United States could no longer justify using so many environmental resources; rearing a generation (or more) of children who cannot read or compute and who are prone to unhealthy and violent behavior; or an economic system where the rich were getting richer, the poor were getting poorer, and the middle class was beginning to diminish.

The third edition focused on practical examples and suggestions for actually becoming involved in the policy process. Both students and teachers were encouraged to use these activities to enhance their theoretical learning.

The fourth edition faces different challenges. We are the generation of leaders. We must harness our will, gather our best minds and spirits, and employ the widest range of technology to make our earth sustainable, beautiful, and safe. We must lead the world in treating our people in a humane, ethical, and moral manner. The ability to work within our government and with other governments, agencies, institutions, and consumers requires exquisite political leadership. We must use our communication skills and our knowledge of policymaking to forge change that will make our country and the world better. We can start by educating ourselves about the full range of the policy process.

The fourth edition has changed in some very important ways. Case studies appear in every chapter, along with discussion questions and relevant activities that will provide a safe place to try out solutions to some of the ideas presented. Current scenarios offer points to consider—remember, there are no right or wrong answers, and posing different outcomes to each situation can help the reader become more flexible in thinking about options or choosing responses to very real circumstances. The 2010 Institute of Medicine report on the *Future of Nursing* will have serious and life-changing challenges for nurses and the recommendations have been discussed in many places throughout this fourth edition.

Dr. Mary Wakefield had to rescind her wonderful chapter on legislation due to some restrictions placed on her in her current position as Director of the Health Resources and Services Administration (HRSA), which makes her the nation's highest-placed nurse. We thank her for her leadership; readers will miss her articulate and readable chapter. Jan Lanier, an experienced nurse attorney, picked up the ball and has written a chapter on how a bill really becomes a law, using her extensive background with state legislatures as a foundation. Jan highlights the political process, a segment of the policy process that we wanted to give a greater focus. Jan also provides us with a unique insight into what it takes to run for elective state office. Dr. Short realized that many nurses confuse economics with finance, so she added a component on finance and spending to her chapter. Dr. Nelson suggested that we replace her chapter on electronic resources (she trusts that most of you know how to maneuver through the maze of resources available today). She recommended the focus but was not able to write because of postretirement commitments. Therefore, two doctoral students (DNS) move the reader to a new level as they focus on the impact of social networking on policymaking by examining how people use the material they find on the Internet with the people with whom we connect. Beth Barnhill is a nurse experienced in informatics and electronic medical records and Troy Spicer is a practicing board-certified FNP. Thanks, Dr. Nelson, for your wisdom. My first and last chapters have been significantly rewritten and, I hope, have greater focus and more relevance. We are excited about the latest changes and hope that you like the book. We welcome your feedback.

TARGET AUDIENCE

This book is intended for several audiences:

- Nurses who work in advanced practice in clinical, education, administrative, research, or consultative settings can use this book as a guide for understanding the full range of the policy components that they did not learn or may have forgotten in graduate school. Components are brought to life through nursing research, real life cases, and theory. This book will help the nurse who is searching for knowledge of how leaders of today influence public policy toward better health care for the future. Nurses in leadership positions clearly articulate nursing's societal mission. Nurses, as the largest group of healthcare workers in the country, realize that the way to make a permanent impact on the delivery of health care is to be a part of the decision-making that occurs at every step of the healthcare policy process.

- Doctoral and master's students in nursing can use this text for in-depth study of the full policy process. Works of scholars in each segment provide a solid foundation for examining each component. This book goes beyond the narrow elementary explanation of legislation and bridges the gap toward an understanding of the broader policy process in which multiple opportunities for involvement exist.

- Faculty in graduate programs and other current nurse leaders can use this book as a reference for their own policy activity. Faculty and other leaders should be mentors for those they teach and for other nurses throughout the profession. Because the entire policy process is so broad, these leaders can track their own experiences through the policy process by referring to the components described in this book.

- Other healthcare professionals who are interested in the area of healthcare policy will find this book useful in directing their thoughts and actions toward the complex issues of both healthcare policy and public policy. Physicians, pharmacists, psychologists, occupational and physical therapists, physicians' assistants, and others will discover parallels with their own practices as they examine case studies and other research. Nurses cannot change huge systems alone; members of the healthcare team can use this book as a vehicle to educate themselves so that, together, everyone in the healthcare profession can influence policymakers.

- Those professionals who do not provide health care directly, but are involved in areas of the environment that produce actual and potential threats to personal and community health and safety, will find this book a valuable resource regarding how a problem becomes known, who decides what to do about it, and what type of governmental response might result. Environmental scientists, public health officials, sociologists, political scientists, anthropologists, and other professionals involved with health problems in the public interest will benefit from the ideas generated in this book.

- Interest groups can use this book as a tool to consider opportunities for becoming involved in public policymaking. Interest groups can be extremely helpful in changing systems because the passion for their causes energizes them to act. Interest groups can become partners in the political activity of nurses by knowing how and when to use their influence to assist APNs at crucial junctures in the policy process.

- Corporate leaders can use this book to gain an understanding of the broad roles within which nurses function. Chief executive officers (CEOs) and other top business administrators must learn that nurses are articulate, assertive, and intelligent experts in health care who have a solid knowledge base and a political agenda. The wise CEO and colleagues will seek out APNs for counsel and collaboration when moving policy ideas forward.

USING THIS BOOK

Each chapter is freestanding; that is, chapters do not rely, or necessarily build, on one another. The sequence of the chapters is presented in a linear fashion, but readers will note immediately that the policy process is not linear. For example, readers of the policy implementation chapter will find reference to scholars and concepts featured in the agenda setting and policy design chapters—such is the nature of the public process of making decisions. The material covered is a small portion of the existing research, argument, and considered thought about policymaking and the broader political, economic, and social concepts and issues. Therefore, readers should use this book as a starting point for their own scholarly inquiry.

This book can be used to initiate discussions about issues of policy and nurses' opportunities and responsibilities throughout the process. The research studies that are presented should raise some questions about what should have happened or why something else did not happen. In this way, the book can serve as a guide through what some think of as a maze of activity with no direction, but is actually a rational, albeit chaotic, system.

The case studies and discussion points and activities are ideal for planning a class or addressing an audience. Many activities are presented, and I hope that they serve to stimulate the readers' own creative thoughts about how to engage others. Gone are the days of the "sage on stage"—the teacher who had all the answers and lectured to students who had no questions. Good teachers always have learned from students and vice versa. Today's teachers and learners are interactive, technically savvy, curious and questioning, and capable of helping learners integrate large amounts of data and information. The manual can serve as a guide and a beginning.

Acknowledgments

Only a few nurses in the United States with master's degrees in nursing also hold doctorates in political science. When I discovered that several of these nurses had researched a different component of the policy process, a book immediately came to mind. The authors realize that there is much more to public decision-making than the process of writing laws and that this knowledge affords them the opportunity and responsibility for contributing seriously to public policy. When I approached these nurses about contributing to this book, each agreed enthusiastically. Therefore, special thanks must go to Dr. Beth Furlong, Dr. Patricia Smart, Dr. Ardith Sudduth, and Dr. Marlene Wilken for their scholarly contributions. We also applaud Dr. Wilken, who recently was awarded a major grant from NIH to study diabetes education in culturally appropriate Talking Circles with the Omaha and Rosebud Native American tribes. The two chapters on government response are a welcome addition because of the importance of the content. Nurses owe a lot to Jan Lanier, who ran for the Ohio State House of Representatives in 2008. In spite of being a Democrat in a decidedly Republican district whose incumbent opponent's position was fairly secure, Jan garnered nearly 40% of the vote—a truly remarkable feat. Jackie Loversidge continues to help us understand one of the most important components of the policy process: regulation. She is completing her dissertation at The Ohio State University where she teaches in the College of Nursing. Nancy Sharp's approach to nursing is so positive and full of life. She always brings a sense of hope and action to others through her writing. Dr. Nancy Short has added a critical perspective for nurses who want to understand government funding and spending. Thanks, Nancy, for your astute appreciation of the difference between economics and finance.

I continue to thank Jones & Bartlett Learning for their encouragement and guidance in writing the fourth edition. Their confidence in all of the contributors has been consistent and unwavering. Rachel Shuster, Sara Bempkins, and Carolyn Rogers have kept the authors on track in meeting deadlines and in providing editorial assistance. I also thank the readers of this book for their interest in the policy and political processes. For those of you who have integrated these components and concepts into your nursing careers, I applaud you. You will continue to contribute to the profession and to the broader society. For those readers who are struggling with how to incorporate one more piece of anything into your role as an advanced practice nurse, remember that you are advancing the cause of your own personal work, the profession, and healthcare delivery in this country and throughout the world every time you use the concepts in this book. Nurses are a powerful force and exercise their many talents to further good public policy, which, ultimately, must improve health care for patients, consumers, and families.

Finally, I acknowledge my forever-cheering section—my four children, their spouses and significant others, and three grandchildren. They are always there for me and provide continuous support, encouragement, and unconditional love. I love you, Kerrin, George, Sunny, and George Biddle; Joan Milstead; Kevin Milstead and Gregg Peace; and Sara, Steve, and Matthew Lott. You are a fun bunch and you make me laugh. And a special thanks to my wonderful late fiancé, Ed Salser, who for nearly three years "rocked my boat" and was a constant source of encouragement and delight.

Jeri A. Milstead

Contributors

Elizabeth Barnhill, MSN, RN, DNS student
Kennesaw State University
Kennesaw, Georgia

Elizabeth Ann Furlong, JD, PhD, RN
Associate Professor, School of Nursing
Faculty Associate, Center for Health Policy and Ethics
Creighton University
Omaha, Nebraska

Janice Kay Lanier, JD, RN
Senior Consultant
Westerville, Ohio

Jacqueline M. Loversidge, PhD(c), MS, RN, C
Assistant Professor
The Ohio State University
Columbus, Ohio

Jeri A. Milstead, PhD, RN, NEA-BC, FAAN
Senior Nurse Consultant
Professor and Dean Emerita
University of Toledo (Ohio) College of Nursing
Dublin, Ohio

Nancy J. Sharp, MSN, RN, FAAN
Senior Nurse Consultant
Bethesda, Maryland

Nancy Munn Short, DrPH, MBA, RN
Associate Professor and Senior Research Fellow
Duke University School of Nursing
Durham, North Carolina

Patricia Smart, PhD, RN, FNP-BC
Professor and Faculty Assistant to the Provost and Assistant to the President
Clemson University
Clemson, South Carolina

Troy Spicer, MS, RN, FNP-BC, DNS student
Kennesaw State University
Coordinator, Student Health Center
Assistant Professor, School of Nursing and Health Sciences
Abraham Baldwin Agricultural College
Tifton, Georgia

Ardith L. Sudduth, PhD, RN, GNP, FNP-BC
Associate Professor
Hamilton Medical Group/BORSF Professorship in Nursing
College of Nursing and Allied Health Professions
University of Louisiana at Lafayette
Lafayette, Louisiana

Marlene Wilken, PhD, MN, RN
NIH Researcher on Native Americans and Diabetes
Associate Professor, School of Nursing
Creighton University
Omaha, Nebraska

CHAPTER 1

Advanced Practice Nurses and Public Policy, Naturally

Jeri A. Milstead

KEY TERMS

Advanced practice nurse (APN): A registered nurse with a master's or doctoral degree in nursing who demonstrates expert knowledge, skills, and attitudes in the practice of nursing.

Nursing's agenda for health: Policy expectations of a vision for nursing practice that includes prevention of illness, promotion of health, empowerment of individuals to assume responsibility for the state of their own health, expertise in the provision of direct nursing care, delegation and supervision of selected care to appropriate individuals, and the political influence to accomplish these goals.

Policy process: The course of bringing problems to government and obtaining a reply. The process includes agenda setting, design, government response, implementation, and evaluation.

Public policy: Actual directives that document government decisions; also, the process of taking problems to government agents and obtaining a decision or reply in the form of a program, law, regulation, or other legal directive.

INTRODUCTION

This book addresses the policy process as a broad range of decision points, strategies, activities, and outcomes that involve elected and appointed government officials and their staffs, bureaucratic agencies, private citizens, and interest groups. The process is dynamic, convoluted, and ongoing, not static, linear, or concise. The idea of "messy" may be uncomfortable to nurses who are known to expect action immediately, but the political arena requires patience, tact, diplomacy, and persistence. Knowledgeable nurses in advanced practice must demonstrate their commitment to action by being a part of relevant decisions that will ensure the delivery of quality health care by appropriate providers in a cost-effective manner. So why would anyone suggest that working at the policy level is "natural" to our profession? Some nurses are experienced in their political activity. They have served as chairs of legislative committees for professional organizations, worked as campaign managers for elected officials, or presented testimony at congressional or state hearings; a few actually have run for office. Still, there is a perception that "legislation" and "policy" are interchangeable, and that perception misses a lot of what policy is about.

Nursing as a practice profession is based on theory and evidence. For many years, that practice has been interpreted as direct, hands-on care of individuals. Although this still is true, the profession has matured to the point where the provision of expert, direct care is not enough. Nurses of the third millennium can stand tall in their multiple roles of provider of care, educator, administrator, consultant, researcher, political activist, and policymaker. The question of how much a nurse in advanced practice can or should take on may be raised. The Information Age continues to present new knowledge exponentially. Nurses have added more and more tasks that seem important to a professional nurse and are essential for the provision of safe care to the client. Is political activism necessary? All health professionals are expected to do more with fewer resources. Realistically, how much can a specialist do?

Drucker (1995), in addressing the need for more general-practitioner physicians rather than specialists, redefined the generalist of today as one who puts multiple specialties together rapidly. Nursing can benefit from that thought. In Drucker's definition, the **advanced practice nurse (APN)** must be a multidimensional generalist/specialist. This means that the APN combines knowledge and skills from a variety of fields or subspecialties effectively to design the new paradigm of healthcare delivery. This also means that the APN must demonstrate competence in the multiple roles in which he or she operates. To function effectively in the role of political activist, the APN must realize the scope of the whole policy process, and the process is much broader than how a bill becomes a law.

It is natural for nurses to talk with bureaucrats, agency staff, legislators, and others in public service about what nurses do, what nurses need, and the extent of their cost-effectiveness and long-term impact on health care in this country. For too long, nurses only talked to each other. Each knew their value, and each told great stories; they "preached to the choir" of other nurses instead of sharing their wisdom with those who could help change the healthcare system for the better. We finally are listening to those who have espoused interprofessional collaboration, and we are realizing that, together with our colleagues in medicine, psychology, pharmacy, allied health, and other professions, we can join forces and make a stronger presence in determining policy. In the end, the patient is the winner.

Today's nurses, especially those in advanced practice who have a solid foundation of focused education and experience, know how to market themselves and their talents and know how to harness their irritations and direct them toward positive resolution. Nurses are embracing the whole range of options available in the various parts of the policy process. Nurses are initiating opportunities to sustain ongoing, meaningful dialogues with those who represent the districts and states and those who administer public programs. Nurses are becoming indispensable to elected and appointed officials, and nurses are demonstrating leadership by becoming those officials and by participating with others in planning and decision-making.

The advanced practice nurse of the third millennium is technically competent; uses critical thinking and decision models; possesses vision that is shared with colleagues, consumers, and policy makers; and functions in a vast array of roles. One of these roles is policy analyst. Although Florence Nightingale demonstrated great political influence in the 19th century (Nightingale, 1859), this aspect of the nurse's role was slow to become integrated into the scope of practice of the advanced practice nurse. Policy and politics is a natural domain for nurses. We are on the brink of an opportunity for the full integration into practice of the impending major changes in the delivery of care in the United States. Nurses have prepared for these changes by initiating new nurse education programs, expanding the number of master's and doctoral programs, and focusing on issues important to patients such as the just and equitable delivery of health care.

CHANGES IN NURSING EDUCATION AND PRACTICE

Education and practice reflect or direct alterations in the delivery of health care. According to a 2008 survey of registered nurses (Health Resources and Services Administration, 2008), there are 3,063,162 registered nurses in the United States, 84.8% of whom are working in nursing. Projections indicate that the long-standing nurse shortage will become worse as baby boomers retire. This group of consumers grew up in a time of abundance and will expect an abundance of health services when they leave the workforce. Nurse education programs recognize the opportunity to expand program enrollment but are faced with a dearth of qualified faculty and appropriate clinical space.

Nurse educators and administrators are using technology to enhance and supplement the learning process. Patient simulators are models that can mimic healthcare problems in a laboratory. These models are very sophisticated and expensive, and can be programmed to mirror a heart attack, congestive heart failure, or any number of health conditions and emergencies. For best effect, students work in teams with colleagues from nursing, medicine, physical therapy, emergency medical technology, medical residents, and others. The lab approach can ease the need for clinical experience because of the focused approach and because a scenario can be analyzed and re-played for different outcomes. Boards of nursing are concerned about how much simulation is appropriate, but it is clear that simulation is an asset to learning. Another benefit of simulation is the experience of working with a team. Interprofessional education is fairly new in most educational programs, although the concept has been discussed for many years. The use of simulators may be a way to implement the idea of interprofessional collaboration.

Online education has become a major force in the United States, as well. Whether described as *distance learning*, *electronic education*, or another similar term, most nurse education programs use at least some form of teaching that is not face-to-face (F2F) in a single classroom. Distance learning was pioneered as "television courses" in the 1960s, in which a group of students met together at a location remote from the customary classroom and were taught by a faculty member in the primary classroom. Today's e-learning affords opportunities to learn in a flexible, "anytime" schedule that is not grounded in geography or time. The sophistication of software systems provides students and faculty with a wide range of presentations.

Telehealth, an outgrowth of e-learning and advanced diagnostic technology, allows patients and providers access to each other's domain without concerns about transportation, time lost from work, childcare during visits, and other major reasons why patients do not make or keep appointments. This sophisticated technology first was tested by military personnel and found to be an effective method for training and for practice. Currently, a physician in Washington, D.C., is testing the use of an Internet-ready cell phone to track disease compliance (Neergaard, 2010). Ethical issues, cost of equipment, and the learning curve of the provider and patient will dictate how much telehealth the public will embrace.

Although the profession has not solved the "entry" problem, there are efforts to move closer to requiring a bachelor of science in nursing (BSN) degree as the beginning point for professional nursing. Aiken, Clark, Cheung, Sloan, and Silber (2003) report that hospitals with higher proportions of baccalaureate-prepared nurses demonstrate decreased patient morbidity and mortality. Over 90 nurse generalist and specialty organizations are on record as supporting the BSN as an entry point to professional nursing. Some states are moving legislation or regulation to require that graduates of hospital diploma and associate degree programs obtain a BSN within 10 years of graduation in order to be relicensed as registered nurses (RNs). Academic institutions have created programs to expand the number of graduates.

Accelerated nurse education programs, recalling similar programs during World War II, have been developed at the bachelor's and master's degree levels. These programs were created to accept applicants with college degrees in fields other than nursing and provide the student with opportunities to graduate with degrees in nursing in an abbreviated time period, and graduates are eligible to sit for the National Council Licensing Exam (NCLEX-RN) to become registered nurses. These popular programs provide new avenues that address the nurse shortage.

A new education model at the master's level was created by the American Association of Colleges of Nursing (AACN), the national organization of deans and directors of baccalaureate and higher-degree nurse programs. During meetings of leaders of AACN, the American Organization of Nurse Executives, and other employers of nurses, AACN asked: Are educational institutions providing appropriate professionals for the workforce? The answer was that the nurses of today and the future should be educated to manage a population of patients/clients (such as a group of diabetics or those with congestive heart failure) both in a hospital setting and after discharge and should be able to make changes at a microsystem (i.e., unit) level. The clinical nurse leader (CNL) master's level program was proposed in 2003 to address those recommendations. In 2011 there are over 100 CNL programs, whose graduates can sit for a national certification exam that provides credibility to employers (Commission on Nurse Certification, 2011).

At about the same time as the CNL program was initiated, much work had been accomplished in moving APNs toward doctoral education as an entry point. Rationale included granting a degree appropriate to the knowledge base and credit hours required in APN programs and placing the advanced practitioner on a level with other health professionals. Note that a physician (MD), dentist (DDS), physical therapist (DPT), occupational therapist (OTD), and audiologist (AuD) require a practice doctorate. In 2004 AACN members voted to establish a Doctor of Nursing Practice (DNP) and to require that all APN education be offered through DNP programs by 2015 (American Association of Colleges of Nursing [AACN], 2010a). The DNP will be an expert in patient care and will design, administer, and evaluate the delivery of complex health care in new organizational arrangements. Areas of concentration are offered in direct care, informatics, executive administration, and health policy. Although some nurse educators still debate AACN's decision (Cronenwett et al., 2011), over 153 DNP programs currently exist. A concern that DNP programs would siphon students from PhD programs was unfounded (AACN, 2011).

The CNL and DNP also reflect a change in how health care is provided. Certified CNLs work at the unit micro level (not the health systems macro level) and provide direct care to groups of patients, which includes teaching with the goal of self-management of their own health problems. Patients learn to notice early indicators of changes in their conditions so that they may seek help before serious symptoms arise, with the goal being to keep patients as healthy as possible and to reduce hospital readmissions. The DNP provides care at the systems level; that is, this provider is alert to problems in the healthcare organization and can seek solutions through policy changes. DNPs develop relationships within and outside the healthcare network in order to facilitate transformation.

Perhaps the greatest potential for change in the education of nurses will be the effect of the report from the Institute of Medicine (IOM) of the National Academies, *The Future of Nursing: Leading Change, Advancing Health* (Institute of Medicine [IOM], 2010). Under the aegis of the IOM and funded by the Robert Wood Johnson Foundation (RWJF), the report recognizes that nurses (the largest healthcare workforce in the United States) must be an integral part of a healthcare team. The report provided four key messages:

1. Nurses should practice to the full extent of their education and training;
2. Nurses should achieve higher levels of education and training through an improved education system that promotes seamless academic progression;
3. Nurses should be full partners with physicians and other healthcare professionals in redesigning health care in the United States; and
4. Effective workforce planning and policy making require better data collection and an improved information infrastructure (IOM, 2010, pp. 1–3).

How the messages will be received by the intended audiences—"policy makers; national, state, and local government leaders; payers; and health care researchers, executives, and professionals—including nurses and other—as well as to licensing bodies, educational institutions, philanthropic organizations, and consumer advocacy organizations" (IOM, 2010, p. 4)—can have a seismic impact on nursing education, practice, administration, and research. Removing barriers to practice, expanding leadership opportunities, doubling the number of nurses with doctorates, and greatly increasing bachelor's degrees to 80 percent of the workforce will require money, commitment, energy, and creativity. As Donna Shalala, chair of the committee that initiated the report, noted at the 2010 annual meeting of the American Academy of Nursing, this report is the most important report on nursing in the past century.

It is now up to nurses to use the report to advance health care so that both patients and professionals will benefit. Nurses must not only reform nurse education and practice, but they must also provide leadership in gathering other healthcare professionals (practitioners and educators) together to begin paradigm-changing discussions to reform the entire system. The new system will focus on sick care, prevention of disease/disability, and health promotion. Research will continue to produce breakthroughs in medical science. Research on outcomes of treatment will become essential. **Exhibit 1-1** compares the old paradigm of sick care and the new paradigm of health care.

Exhibit 1-1 Comparison of Old Sick Care Paradigm with New Healthcare Paradigm

Old Paradigm	New Paradigm
Hospital-based acute care	Short-term hospital, outpatient surgery, mobile/satellite clinics, telehealth/telemedicine
Physician in charge	Team approach
Nurse as subordinate	Nurse as full team member
Physician as primary decision maker	Relevant professionals and patient make treatment decisions
Segmented care focused on separate body parts/systems	Seamless, coordinated, holistic care
Primary care physician and specialist separated	Patient-centered home health
Paper records; some electronic health records (EHRs)	HER systems that generate data used for change
Fee-for-service	Mix of reimbursement packages
Hierarchical organizations	Value-based organizations
Positivist, linear thinking	Complexity science: patterns noted in chaos, networks essential, quantum principles

There has been talk for decades about reforming the U.S. healthcare system. In the 1990s, President Clinton established a group that made major recommendations, but the constant pressure of special interest groups, such as pharmaceutical and insurance companies that protected their own interests, delayed and ultimately de-railed any serious attempt at overhauling this huge system. During the George W. Bush Administration, defense was the number one issue on the agenda and health care was not a priority.

Today's policymakers seem to be more polarized than at any time in recent history; choices often are dichotomous or mutually exclusive and rulings follow a strict party line. Compromise can be perceived as losing power, and power seems to be revered over common sense or the common good. Splinter groups or loose arrangements of radical thinkers have appeared on the political scene and are challenging the traditional two- or three-party system. A long-time congressperson told this author that she has never seen this much bitterness and antagonism in her 30+ years of elected office. Nurses will have to be especially sensitive to the political positions of all policymakers when working in this arena. Communications techniques learned in basic baccalaureate and graduate programs will enable the nurse to transcend some of the pressures encountered in working through the political process.

The healthcare system in the United States is on the brink of huge changes. Many health problems are the result of lifestyles that do not support health. Obesity, hypertension, and cardiovascular illnesses are only three that are mentioned frequently. In order to promote a healthy population, we are in the early phases of a move toward prevention of illness and disability and promotion of healthy living. Many people know how to live a healthy life, but just as many do not actually engage in healthy practices. Healthcare professionals are changing the way they assess, diagnose, counsel, and treat patients.

People are living longer and are encountering many chronic problems. Who would have thought five years ago that cancer today is considered a chronic disease? Surgery has made great strides, especially as minimally-invasive methods and robotics are perfected. Genetics has opened up a whole discipline that incorporates gene splicing and manipulation, genetic testing and counseling, and many other approaches to what have been considered irreversible or inevitable conditions. The use of prosthetics in many forms and for many body parts is maturing into a fast-growing business, especially with the recovery and return of military personnel from wars. Body parts grown in laboratories from stem cells taken from a recipient will reduce the probability of autorejection. Ethical questions are integral to policy arguments, especially as appropriations are examined with a critical eye toward costs.

Federal reform has mandated programs and policies that will demand action that is different from what is available today. The Patient Protection and Affordable Care Act of 2010 (commonly known as the Affordable Care Act, or ACA) is a federal law that will transform how, where, and by whom health care is provided. Whether or not the programs envisioned in the law will succeed (i.e., meet the needs of the populace and be politically acceptable) will be played out through federal and state legislatures, presidential influence, and judicial decisions. Already in 2011, bills have been introduced to seriously amend and terminate the law. Nurses and nurse organizations will be strong voices in the debates that will have lasting influence on health care in this country.

Hospitals are concerned with staffing the workforce with nurses and other healthcare providers. Staffing levels have become a huge issue, with two opposing camps: one supports actual numbers of nurses per patient or per unit and the other supports principles of staffing rather than actual numbers. The California Nurses Association (CNA), originally a state affiliate of the American Nurses Association, broke from ANA mainly over staffing issues. The CNA (the group kept the name), under the umbrella of the National Nurses Organizing Committee (NNOC), became politically active in several states in their requirements to establish legal, specific, numerical nurse-to-patient ratios. ANA, in contrast, established "principles of staffing" that required including patient acuity, diagnosis, type of nursing unit, and other considerations rather than specific numbers. Buerhaus (2008, 2009) presents data and thoughtful discussion to support the need for nurses as the primary workforce in the United States.

Most care providers recognize the problems inherent in offering care to the uninsured and underinsured. The disparity in care seen in low socioeconomic groups and vulnerable populations (e.g., children, the elderly) and groups with specific health concerns (e.g., diabetics, smokers) presents enormous challenges. Nurses have proffered solutions that have not been taken seriously by major policy players.

For some policymakers, this seems as if nurses are trying to expand the scope of their practice. This often comes as a reflection that policymakers do not know what nurses do or the actual dimensions of their roles. The nurse of today and the future is "not your mother's nurse," to paraphrase an automobile commercial. Haas's (1964) early study of nurses clarified that their role had four dimensions: task, authority or power, deference or prestige, and affect or feelings. Each of those dimensions has changed drastically over the past 10 years. Nurses simply want to practice at the level of their education and within legal and professional definitions.

Expanding the boundaries of historical nursing takes skill in negotiation, diplomacy, assertiveness, expert communication, and leadership. Sometimes physician and nurse colleagues are threatened by these behaviors, and it takes persistence and certainty of purpose to proceed. Nurses must speak out as articulate, knowledgeable, caring professionals who contribute to the whole **health agenda** and who advocate for their patients and the community.

The American Academy of Nursing (AAN), a prestigious organization of approximately 1500 select nurse leaders, created a Raise the Voice campaign that "provides a platform to inform policymakers, the media, health providers and consumers about nurse-driven activities and solutions for an ailing health care system" (American Academy of Nursing, 2010, p. 1). This program, funded by a grant from the Robert Wood Johnson Foundation, cites "Edge Runners"—nurses who are leading the way to healthcare reform by creating models of care that "demonstrate significant clinical and financial outcomes" (p. 2). AAN members are committed to transforming the healthcare system from the "current hospital-based, acuity-oriented, physician-dependent paradigm towards a patient-centered, convenient, helpful, and affordable system" (p. 1).

A major influence in how health care is delivered is occurring as more and more people use social media. Patients bring articles about diseases and conditions to their healthcare providers. Providers surf the Internet and other social networks in search of accurate information. The expansion of knowledge and the rapidity with which it can be disseminated has grown exponentially in ways that were not possible even five years ago. A unique resource, *The Nurse's Social Media Advantage* (Fraser, 2011), explains social media and, more importantly, discusses the necessity for nurses to understand how to use media resources in order to practice effectively in a fast-changing world.

DEVELOPING A MORE SOPHISTICATED POLITICAL ROLE FOR NURSES

There has been a major shift in the roles that nurses assume. In addition to clinical experts, nurses are entrepreneurs, decision makers, and political activists. The nurse's role must be examined to determine if there is a power differential, what the unwritten rules are that acknowledge deference, and how both actors exhibit or control feelings. Many nurses realize that to control practice and move the profession of nursing forward as a major player in the healthcare arena, nurses have to be involved in the legal decisions about the health and welfare of the public, decisions that often are made in the governmental arena.

For many nurses, political activism used to mean letting someone else get involved. Today's nurse "tunes in" to bills that reflect a particular passion (e.g., driving and texting), disease entity (e.g., diabetes), or population (e.g., childhood obesity). Although this activity indicates a greater involvement in the political process, it still misses a broader comprehension of the whole policymaking process that provides many opportunities for nurse input before and after legislation occurs.

Nurses who are serious about political activity realize that the key to establishing contacts with legislators and agency directors is through ongoing relationships with elected and appointed officials and their staffs. By developing credibility with those active in the political process and demonstrating integrity and moral purpose as client advocates, nurses are becoming players in the complex process of policymaking.

Nurses have learned that by using nursing knowledge and skill they could gain the confidence of government actors. Communications skills that were learned in basic skills classes or in psychiatric nursing classes are critical in listening to the discussion of larger health issues and in being able to present nursing's agenda. Personal stories gained from professional nurses' experience anchor altruistic conversations with legislators and their staffs in an important emotional link toward policy design. Nurses' vast network of clinical experts produces nurses in direct care who provide persuasive, articulate arguments with people "on the Hill" during appropriations committee hearings and informal meetings.

Nurses participate in formal, short-term internship programs with elected officials and in bureaucratic agencies. Most of the programs were created by nurse organizations that were convinced of the importance of political involvement. The interns and fellows learn how to handle constituent concerns, how to write legislation, how to argue with opponents yet remain colleagues, and how to maneuver through the bureaucracy. They carry the message of the necessity of the political process to the larger profession, although the rank and file still are not active in this role.

As nurses move into advanced practice and advanced practice demands master's and doctoral degree preparation, the role of the nurse in the **policy process** has become clearer. Through the influence of nurses with their legislators, clinical nurse specialists, certified nurse midwives, certified registered nurse anesthetists, and certified nurse practitioners are named in several pieces of federal legislation as duly authorized providers of health care. The process has been slow; however, the deliberate way of including more nurse groups over time demonstrates that "getting a foot in the door" is an effective method of instituting change in the seemingly slow processes of government. Some groups of nurses do not understand the political implications of incrementalism (the process of making changes gradually) and want all nurse groups named as providers at one time. They do not understand that most legislators do not have any idea what registered nurses do. Those nurse lobbyists who worked directly with legislators and their staff in early efforts bore the brunt of discontent within the profession and worked diligently and purposefully to provide a unified front on the Hill and to expand the definition of provider at every opportunity. The designation of advanced practice nurses as providers was an entry to federal reimbursement for some nursing services, a major move toward improved client and family access and health care. Advanced practice nurses became acutely aware of the critical importance of the role of political activist. Not only did APNs need the basic knowledge, they understood the necessity of practicing the role, developing contacts, working with professional organizations, writing fact sheets, testifying at hearings, and maintaining the momentum and persistence to move an idea forward.

However, many nurses still focus their political efforts and skills on the legislative process. They understand the comprehensiveness of the policy process, the much broader process that precedes and follows legislation. For APNs to integrate the policy role into the character of expert nurse, they must recognize the many opportunities for action. APNs cannot afford to "do their own thing"—that is, only provide direct patient care. They cannot ignore the political aspects of any issue. Nurses who have fought the battles for recognition as professionals, for acknowledgment of autonomy, and for formal acceptance of clinical expertise worthy of payment for services have enabled APNs today to provide reimbursable, quality services to this nation's residents.

The American Association of Colleges of Nursing continues to emphasize the importance of understanding and becoming involved in policy formation, and the organization and financing of health care for the registered nurse and the APN through documents on essential components of baccalaureate, master's, and doctoral education in nursing. Content essential at the undergraduate level includes "policy development . . . legislation and regulatory processes . . . social policy/public policy . . . and political activism and professional organizations" (AACN, 2008a, p. 21). Content at the master's level for all students, regardless of their specialty or functional area, includes "policy, organization, and finance of health care" (AACN, 2008b, p. 6). Required content for doctoral students in advanced practice includes behaviors to "critically analyze . . . demonstrate leadership . . . inform policy makers . . . educate others . . . advocate for the profession" (AACN, 2006, p. 13).

Today's nurses have a much clearer understanding of what constitutes nursing and how nurses must integrate political processes into their practices to further the decisions made by policymakers. Nurses continue to focus on the individual, family, community, and special populations in the provision of care to the sick and infirm and on the activities that surround health promotion and the prevention of disease and disability. Advanced practice nurses have a foundation in expert clinical practice and can translate that knowledge into understandable language for elected and appointed officials as the officials respond to problems that are beyond the scale or impact of individual healthcare providers. As nurses continue to refine the art and science of nursing, forces external to the profession compel the nursing community to consider another aspect— the business of nursing—that is paradoxical to the long history of altruism.

21ST CENTURY ORGANIZATIONS

The whole economic basis of capitalism—that is, the manufacturing system—had become rapidly outdated by the beginning of the 21st century. The new paradigm for organizations in the 21st century began with changes within one's head with a move to a perspective that is outside the usual way of thinking. What work is done, where it is done, how it is done, and what it costs are mundane questions that demand creative answers.

Complexity science acknowledges patterns in chaos, complex adaptive systems, and principles of self-organization and has great applicability to nursing (Curtin, 2010; Lindberg, Nash, & Lindberg, 2008). "The quantum concept of a matrix or field . . . that connects everything together" (Curtin, 2011) informs us that nurses are focused masses of energy who direct their behaviors and actions with patients in an intentional way towards accomplishing healthy states. The nurse–patient (or nurse–provider) relationship is not incidental or haphazard, but fully cognizant of purpose (Curtin, 2010; Husted & Husted, 2008).

Quantum thinking also is crucial to the effectiveness of an organization in the 21st century (Porter-O'Grady & Malloch, 2011). Partnerships are valued over competition, and the old rules of business that rewarded power and ownership have given way to accountability and shared risk. Transforming the old systems to the new systems does not mean merely automating processes or restructuring the organizational chart. Transformation involves a radical, cross-functional, futuristic change in the way people think. Long-term planning is balanced with strategic planning, and vertical work relationships are replaced with networks and webs of people and knowledge. All workers at all levels share a commitment to the organization and an accountability to define and produce quality work. Rhoades, Covery, and Shepherdson (2011) are "convinced that positive, people-centered cultural values lead to higher performance" (p. 1). All workers share responsibility for self-governance, from which both the organization and the worker benefit (Porter-O'Grady, Hawkins, & Parker, 1997). Control is replaced by leadership. The new leader does not use policing techniques of supervision, but enables and empowers colleagues through vision, trust, and respect (Bennis & Nanus, 1985; Kouzes & Posner, 2007; Porter-O'Grady & Wilson, 1999). Encouragement, appreciation, and personal recognition are celebrated together in an effective organization (Kouzes & Posner, 1999).

WHAT IS PUBLIC POLICY?

So, what do the changes in education, practice, and organizations have to do with policymaking, especially in the public arena? A brief overview of the entire policy process will clarify what policy is and how influencing government policies has become crucial to the profession of nursing.

In this chapter, *policy* is an overarching term used to define both an entity and a process. The purpose of **public policy** is to direct problems to government and secure government's response, while politics is the use of influence to direct the responses toward goals. Although there has been much discussion about the boundaries and domain of government and the extent of difference between the public and private sectors, that debate is beyond the scope of this chapter.

The definition of public policy is important because it clarifies common misconceptions about what constitutes policy. In this book, the terms *public policy* and *policy* are interchangeable. The process of creating policy can be focused in many arenas and most of these are interwoven. For example, environmental policy deals with health issues such as hazardous material, particulate matter in the air or water, and safety standards in the workplace. Education policy, more than tangentially, is related to health—just ask school nurses. Regulations define who can administer medication to students; state laws dictate what type of sex education can be taught. Defense policy is related to health policy when developing, investigating, or testing biological and chemical weapons. Health policy directly addresses health problems and is the specific focus of this book.

Policy as an Entity

As an entity, policy is seen in many forms as the "standing decisions" of an organization (Eulau & Prewitt, 1973, p. 495). As formal documented directives of an organization, official government policies reflect the beliefs of the administration in power and provide direction for the philosophy and mission of government organizations. Specific policies usually serve as the "shoulds" and "thou shalts" of agencies. Some policies, known as position statements, report the opinions of organizations about issues that members believe are important. For example, state boards of nursing (government agencies created by legislatures to protect the public through the regulation of nursing practice) publish advisory opinions on what constitutes competent and safe nursing practice.

Agency policies can be broad and general, such as those that describe the relationship of an agency to other governmental groups. Procedure manuals in government hospitals that detail steps in performing certain nursing tasks are examples of the results of policy directives, but are not considered policies. Policies serve as guidelines for employee behavior within an institution. Although policies and procedures often are used interchangeably, policies are considered broader and reflect the values of the administration.

Laws are types of policy entities. As legal directives for public and private behavior, laws serve to define action that reflects the will of society—or at least a segment of society. Laws are made at the international, federal, state, and local levels and have the impact of primary place in guiding conduct. Lawmaking usually is the purview of the legislative branch of government in the United States, although presidential vetoes, executive orders, and judicial interpretations of laws have the force of law.

Judicial interpretation is noted in three ways. First, courts may interpret the meaning of laws that are written broadly or with some vagueness, though laws often are written deliberately with language that addresses broad situations. Agencies that implement the laws then write regulations that are more specific and that guide the implementation. However, courts may be asked to determine questions in which the law is unclear or controversial (Williams & Torrens, 1988). For example, the 1973 Rehabilitation Act prohibited discrimination against the handicapped by any program that received federal assistance. Although this may have seemed fair and reasonable at the outset, courts were asked to adjudicate questions of how much accommodation is "fair" (Wilson, 1989). Second, courts can determine how some laws are applied. Courts are idealized as being above the political activity that surrounds the legislature. Courts also are considered beyond the influence of politically-active interest groups. The court system, especially the federal court system, has been called upon to resolve conflicts between levels of government (state and federal) and between laws enacted by the legislature and their interpretation by powerful interest groups. For example, courts may determine who is eligible or who is excluded from participation in a program. In this way, special interest groups that sue to be included in a program can receive "durable protection" from favorable court decisions (Feldstein, 1988, p. 32). Third, courts can declare the laws made by Congress or the states unconstitutional, thereby nullifying the statues entirely (Litman & Robins, 1991). Courts also interpret the Constitution, sometimes by restricting what the government (not private enterprise) may do (Wilson, 1989).

Regulations are another type of policy initiative. Although they often are included in discussions of laws, regulations are different. Once a law is enacted by the legislative branch, the executive branch of government is charged with administrative responsibility for implementing the law. The executive branch consists of the president and all of the bureaucratic agencies, commissions, and departments that carry out the work for the public benefit. Agencies in the government formulate regulations that achieve the intent of the statute. On the whole, laws are written in general terms, and regulations are written more specifically to guide the interpretation, administration, and enforcement of the law. The Administrative Procedures Act (APA) was created to provide opportunity for citizen review and input throughout the process of developing regulations. The APA ensures a structure and process that is published and open, in the spirit of the founding fathers, so that the average constituent can participate in the process of public decision-making.

All of these entities evolve over time and are accomplished through the efforts of a variety of actors or players. Although commonly used, the terms *position statement, resolution, goal, objective, program, procedure, law,* and *regulation* really are not interchangeable with the word *policy*. Rather, they are the formal expressions of policy decisions. For the purposes of understanding just what policy is, nurses must grasp policy as a process.

Policy as a Process

In viewing policy as a guide to government action, nurses can study the process of policymaking over time. Milio (1989) presents four major stages in which decisions are made that translate to government policies: 1) agenda setting, 2) legislation and regulation, 3) implementation, and 4) evaluation. Agenda setting is concerned with identifying a societal problem and bringing it to the attention of government. Legislation and regulation are formal responses to a problem. Implementation is the execution of policies or programs toward the achievement of goals. Evaluation is the appraisal of policy performance or program outcomes.

In each stage, formal and informal relationships are developed among actors both within and outside of government. Actors can be individuals, such as a legislator, a bureaucrat, or a citizen, but they also can be institutions, such as the presidency, the courts, political parties, or special-interest groups. A series of activities occurs that brings a problem to government, which results in direct action by the government to address the problem. Governmental responses are political; that is, the decisions about who gets what, when, and how are made within a framework of power and influence, negotiation, and bargaining (Lasswell, 1958).

Even as this book explains each of the stages of the policy process and explores them for areas in which nurses can provide influence, one must recognize that the policy process is not necessarily sequential or logical. The definition of a problem, which usually occurs in the agenda-setting phase, may change during legislation. Program design may be altered significantly during implementation. Evaluation of a policy or program (often considered the last phase of the process) may propel onto the national agenda (often considered the first phase of the process) a problem that differs from the original. However, for the purpose of organizing one's thoughts and conceptualizing the policy process, the policy process is examined from the linear perspective of stages.

Even before the process itself can be studied, nurses must understand why it is so important to be knowledgeable about the components and the functions of the process and how this public arena has become an integral part of the practice of advanced nursing.

WHY NURSES AND PUBLIC POLICY?

Registered professional nurses have studied the basics of how a bill becomes a law in their baccalaureate programs. An extension of the focus on legislation usually is provided in graduate schools. However, most nurses (and most nurse educators) do not have a clear understanding of the total policy process. To focus on legislation misses a whole range of governmental and political activities—activities in which professional nurses should have a central place.

Nurses and nursing are at the center of issues of tremendous and long-lasting impact, such as access to providers, quality of care, and reasonable cost. Issues crucial to the profession are being decided, such as who is eligible for government reimbursement for services and what is the appropriate scope of practice of registered nurses in advanced practice. If nurses wait until legislation is being voted on before they become involved, it is too late to affect decisions.

Nurses have learned the legislative process. Nurses have written letters and made visits to their legislators. Now nurses must move forward and apply the knowledge of the whole policy process by speaking out to a variety of appropriate governmental actors and institutions so that nurses can move issues onto the national agenda, lobby Congress with alternative solutions, and provide nursing expertise as policies and programs are being designed. In addition, nurses must be the watchdogs as programs are implemented so that target groups are served and services are appropriate. Nurses should be experts at program evaluation and continuing feedback to ensure that old problems are being addressed, new problems are being identified, and appropriate solutions are being considered.

The opportunities for nurse input throughout the policy process are unlimited and certainly not confined narrowly to the legislative process. Nurses are articulate experts who can address both the rational shaping of policy and the emotional aspects of the process. Nurses cannot afford to limit their actions to monitoring bills; they must seize the initiative and use their considerable collective and individual influence to ensure the health, welfare, and protection of the public and healthcare professionals.

AN OVERVIEW OF THE POLICY PROCESS

Most of the chapters in this book address specific components of the policy process in depth and from a theoretical perspective. However, at the outset, advanced practice nurses should have an overview of the total process so that they do not get stuck on legislation. Many useful articles and books have been written about policy in general and even about specific policies, but few have addressed the scope of the policy process or defined the components. The elements of agenda setting (including problem definition), government response (legislation, regulation, or programs), and policy and program implementation and evaluation are distinct entities, but are connected as parts of a whole tapestry in the process of public decision making.

Agenda Setting

Getting a healthcare problem to the attention of government can be a tremendous first step in getting relief. The actual mechanism of defining a healthcare problem is a major political issue. APNs have the capacity and opportunity to identify and frame problems from multiple sources.

The choice of a clinical problem on which to focus one's energy is a major decision. A nurse may be working in a specialized area and may see a need for more research or alternatives to existing treatment options; for example, those who work with patients and families with breast cancer already may have a passion for issues critical to this area. Other topics receiving attention include diabetes, obesity, AIDS, early detection and treatment of prostate cancer, child and parent abuse, cardiac problems in women, and empowering caregivers (Hash & Cramer, 2003; Pierce & Steiner, 2003).

Professional problems that are especially critical to nurses in advanced practice include reducing barriers to autonomy and reimbursement for nursing services. Workplace issues include advocacy for workplace safety and management strategies for training and redeploying nurses as work sites change. Related social problems that affect nurses include the increase of street violence and bioterrorism. A plethora of problems and "irritations" can arouse the passion of a nurse in advanced practice.

APNs must come to understand the concepts of windows of opportunity, policy entrepreneurs, and political elites. "Sound bites" and "word bites" are tools that are used to gain the attention of viewers and readers and serve as a shortcut or an abbreviated version of a statement. Originally created as off-hand remarks, these oral and written snippets have become planned tactics. For example, a nurse who speaks at a press conference or who delivers a message to a politician should have a written message that includes bulleted sound or word bites that underscore the message and that emphasize the important points. These brief, focused points can serve as references for the media or a politician as they consider the message later.

Government Response

The government response to public problems often emanates from the legislative branch and usually comes in three forms: 1) laws, 2) rules and regulations, and 3) programs. Because only senators and representatives can introduce legislation (not even the president can bring a bill to the floor of either house), these elected officials command respect and attention. The work of legislation is not clear-cut or linear. Informal communication and influence are the coin of the realm when trying to construct a program or law from the often vague wishes of disparate groups. The committee structure of both houses is a powerful method of accomplishing the work of government. Conference committees are known as the "Third House of Congress" (*How Our Laws Are Made,* 1990) because of their power to force compromise and bring about new legislation. APNs must appreciate the difference between the authorization and appropriations processes and seek influence in both arenas. Becoming involved directly with legislators and their staffs has been a training ground for many APNs. Supporting or opposing passage of a bill often has served as the first contact with the political process for many nurses, but this place often has been the stopping point for many nurses because they were unaware of other avenues of involvement, such as the follow-up process of regulations and rulemaking.

Lowi (1969) notes that administrative rulemaking is often an effort to bring about order in environments that are unstable and full of conflict. Some regulations codify precedent; others break new ground and address issues not previously explicated. An example of the latter is the Federal Trade Commission's (FTC) Trade Regulation Rules. In 1964, the FTC, whose mission is to protect the consumer and enforce antitrust legislation, wrote regulations requiring health warnings on cigarette packages. The tobacco industry reacted so fiercely that Congress quickly passed a law that nullified the regulations and replaced them with less stringent ones (West, 1982). Decades passed before no-smoking rules actually were mandated in public places. Other ways to sanction agencies whose rules are viewed as too restrictive are to reduce budget allocations and increase the number of adjudications or trial-like reviews. Advanced practice nurses must become knowledgeable about the regulatory process so that they can spot opportunities to contribute or intervene prior to final rulemaking ("The Regulatory Process," 1992).

Programs are concrete manifestations of solutions to problems. Program design often is a joint effort of legislative intent, budgetary expediency, and political feasibility. There are many opportunities for nurses in advanced practice to become involved in the design phase of a program. Selecting an agency to administer the program, choosing the goals, and selecting the tools that will ensure eligibility and participation are all decisions in which the APN should offer input.

Policy and Program Implementation

It is important that APNs keep reminding their colleagues that the phases of the policy process are not linear and that policy activities are fluid and move within and among the phases in dynamic processes. The implementation phase includes those activities in which legislative mandates are carried out, most often through programmatic means. The implementation stage also includes a planning ingredient. Problems occur in program planning if technological expertise is not available. This is particularly important to nurses, who are experts in the delivery of health care in the broadest sense.

If government officials do not know qualified, appropriate experts, decisions about program planning and design often are determined by legislators, bureaucrats, or staff who know little or nothing about the problem or the solutions. As excellent problem solvers, APNs have many opportunities to offer ideas and solutions. One strategy is to employ second-order change to reframe situations and recommend pragmatic alternatives to implementers (de Chesnay, 1983; Watzlawick, Weakland, & Fisch, 1974). Bowen (1982) uses probability theory to demonstrate how program success could be improved. She suggests putting several clearance points (instances where major decisions are made) together so that they could be negotiated as a package deal. She also advocates beginning the bargaining process with alternatives that have the greatest chance for success and using that success as a foundation for building more successes, a strategy she refers to as a "bandwagon approach" (p. 10). In the past, nurses have done the opposite: focused on failure and perceived lack of nursing power. APNs have begun to note successes in the political arena and are building a new level of success and esteem. The nurse in advanced practice today uses the strategies of packaging, success begets success, and persistence in a deliberate way so that nurses can increase their effective impact in the implementation of social programs.

Although nurses most often work toward positive impact, they have found that opposition to an unsound program can have a paradoxical positive effect. Although not in the public arena, an example of phenomenal success in the judicious use of opposition occurred when the professional body of nursing rose up as one against the American Medical Association's 1986 proposal to create a new type of low-level healthcare worker called a registered care technician. The power emerged as more than 40 nurse organizations stood together in opposition to an ill-conceived proposal that would have placed patients in jeopardy and created dead-end jobs.

Policy and Program Evaluation

For nurses who have worked beyond the nursing process through the process of clinical reasoning (Pesut & Herman, 1999), evaluation seems to be a logical component of the policy process. Evaluation is the systematic application of methods of social research to public policies and programs. Evaluation is conducted "to benefit the human condition to improve profit, to amass influence and power, or to achieve other goals" (Rossi & Freeman, 1995, p. 6). Evaluation research is a powerful tool for defending viable programs, for altering structures and processes to strengthen programs, and for providing rationale for program failure. Goggin, Bowman, Lester, & O'Toole (1990) propose that researchers investigate program implementation within an analytical framework rather than a descriptive one. They argue that a "third generation" of research established within a sound theory would strengthen the body of knowledge of the policy process. APNs can contribute to both the theory and the method of evaluation.

Evaluation should be started early and continued throughout a program. An unconscionable example of a program that should have been stopped even before it was begun is the Tuskegee "experiment." From 1932 to 1972, a group of African Americans was used as a control group and denied antibiotic treatment for syphilis, even after treatment was known to be successful (Thomas & Quinn, 1991). Beyond evaluation research, this study clearly points out the moral and ethical concerns that are mandated when researchers work with human beings. Should a study or program be started at all? At what point should it be stopped? What is involved in "informed consent"? If a program involves experimental therapy, what are the methods for presenting subjects with relevant data so that participation preferences are clear (Bell, Raiffa, & Tversky, 1988)? These kinds of questions should be considered automatically by today's researchers, but it is the responsibility of APNs as consumer agents to ask the questions if they have not been asked or if there is any doubt about the answers.

A BRIGHT FUTURE

The multiple roles of the APN—provider of direct care, researcher, consultant, educator, administrator, consumer advocate, and political activist—reflect the changing and expanding character of the professional nurse. Today is the future; nurse action today sets the direction for what health care becomes for coming generations. As true professionals with a societal mandate and a comprehensive body of knowledge, nurses function as visionaries who are grounded in education, research, and experience. APNs serve as the link between human responses to actual and potential health problems and the solutions that may be addressed in the government arena.

Full integration of the policy process becomes evident when professional nurses discern early the social implications of health problems, seize the opportunity to inform public officials with whom the nurses have credible relationships, provide objective data and subjective personal stories that help translate big problems down to a level of understanding, propose alternative solutions that acknowledge reality, and participate in the evaluation process to determine the effectiveness and efficiency of the outcomes.

Educating Our Political Selves

Nurses in advanced practice must be politically active. Basic content in undergraduate nursing programs must be reexamined in light of the needs of the profession. Educators must do more than plant the seeds of interest and excitement in baccalaureate students; they must model activism by talking about the bills they are supporting or opposing, by organizing students to assist in election campaigns, and by demanding not only that students write letters to officials but that they mail them and provide follow-up.

Educators can develop games in which students maneuver through a virtual bureaucracy to move a health problem onto the agenda. Brainstorming techniques can lead students to discover innovative alternative solutions. Baccalaureate students can analyze policy tools to discover how and when to use them. Teachers of research methods and processes can use political scenarios to point out how to phrase clinical questions so that legislators will pay attention. Program effectiveness can be studied in research and clinical courses. The theoretical components taught in class and followed by practical application through participation in political and legislative committees in professional organizations must serve as "basic training" for the registered nurse.

Graduate education must demand demonstrated knowledge and application of more extensive and sophisticated political processes. All graduate program faculty should serve as models for political activism. The atmosphere in master's and doctoral programs should heighten the awareness of students who are potential leaders.

Faculty can motivate students by displaying posters that announce political events and by including students in discussions of nursing issues framed in a policy context. Students who spot educators at rallies and other political and policy occasions are learning by example, so faculty should advertise their experiences as delegates to political and professional conventions. A few faculty can serve as mentors for students who need to move from informal to sustained, formal contact with policymakers and who have a policy track in their career trajectories. Both faculty and students should consider actual experience in government offices as a means of learning the nitty-gritty of how government functions and of demonstrating their own leadership capabilities.

If students hesitate and seem passive about involvement, educators must help these nurses determine where their passions are, which may help students focus on where they might start. Often the novice can be enticed by centering on a clinical problem. Every nurse cannot assume responsibility for all of the profession's problems or work on every healthcare issue. Issues can be at the practice level or the systems level (e.g., funding for nurse education or nurse-led research). Each nurse must choose the issue on which to invest energy, time, and other resources. Nurses can make a difference in the new healthcare system.

Strengthening Organized Nursing

The most productive and efficient way to act together is through a strong professional organization. As organizations in general have restructured and reengineered for more efficient operation, so will the professional associations. APNs have a knowledge base that includes an understanding of how organizations develop and change. This theoretical knowledge must serve as a foundation for leadership in directing new organizational structures that are responsive to members and other important bodies. National leaders must talk with state and local leaders as new configurations are conceived. States must confer among themselves to share innovations and knowledge about what works and what does not.

Issues such as the role of collective bargaining units within the total organizational structure, the position of individual membership vis-à-vis state membership, the political role of a specialized interest group (nurses) in creating public policy, and the issue of international influence in nursing and health care require wisdom and leadership that APNs must exert as the American Nurses Association addresses its place as a major voice of this country's nurses. The National League for Nursing (NLN) will exert leadership as nurse education programs move toward baccalaureate programs. Accrediting agencies (e.g., Commission for Credentialing in Nursing Education and the NLN Accrediting Commission) must continue to be visionary and flexible in developing criteria and processes for accreditation. Boards of Nursing must not become trapped in the slowness with which government bureaucracy can be mired, but must be on the forefront of developing regulations that protect the public and allow nurses to work at their top capacity.

Issues inherent in multistate licensure are being debated today, and the outcome will reflect the extent to which nurses will use concepts of telehealth in their practices. Because APNs already are eligible for Medicare reimbursement for telehealth services that are provided in specified rural areas (Burtt, 1997), these nurses are rich resources and must be included in reasoned discussions on this issue. State boards of nursing in every state and jurisdiction face issues of appropriate methods of recognizing advanced nursing practice, the role of the government agency in regulating nursing and other professions, and the analysis of educationally sound and legally defensible examinations for candidates.

Nurses who have been reluctant to become political cannot afford to ignore their obligations any longer. Each nurse counts, and, collectively, nursing is a major actor in the effort to ensure the country's healthy future. Nurses have expanded their conception of what nursing is and how it is practiced to include active political participation. A nurse must choose the governmental level on which to focus: federal, regional, state, or local. The process is similar at each level: Identify the problem and become part of the solution.

Advanced practice nurses understand the scope of service delivery, continuity of care, appropriate mix of caregivers, and the expertise that can be provided by multidisciplinary teams. By being at the forefront of understanding, nurses have a moral and ethical mandate to lead the public-policy process. Dynamic political action is as much a part of the advanced practice of nursing as is expert direct care.

Working with the Political System

By now, many APNs have developed contacts with legislators, appointed officials, and their staffs. A new group that holds great potential for nurse interaction is the Senate Nursing Caucus (AACN, 2010b). Established in March 2010, this group will provide a forum for educating senators on issues important to nurses, as well as for hearing concerns of the senators. Four senators established the caucus: Jeff Merkley (D-OR),

Mike Johanns (R-NE), Barbara Mikulski (D-MD), and Olympia Snowe (R-ME). The Senate Nursing Caucus follows the lead of the Congressional Nursing Caucus in the U.S. House of Representatives, begun in 2003 by Representatives Lois Capps (D-CA) and Ed Whitfield (R-KY) (American Nurses Association, 2003). Members hold briefings on the nurse shortage, patient and nurse safety issues, preparedness for bioterrorism, and other relevant and pertinent issues and concerns.

APNs must stay alert to issues and be assertive in bringing problems to the attention of policymakers. It is important to bring success stories to legislators and officials—they need to hear what good nurses do and how well they practice. Sharing positive information will keep the image of nurses in an affirmative and constructive picture. Legislators must run for office (and U.S. Representatives do this every 2 years), so media coverage with an APN who is pursuing noteworthy accomplishments is usually welcomed eagerly.

Nurses absolutely must "get their act together" and work toward a unified voice on issues that affect the public health and the nursing profession. Whatever their differences in the past—anger from entry-into-practice arguments that have dragged on for over half a century; disparagement and animosity among those with varied levels of education; cerebral and pragmatic concerns about gaps between education and practice, practice and administration; or administration and education—nurses must put these kinds of divisive, emotional issues behind them if they expect to be taken seriously as professionals by elected and appointed public officials and policymakers.

Nurses cannot afford to stop arguing critical issues internally, but they must learn how to argue heatedly among themselves—and then go to lunch together. Nurses can learn lessons from television shows such as *Meet the Press, This Week, The O'Reilly Factor,* and *The McLaughlin Group* about how to challenge, contest, dispute, contend, and debate issues passionately, then shake hands and respect the opponent's position. Passionate issues must not polarize the profession any longer and, more important, must not stand in the way of a unified voice to the public.

CONCLUSION

Nurses in advanced practice must have expert knowledge and skill in change, conflict resolution, assertiveness, communication, negotiation, and group process to function appropriately in the policy arena. Professional autonomy and collaborative interdependence are possible within a political system in which consumers can choose access to quality health care that is provided by competent practitioners at a reasonable cost. Nurses in advanced practice have a strong, persistent voice in designing such a healthcare system for today and for the future.

The policy process is much broader and more comprehensive than the legislative process. Although individual components can be identified for analytical study, the policy process is fluid, nonlinear, and dynamic. There are many opportunities for nurses in advanced practice to participate throughout the policy process. The question is not whether nurses should become involved in the political system, but to what extent. In the whole policy arena, nurses must be involved with every aspect. Knowing all of the components and issues that must be addressed in each phase, the nurse in advanced practice finds many opportunities for providing expert advice. APNs can use the policy process, individual components, and models as a framework to analyze issues and participate in alternative solutions.

Nursing has a rich history. The professional nurse's values of altruism, respect, integrity, and accountability to consumers remain strong. In some ways, the evolution of nursing roles has come full circle, from the political influence recognized and exercised by Nightingale to the influence of current nurse leaders with elected and appointed public officials. The APN of the 21st century practices with a solid political heritage and a mandate for consistent and powerful involvement in the entire policy process.

DISCUSSION POINTS AND ACTIVITIES

1. Read Nightingale's *Notes on Nursing* and other historical sources of the mid-1800s and discuss how Nightingale's personal and family influence moved her agenda for the Crimea and for nursing education, and how this has implications for the future.
2. Discuss implications of the "BSN in 10" movement in relation to your own education. Research opportunities for BSNs and for APNs. Dream about positions that might not be available today.
3. Compare the definition of nursing according to Nightingale, Henderson, the ANA, and your own state nurse practice act. What are the differences in a legal definition versus a professional definition? What are the similarities? What did definitions include or not include that reflected the state of nursing at the time? Construct a definition of nursing for today and for 10 years from now.
4. Discuss the role of research in nursing. What has been the focus over the past century? What is the pattern of nursing research vis-à-vis topic, methodology, and relevance? To what extent do you think nursing research has had an impact on nursing care? Cite examples.
5. Trace the amount of federal funding for nursing research. Do not limit your search to federal health-related agencies; that is, investigate departments (commerce, environment, transportation, etc.), military services, and the Veterans Administration. What funding opportunities exist for nurse scientists?
6. Read books and articles about the changing paradigm in healthcare delivery systems. Discuss the change in nursing as an occupation and nursing as a profession. What does this mean in today's transformational paradigm?
7. Consider a thesis, graduate project, or dissertation on a specific topic (e.g., clinical problems, healthcare issues) using the policy process as a framework.

8. Identify policies within public agencies and discuss how they were developed. Interview members of an agency policy committee to discover how policies are changed.

9. Have faculty and students bring to class official governmental policies. What governmental agency is responsible for developing the policy? For enforcing the policy? How has the policy changed over time? What are the consequences of not complying with the policy?

10. Identify nurses who are elected officials at the local, state, or national level. Interview these officials to determine how the nurses were elected, what their objectives are, and to what extent they use their nurse knowledge in their official capacities. Ask the officials if they tapped into nurse groups during their campaigns. If so, what did the nurses contribute? If not, why?

11. Discuss the major components of the policy process and discuss the fluidity of the process. Point out how players move among the components in a nonlinear way.

12. Using Exhibit 1-1 as a framework, construct a healthcare organization in which access is provided and quality care is assured. What are the barriers to this type of paradigm?

13. Develop an assessment tool by which students can determine their own level of knowledge and involvement in the policy process. Reminder: Stretch your thinking beyond legislative activity.

14. Watch television programs in which participants discuss national and international issues, then analyze the verbal and nonverbal communication patterns, pro-and-con arguments, and other methods of discussion. Discuss your analysis within the framework of gender differences in communication and utility in the political arena.

15. Construct a list of ways in which nurses can become more knowledgeable about the policy process. Choose at least three activities in which you will participate. Develop a tool for evaluating the activity and your knowledge and involvement.

16. Select at least one problem or irritation in a clinical area and brainstorm with other APNs or graduate students on how to approach a solution. Discuss funding sources; be creative.

17. Attend a meeting of the state board of nursing, the district or state nurses association, or a professional convention. Identify issues discussed, resources used, communication techniques, and rules observed. Evaluate the usefulness of the session to your practice.

18. Discuss what skills (task, interpersonal, etc.) and attitudes are required for the nurse in the new paradigm. Who is best prepared to teach these skills, and what teaching techniques should be used? How will they be evaluated? Develop a worksheet to facilitate planning.

19. Discuss at least five strategies for helping nurses integrate these skills into their practices.

For a full suite of assignments and additional learning activities, use the access code located in the front of your book to visit this exclusive website: http://go.jblearning.com/milstead. If you do not have an access code, you can obtain one at the site.

REFERENCES

Aiken, L. H., Clarke, S. R., Cheung, R. B., Sloan, D. M., & Silber, J. H. (2003). Hospital nurse staffing and patient mortality, nurse burnout, and job dissatisfaction. *Journal of the American Medical Association, 290*(12), 1617–1623.

American Acadamy of Nursing. (2010). *Raise the voice.* Retrieved from http://www.aannet.org/i4a/pages/Index.cfm?pageid=3301

American Association of Colleges of Nursing. (2006). *Essentials of doctoral education for advanced nursing practice.* Washington, DC: Author.

American Association of Colleges of Nursing. (2008a). *Essentials of baccalaureate education for professional nursing practice.* Washington, DC: Author.

American Association of Colleges of Nursing. (2008b). *Essentials of master's education for advanced practice nursing.* Washington, DC: Author.

American Association of Colleges of Nursing. (2010a). Fact sheet: The doctor of nursing practice. Retrieved from http://www.aacn.nche.edu/media/FactSheets/dnp.htm

American Association of Colleges of Nursing. (2010b). Senate nursing caucus. Retrieved from http://www.aacn.nche.edu/Government/SenNursingCaucus.htm

American Association of Colleges of Nursing. (2011). Press release: Despite educational challenges facing schools of nursing, new AACN data confirm sizable growth in doctoral nursing programs. Retrieved from http://www.aacn.nche.edu/media/NewsReleases/2011/enrollsurge.html

American Nurses Association. (2003, March 19). American Nurses Association commends Reps. Capps, Whitfield for forming congressional nursing caucus. Retrieved from http://www.nursingworld.org/pressrel/2003/pr0319.htm

Bell, D. E., Raiffa, H., & Tversky, A. (1988). *Decision making.* Cambridge, MA: Cambridge University Press.

Bennis, W., & Nanus, B. (1985). *Leaders.* New York: Harper and Row.

Bowen, E. (1982). The Pressman-Wildavsky paradox: Four addenda on why models based on probability theory can predict implementation success and suggest useful tactical advice for implementers. *Journal of Public Policy, 2*(1), 1–22.

Buerhaus, P. (2008). The future of the nursing workforce in the United States: Data, trends, and implications. *Journal of the American Medical Association, 300*(16), 1950.

Buerhaus, P. I. (2009). Messages for thought leaders and health policy makers. *Nursing Economic$, 2*(2), 125–127.

Burtt, K. (1997). Nurses use telehealth to address rural health care needs, prevent hospitalizations. *The American Nurse, 29*(6), 21.

Commission on Nurse Certification. (2011). History of CNL certification. Retrieved from http://www.aacn.nche.edu/CNC/pdf/history.pdf

Cronenwett, L., Dracup, K., Grey, M., McCauley, L., Meleis, A., & Salman, M. (2011). The doctor of nursing practice: A national workforce perspective. *Nursing Outlook, 59*(1), 9–17.

Curtin, L. (2010). Quantum nursing. *American Nurse Today, 5*(9), 47–48.

Curtin, L. (2011). Quantum nursing II: Our field of influence. *American Nurse Today, 6*(1), 56.

de Chesnay, M. (1983). The creation and dissolution of paradoxes in nursing practice. *Topics in Clinical Nursing, 5*(3), 71–80.

Drucker, P. F. (1995). The age of social transformation. *Quality Digest,* 36–39.

Eulau, H., & Prewitt, K. (1973). *Labyrinths of democracy.* Indianapolis, IN: Bobbs-Merrill.

Feldstein, P. J. (1988). *The politics of health legislation.* Ann Arbor, MI: Health Administration Press.

Fraser, R. (2011). *The nurse's social media advantage.* Indianapolis, IN: Sigma Theta Tau International.

Goggin, M. L., Bowman, A. O'M., Lester, J. P., & O'Toole, L. J., Jr. (1990). *Implementation theory and practice: Toward a third generation.* New York: HarperCollins.

Haas, J. E. (1964). *Role conception and group consensus* (Research Monograph No. 17). Columbus, OH: The Ohio State University, Bureau of Business Research.

Hash, K. M., & Cramer, E. P. (2003). Empowering gay and lesbian caregivers and uncovering their unique experiences through the use of qualitative methods. *Journal of Gay and Lesbian Social Services, 15*(1/2), 47–64.

Health Resources and Services Administration. (2008). The RN population: Findings from the 2008 national sample survey of registered nurses. Retrieved from http://bhpr.hrsa.gov/healthworkforce/rnsurveys/rnsurveyinitial2008.pdf

How our laws are made. (1990). (House Document 101–139). Washington, DC: U.S. Government Printing Office.

Husted, J., & Husted, G. L. (2008). Bioethical decision making in nursing and health care: A symphonological approach (4th ed.). New York, NY: Springer.

Institute of Medicine. (2010). *The future of nursing: Leading change, advancing health.* Washington, DC: Author.

Kouzes, J., & Posner, B. (2007). *The leadership challenge* (4th ed.). San Francisco, CA: Jossey-Bass.

Kouzes, J., & Posner, B. (1999). *Encouraging the heart: A leader's guide to rewarding and recognizing others.* San Francisco, CA: Jossey-Bass.

Lasswell, H. D. (1958). *Politics: Who gets what, when, how.* New York: Meridian Books.

Lindberg, C., Nash, S., & Lindberg, C. (2008). *On the edge: Nursing in the age of complexity.* Medford, NJ: Plexus Press.

Litman, T. J., & Robins, L. S. (1991). *Health politics and policy* (2nd ed.). Albany, NY: Delmar.

Lowi, T. (1969). *The end of liberalism.* New York: Norton.

Milio, N. (1989). Developing nursing leadership in health policy. *Journal of Professional Nursing, 5*(6), 315.

Neergaard, L. (2010, July 26). Cell phone doctoring. *The Columbus Dispatch.* Retrieved from http://www.dispatch.com/content/stories/business/2010/07/26/cell-phone-doctoring.html

Nightingale, F. (1859). *Notes on nursing.* Cambridge, England: Cambridge University Press.

Patient Protection and Affordable Care Act of 2010. (2010). Pub. L. No. 111-148, 124 Stat. 119.

Pesut, D., & Herman, J. (1999). *Clinical reasoning: The art and science of critical and creative thinking* (2nd ed.). Albany, NY: Delmar Learning.

Pierce, L., & Steiner, V. (2003). The male caregiving experience: Three case studies. *Stroke, 34*(1), 315.

Porter-O'Grady, T., Hawkins, M.A., & Parker, M. L. (1997). *Whole-systems shared governance: Architecture for integration.* Gaithersburg, MD: Aspen.

Porter-O'Grady, T. & Malloch, K. (2011). *Quantum leadership: Advancing innovation, transforming health care* (3rd ed.). Sudbury, MA: Jones and Bartlett Learning.

Porter-O'Grady, T., & Wilson, C. K. (1995). *The leadership revolution in health care: Altering systems, changing behaviors.* Gaithersburg, MD: Aspen.

The regulatory process. (1992, December 4). *Capitol Update, 10*(23), 1.

Rhoades, A., Covery, S. R., & Shepherdson, N. (2011). *Building values: Creating an equitable culture that outperforms the competition.* San Francisco, CA: Jossey-Bass.

Rossi, P. H., & Freeman, H. E. (1995). *Evaluation: A systematic approach* (5th ed.). Beverly Hills, CA: Sage.

Thomas, S. B., & Quinn, S. C. (1991). The Tuskegee syphilis study, 1932 to 1972: Implications for HIV education and AIDS risk reduction education programs in the black community. *American Journal of Public Health, 8*(11), 1498–1505.

Watzlawick, R., Weakland, C. E., & Fisch, R. (1974). *Change.* New York: W. W. Norton.

West, W. F. (1982, September/October). The politics of administrative rulemaking. *Public Administration Review,* 420–426.

Williams, S. J., & Torrens, P. R. (Eds.). (1988). *Introduction to health services* (3rd ed.). Albany, NY: Delmar.

Wilson, J. Q. (1989). *American government institutions and policies* (4th ed.). Lexington, MA: D. C. Heath.

CHAPTER 2

Agenda Setting

Elizabeth Ann Furlong

KEY TERMS

Contextual dimensions: Studying issues in the real world, in the circumstances or settings of what is happening at the time.

Iron triangle: Legislators or their committees, interest groups, and administrative agencies that work together on a policy issue that will benefit all parties.

Stakeholders: Policy actors, policy communities, and policy networks; people and groups that have a say in what goes on.

Streams: Kingdon's concept of the interaction of public problems, policies, and politics that couple and uncouple throughout the process of agenda setting.

Window of opportunity: Limited time frame for action.

INTRODUCTION

This chapter will emphasize the agenda-setting aspect of policy by using exemplar case studies at both the state and national levels. Agenda setting is the process of moving a problem to the attention of government so that solutions can be considered. Advanced practice nurses can apply the knowledge from these case studies to the many current concerns they face.

"At the end of my pilgrimage, I have come to the conclusion that among the sins of modern political science, the greatest of all has been the omission of passion" (Lowi, 1992, p. 6). This criticism does not apply to public policy researchers' current scholarly interest in agenda setting, policy design, and alternative formulation, nor does it apply to certain policy communities who push for selected public policies. The passion of the former group, the researchers, is seen in their search and inquiry for a better understanding of public policy. The passion of the latter, policy communities, is reflected in their tenacity on policy design, in pushing to make sure that a policy is put into practice as it was intended.

Advanced practice nurses, as well as policymakers and citizens, are interested in the best public policy to address society's concerns. In the past, political science researchers have mostly studied the latter steps of policymaking—implementation and evaluation—to gain an understanding of public policy and knowledge that could be used by policymakers to create better public policy. Although all stages of the policy process have been studied, the need for more research on the earlier parts of policymaking—agenda setting, policy formulation, and policy design—has been drawing more discussion (Bosso, 1992; Ingraham, 1987; May, 1991). Thus, research interest in these latter areas grew during the 1980s and 1990s and it continues into the 21st century.

In this chapter, examples will be given of agenda setting at both the state and the federal level. First, the state example will be discussed. By discussing this case study, APNs can learn ways that issues can get on the legislative state agenda, how interest groups both propose and block such agenda issues, how such interest groups persist over years to accomplish their goals, and how opponents plan strategies to prevent such agenda items. Following the state agenda setting example, a classic national legislative example will be given.

CASE STUDY 1: Immigration and Perinatal Care

For APNs (and all nurses, health providers, and the lay public), a major concern in the United States is how nondocumented immigrants are treated relative to healthcare access and other human rights issues. At the time of the submission of this chapter (Spring 2011), Nebraska is facing an outlier state policy dictated and implemented by Governor Heineman in Spring 2010 that states that nondocumented pregnant women would no longer receive government-reimbursed health care through Medicaid or other state programs. The outlier aspect of this policy was noted by the author when attending a conference forum presented by an expert on immigration issues in the United States, who mentioned the outlier prenatal care policy of Nebraska. This ruling was implemented through the Nebraska Health and Human Services administrative office. When this new policy was promulgated during Spring 2010, Senator Kathy Campbell attempted a legislative change to prevent this, but was unable to obtain the necessary 30 votes (Senator K. Campbell, personal communication, January 2011). She (and others) had attempted many strategies, including the available option of an administrative agency nonlegislative strategy, i.e., a transfer of money from one financial area to another area that would allow the program to continue. Further, she and many others worked at negotiation with the governor. None of the above strategies was successful. For one year, nondocumented, pregnant women have been and continue to be placed at health risk in one midwestern state.

APNs in Nebraska responded in three ways: 1) being active lobbyists throughout the state with their respective state senators; 2) responding directly by providing perinatal care to these women in selected settings; and 3) collecting data of unmet needs for Senator Campbell's office for the January 2011 Unicameral Session. One example of the second response is what APNs and other health providers did at one federally funded community health center in Omaha, Nebraska. At the One World

Community Health Centers, the APNs and others created a new program titled Every Baby Matters, putting into place a new volunteer clinic that was open one night a week for these women. APNs, physicians, physician assistants, and other health providers donated their time and expertise to this population of women, and that care has now been integrated into their regular clinic (B. Buschkemper, personal communication, February 26, 2011).

"Politicians and the media may occasionally pander to some greedy, fearful, narrow-mindedness within us" (Lowney, 2009, p. 193). This is the analysis by those who are opposed to Governor Heineman's Spring 2010 policy. Previously, the non-documented women could receive health care based on the Medicaid eligibility of their unborn children. During a December 2010 vigil at the Lincoln, Nebraska, state capitol, speakers noted that 5 infants had died since implementation of the policy and 1500 women were denied health care; 840 of these women were non-documented (Stoddard, 2010). The above "pandering" to fear is ascribed partly to how this issue got on the policy agenda. The above policy is one of several policies introduced in Nebraska that are anti-immigrant in purpose.

Another major bill that was introduced in January 2011 was an Arizona-type anti-immigrant law that required showing documentation during a lawful stop. A third example is a bill, resubmitted in 2011 (not passed during the last 2-year legislative session) that attempts to deny certain college privileges to children of immigrants. Political analysts note the conservative ideology of many Nebraskans and acknowledge that many individuals in the state support such anti-immigrant policies. Another variable that affects the issue is the decline of the economy in the past three years, the fear that this downturn generated, and the seeking of victims to blame. There are legislative structural variables (term limits) and partisan political reasons why the governor has major influence on the predominantly Republican legislature and their voting patterns (such as members' concern about their political ambitions).

The political actors (**stakeholders**) supporting the "no prenatal care policy" have been Governor Heineman, many Republicans, and many citizens. The actors opposed to the policy have been some senators, the healthcare-provider communities (including APNs), the Nebraska Catholic Conference (the dioceses of Nebraska), Voices for Children (a major state child advocacy organization), Nebraska Appleseed for Law in the Public Interest, concerned citizens, and federally funded community health centers throughout the state.

There have been many strategies by the above policy opposition groups to reobtain pregnancy coverage for the women. In January 2011, Senator Campbell introduced LB 599 to make such coverage possible. This author notes that the public hearing at the committee level did not occur until March 16th, 2011 (the third to last day for all public hearings), and such late hearings do not bode well for passage of a bill during that particular legislative session. Further, only two additional senators have signed on as cosponsors of this bill; bills have a better chance of passage when there are many cosponsors.

As this chapter goes to press, APNs in Nebraska are proud of how they have responded to the needs of prenatal women, whether or not they are "documented." They are proud of their policy activity, their practice skills, their research skills, and their living by the American Nurses Association Code of Ethics.

CASE STUDY 2: The National Center for Nursing Research Amendment

Victor Hugo wrote, "Greater than the tread of mighty armies is an idea whose time has come" (Kingdon, 1995, p. 1). For nurses, one example of this was the initiation of legislation in 1983 that increased the funding base for nursing research. An amendment to the 1985 Health Research Extension Act, which created the National Center for Nursing Research (NCNR) on the campus of the National Institutes of Health (NIH), is the focus of this chapter's national example of agenda setting.

Creation of the NCNR came about because a group of nurse leaders wanted to create a national institute of nursing within the NIH. In order to pass the legislation in 1985, a political compromise was made with legislators to create a center instead of an institute. However, in 1993 the NCNR was changed to an institute, and today the agency continues as the National Institute of Nursing Research (NINR). Discussion in this chapter of the NCNR amendment focuses on the agenda setting and policy formulation that occurred from 1983 to 1985.

The Influence of National Nurse Groups

The creation of the National Center for Nursing Research on the campus of the National Institutes of Health was a policy victory for national nurse organizations. But, despite this victory, those organizations still need a better understanding of agenda setting, policy formulation, and policy design as they work for other policy changes in the future. Although nurses' groups traditionally have not been considered strong political actors, these groups recognize the importance of political activity to bring about public policies that enhance patient care (Warner, 2003). In the last decade of the 20th century, nurse groups were just emerging as actors in policy networks; however, "a full cadre of nurse leaders who are knowledgeable and experienced in the public arena, who fully understand the design of public policy, and who are conversant with consumer, business and provider groups does not yet exist" (DeBack, 1990, p. 69).

In a study of national health organizations that play a key role in the health policy-making area (Laumann, Heinz, Nelson, & Salisbury, 1991), no nurse organizations were cited. The scope and nature of nursing care and certain restrictions to providing that care are closely related to public policy. APNs are well aware of this, as state legislative and regulatory activity affects their professional practice on a daily basis. Raudonis and Griffith (1991) and Warner (2003) are three of the many nurse leaders who challenged nurses to be more knowledgeable about health policy. These leaders also urged nurses to become more empowered on health policy issues; if nurses were to become more involved in policymaking, public policy could better reflect the contributions of nurses to patient care, to the health of citizens, and to cost-effective quality solutions for the financial crisis of the healthcare system. Nagelkerk and Henry echoed this concern: "To date, few studies in nursing can be classified as policy research. Leaders in our field, therefore, have identified this type of undertaking as a priority" (1991, p. 20).

Research on the NCNR amendment is important because it studies political actors who are not generally studied (e.g., nurses' interest groups), and so this research contributes to public policy scholars' knowledge of all actors in policy networks. Laumann et al. acknowledged that "we may even run a risk of misrepresenting the sorts of actors who come to be influential in policy deliberation" (1991, p. 67). The significance of this research becomes obvious when the Schneider and Ingram model of social construction of target populations in policy design is applied to the nurse interest groups (1993a). For example, how nurses were viewed by policymakers—the social construction of nurses as a target population—influenced not only the policy that nurses were interested in, but also passage of the total NIH reauthorization bill.

Dohler (1991) compared health policy actors in the United States, Great Britain, and Germany, and found that it is much easier to have new political actors in the United States because there are multiple ways to become involved, and he has written of the great increase in new actors since 1970. Baumgartner and Jones (1993) also described multiple paths of access to becoming involved.

OVERVIEW OF MODELS AND DIMENSIONS

Several researchers have developed models of agenda setting and policy formulation (Baumgartner & Jones, 1993; Cobb & Elder, 1983; Kingdon, 1995), and several political scientists are developing theoretical modeling of policy design (Hedge & Mok, 1987). Ingraham is one of several authors who have noted the lack of one design, one theory, or one model in policy design (1987). Meanwhile, public policy scholars are pushing for more empirical study of agenda setting, alternative formulation, and policy design (Schneider & Ingram, 1993a).

Data analysis reveals the importance of the Schneider and Ingram model (1993a) of the social construction of target populations, and of the Kingdon model (1995) for an understanding of the agenda-setting process of this amendment to the NIH reauthorizing legislative bill. Analysis of this legislation over the period of a decade also underscores the importance of the Dryzek (1983) definition of policy design. An analysis of the legislation supported the importance of studying the **contextual dimension** that has been advocated by Bobrow and Dryzek (1987), Bosso (1992), deLeon (1988–1989), Ingraham and White (1988–1989), May (1991), and Schneider and Ingram (1993b). The value of other models—institutional, representational communities and institutional approach, and the congressional motivational model—is addressed as these models contribute to an understanding of this example. During the study of interest groups opposed to this legislation, the researcher noted two occurrences of **iron triangles** in the early 1980s. These findings will be discussed in more detail.

Kingdon Model

One model that was explanatory for this research was the Kingdon model (1995), which explains how issues get on the political agenda, and, once there, how alternative solutions are devised. The four important concepts are the three **streams** (policy, problem, and political) and the **window of opportunity**. A problem stream can be marked by systematic indicators of a problem, by a sudden crisis, or by feedback that a program is not working as intended. A practical application for APNs is that they can be attentive to these indicators and maximize such opportunities to get an issue on the agenda. A policy stream relates to those policy actors and communities who attach their solutions (policies) to emerging problems. This concept also relates to the actual policy being promoted, and so APNs can be attentive to identifying problems and framing their solutions to such concerns. The third stream of Kingdon's model is the political stream, which consists of the public mood, pressure group campaigns, election results, partisan or ideological distributions in Congress, and changes in administration. Other factors include committee jurisdictional boundaries and turf concerns among agencies and government branches. Thus, APNs need to be constantly attentive to all of these political factors, which can integrate with the fourth concept, the "window of opportunity." This is when the above three streams integrate at a time that is favorable to solve a problem with one's preferred policy and with least resistance. This window of opportunity is most usually affected by the problem and political streams.

Interview data and a review of the literature showed many ways in which the Kingdon model explained the agenda setting for this bill. For example, for the problem stream, these were variables: 1) the need for nursing research was recognized by many (e.g., Rep. Madigan (R-IL), legislative staffers, and national nurse leaders); 2) there were data about financial disparity in funding for nurses; and 3) the timing of an Institute of Medicine (IOM) report (Cantelon, 2010) on this problem. For the political stream, these were the variables: 1) this policy would be valuable for Rep. Madigan's re-election and 2) this was an important policy proposal for the Republican Party to secure increased voting by women voters. For the policy stream, it was sound public policy. There was a window of opportunity; the release of the IOM report in conjunction with the election cycle, the presence of many national nurse leaders who were policy and politically knowledgeable, and a U.S. representative who initiated the idea for this bill all came together quickly and at an opportune time. In summarizing these findings in relation to the Kingdon model, this example validated the importance of the political and problem streams. However, the NCNR amendment was passed without meeting the policy stream processes described by Kingdon, in that it did not go through a softening-up phase.

Advanced practice nurses may be able to apply the Kingdon model to ongoing priority practice issues with which they are concerned. For example, APNs can be attentive to the three streams (policy, problem, and political) and a window of opportunity in which to move forward their agenda. Every year a legislative update is printed in *The Nurse Practitioner*, and this is one way to recognize the advances made in state policies in the areas of scope of practice, prescriptive authority, reimbursement practices, title protection, and emerging issues.

Although one of the exemplar case studies used in this chapter is that of the National Institute of Nursing Research getting on the political agenda and being passed as national legislation, APNs also need to be aware that taking political activity in regulatory agencies could also be an ideal way to problem solve. Nurse practitioners are finding increased difficulty in having mail-order pharmacies recognize and fill their prescriptions (Edmunds, 2003). Two nurse practitioners from New York and South Carolina addressed this problem stream by working with the Food and Drug Administration and the Federal Trade Commission. They recognized that the value of working through regulatory agencies was the best initial solution for this problem (Edmunds, 2003).

Importance of Contextual Dimensions

Some authors, notably Bobrow and Dryzek (1987), Bosso (1992), deLeon (1988–1989), Ingraham and White (1988–1989), May (1991), and Schneider and Ingram (1993b), have emphasized the need to analyze the political context in which policies get on the agenda, alternatives are formulated, and policies are put into effect. Although neither a definitive nor an exhaustive list, five contextual dimensions are suggested by Bobrow and Dryzek (1987) for studying the success or failure of any designed policy: 1) complexity and uncertainty of the decision–system environment; 2) feedback potential; 3) control of design by an actor or group of actors; 4) stability of policy actors over time; and 5) the audience must be stirred into action. deLeon writes that sometimes researchers, because of their unstructured environment, have chosen to study approaches and methodologies that may meet scientific rigor better, but in doing so come "dangerously close to rendering the policy sciences all-but-useless in the real-life political arenas" (1988–1989, p. 300).

deLeon notes that it is difficult to impossible for researchers to "structure analytically the contextual environment in which their recommended analyses must operate" (1988–1989, p. 300). Researchers have to work in a world with great social complexity, extreme political competition, and limited resources. Of these writers, Bosso and May are especially strong in their advocacy of this contextual approach to the study of public policy. Bosso (1992) echoes deLeon's concern: "In many ways, the healthiest trend is the admission, albeit a grudging one for many, that policymaking is not engineering and the study of policy formation cannot be a laboratory science. In policy making contexts do matter, people don't always act according to narrow self-interest, and decisions are made on the basis of incomplete or biased information" (p. 23).

Data from congressional documents, archival sources, and personal and telephone interviews show the importance of the political context to all aspects of policy design—how the policy arrived on the agenda; how policy alternatives were formulated; the legislative process; implementation; and redesign of the legislation eight years later, resulting in new legislation within two years to accomplish the original goal (Bobrow & Dryzek, 1987; Bosso, 1992; deLeon, 1988–1989; Ingraham & White, 1988–1989; May, 1991; Schneider & Ingram, 1993b).

Examples of Political Contextual Influence

First, partisan political party conflict within Congress influenced the initial agenda setting of the amendment and the legislative process throughout the two years. Opposition to Rep. Waxman's (D-CA) NIH bill in the spring and summer of 1983 resulted in Rep. Madigan's initiating a substitute policy. As noted by two congressional staffers, this was an example of partisan conflict. Another example of partisanship, noted by an interviewee, was that the appointment of Dr. Ada Sue Hinshaw as the first director of the NCNR was made easier because she was Republican. (The administration at the time was Republican.)

Second, a U.S. representative's concern with his reelection chances influenced the initial agenda setting because of the congressional perception that nurses were a target population that could help his reelection chances. Several respondents noted that this was an important factor in the initial decision for this type of public policy.

A third contextual dimension was the bipartisan negotiation to enact policy. Such negotiations by Rep. Waxman and Rep. Madigan in early Fall 1983 resulted in a firm resolve during the 97th and 98th Congresses to stay with the proposed NINR policy and during the 99th Congress to accept a compromise of an NCNR. Another example of bipartisan negotiation was the early committee work by Rep. Madigan, Rep. Broyhill (R-NC), and Rep. Shelby (D-AL) to forge a simple bipartisan amendment that was four lines long. The bipartisan effort of these three representatives smoothed the way for passage of this amendment by the subcommittee. If there is bipartisan support for issues, there is a greater chance for passage of legislation. Legislators used this strategy early in the legislative process.

Fourth, interest-group unity on the policy was a factor. Such unity by nurse groups was considered by many interviewees to be a crucial factor in the bill's passage, and this unity also was important in explaining why no other policy alternatives were pursued. Because the decision to support Rep. Madigan was officially made by the Tri-Council in the summer of 1983, and although other policy alternatives were considered after that, the priority of presenting unity with Rep. Madigan was maintained. Dohler (1991) reported on the importance of the unity of policy communities. He concluded that the deregulation of two organizations, the Professional Standards Review Organization and the Health Systems Agencies, occurred because of the "weakened stability of the network segment" (p. 267). Dohler also determined that if there is not a stable, united policy community, programs falter. If there is such stability (as with the nursing community in this research), there is an increased chance of success.

Fifth, lack of interest group unity with a congressperson was seen as a negative factor. Such behavior by the American Association of Medical Colleges had disillusioned Rep. Madigan and increased his interest in initiating the NINR policy.

Sixth, partisan conflict between the White House and an interest group (nurses) that generally supported Democratic presidential and vice presidential candidates had an influence on this legislation's history. This campaign support by the American Nurses Association (ANA) for the Democratic candidates was evaluated as the reason for the 1984 Republican presidential veto of the NINR amendment and the NIH bill that had passed Congress. Interviewee data reported one congressperson's concern with how the ANA Political Action Committee (PAC) distributed its money—mainly to Democratic candidates. Research by Makinson (1992) a decade later on the 1990 election reflected that the ANA PAC gave 85 percent of its money to Democratic candidates.

Seventh, ideological and partisan conflicts over other issues within the larger NIH bill affected the bill's legislative history. Concerns about fetal tissue research and animal rights research caused much difficulty in the early 1980s, while concerns about immigration laws and immigrants with HIV infection raised concerns in the 1990s and affected compromises and passage of the bills. Such other issues, although not about the NINR amendment, had a major effect on the bill's legislative history. APNs need to understand bills in their holistic content and the many pressures on a particular bill.

Eighth, concerns with the federal deficit influenced discussion of the bill and decision making. There was opposition to the creation of new federal entities because of the deficit concern, and President Reagan consistently used this argument as a reason not to create a NINR.

Ninth, legislation passed during a lame-duck presidential term was a factor. The NIH bill with the NCNR amendment was passed in 1985 when President Reagan was beginning his second term. Republican congresspeople did not feel as constrained to vote along party lines, and that was reflected in the 1985 legislative vote and the override vote. Thus, the timing of this vote in President Reagan's lame-duck term helped the bill's passage. When the president vetoes legislation, another option for passage is for Congress to secure the necessary number of votes and override the president's decision. As will be explained in the thirteenth contextual variable, this was a significant political event for this nursing issue.

Tenth, the history of Congress with selected administrative agencies influenced the political context. Rep. Waxman's attempted control of NIH was a factor in Rep. Madigan's initiation of NIH legislation during the summer of 1983. Data support the analysis that of all administrative agencies, the NIH consistently was regarded positively by Congress members, and this was reflected in ample funding levels on a consistent basis. Contrary to this usual positive regard was the negative situation between Rep. Dingell (D-MI) and the NIH. He had "captured" letters sent by NIH officials to research scientists asking them to lobby their Congress members for increased funding. Rep. Dingell reminded NIH officials that this activity violated law. Further, this situation led Rep. Dingell and other congresspeople to ask: Who was and who should be in charge of the NIH?

Eleventh, the interaction of Congress, administrative agencies, and the Office of Management and Budget (OMB) also influenced the political context. The congressional funding pattern identified in the 10th factor changed somewhat in the early 1980s. NIH officials became anxious when OMB dictated that NIH make a last-minute revised budget to honor a 1980 promise to fund 5000 new grants yearly. This mandated division of NIH's economic pie contributed to NIH officials' not wanting new research entities on their campus that would further erode current programs and projects. A second similar budgetary crisis occurred at NIH in Spring 1985 that again caused much consternation for NIH officials and research scientists.

Twelfth, the internal political dynamics of Congress also influenced this legislation. Rep. Waxman was a member of the congressional class of 1974, when the dynamic in Congress was a decentralization of power and an increasing congressional class. (A congressional class refers to that cohort of elected officials in a certain election.) The data revealed that Rep. Waxman was interested in gaining more power and control over NIH. Although his committee had authorizing power over NIH, it did not have the greater power of the appropriations committee that was responsible for funding. However, with his ability to authorize legislation, Rep. Waxman had leverage to gain more power. Waxman's attempt to micromanage NIH resulted in Rep. Madigan's initiating substitute policy.

Thirteenth, interaction between the White House and Congress affected the legislation. For example, President Reagan publicly vetoed the legislation in 1984, although he could have done it quietly by not signing the bill. This was done to alert Congress to expect conflict the following year if the bill's provisions were kept the same. An example of the negative relationship between the White House and Congress related to the override vote in 1985. Data showed that members of Congress (and many of the president's party) felt betrayed over their work on this legislation and over what they thought their communication had been with the president about passing this policy and putting it into effect. This sense of betrayal spurred their work in securing the veto override vote. Another example of the relationship between the White House and Congress was the number of presidential vetoes by President Reagan of congressional legislation and the few veto-override votes. Since his inauguration, President Reagan had vetoed 41 legislative bills; this override of the NIH bill veto was the fifth successful override vote since 1981 (Congressional Quarterly, 1985).

Fourteenth, even international political relations were a consideration. During Fall 1985, the Senate waited until the Geneva Summit was finished before beginning the veto-override vote. This was done to keep President Reagan from losing any credibility during the summit meeting because the Soviet leader would be aware of the veto-override vote.

Fifteenth, the skills and abilities of an interest group in furthering its intended policy had an influence on the context of legislation. Data revealed that in the early 1980s, many factors influenced the ability of the nurse interest group to promote this policy once it was on the agenda. These influences were: 1) the formation of the Tri-Council; 2) a special interest in public policy of the executive director of the National League for Nursing (NLN); 3) the coming need to reauthorize the Nurse Education Act; 4) many deans of nursing education programs who were policy oriented; 5) a combination of people who saw the need; 6) much networking by nurses; (7) the presence of highly motivated people who were interested in furthering the nurse profession; 8) nurses appointed to positions within the White House; 9) more nurses working on the Hill; and 10) the study conducted by Dr. Joanne Stevenson (personal communication, 1990) on nurse researchers' inability to obtain NIH grants. These 10 factors were obtained from interview data. Many of these influences demonstrate the increased numbers of nurses who were active in policy and politics in many dimensions and in many places: state and national governmental levels, professional associations, executive and legislative branches of the government, schools of nursing, and networking circles. Further, the research by Dr. Stevenson had shown that nurses had an increased opportunity of receiving NIH grants when they omitted their RN credential on their grant and only listed their PhD.

Sixteenth, the adage that "all politics is personal" influenced the legislation at various points. Data revealed the importance of personal relationships in getting the idea on the agenda, in gaining strategic information, in sharing needed information, and in making requests. For example, strategic networking at certain cocktail parties helped, as did carpooling with selected political actors. Savvy nurse leaders facilitated other nurses meeting with legislators and legislative aides in these settings so nurses could lobby effectively. The importance of congressional staffers to the initiation and passage of legislation must be noted. Several interviewees spoke of the importance of certain staffers in their tenacity to ensure that the NCNR amendment was passed. Other staffers noted the importance of the professional education background and socialization of staffers in influencing the types of policy options that are initiated and worked on with vigor. Interview data attested to the tenacity of one Capitol Hill staffer during the conference committee.

Two of Bobrow and Dryzek's (1987) five contextual dimensions were in evidence and contributed to the success of this policy, both because the NCNR was passed as legislation in 1985 and because the NCNR became a national institute of nursing research in 1993. The two criteria are related in this instance: the control of design by an actor or group of actors and the stability of policy actors over time. Once this policy was on the agenda and once nurses were united, the nurse interest group was committed to it. The nurse interest group showed unity in working with Rep. Madigan and staying the course. Although there were other policy alternatives discussed, they were never vigorously pursued by the nurse interest group. Once the compromise for NCNR was made in 1985, the nurse interest group found it acceptable because they knew they had a "foot in the door" and because they planned to accomplish their original design (an NINR) at a later date.

Stability of Policy Actors

The second dimension, stability of policy actors, also relates to the nurse interest group. This group of nurse leaders was stable for over a decade and kept tenaciously to its goal. Although the policy arrived on the formal agenda because of Rep. Madigan, a very stable group of nurse actors worked for over a decade to see that the original policy design eventually was enacted (change from an NCNR to an NINR).

May (1991) writes that regardless of how one defines policy design, there is the "emphasis on matching content of a given policy to the political context in which the policy is formulated and implemented" (p. 188). This statement describes the contextual dimension of how this public policy arrived on the formal agenda. Rep. Madigan was going to introduce substitute legislation for Rep. Waxman's NIH bill. Rep. Madigan's NINR amendment was based on an appraisal of what policy content would best work in that political context.

Ingraham and White wrote: "Politics can influence both design process and design outcome in a number of ways. It can constrain problem definition and the range of alternative solutions available for consideration. . . . It can, in fact, eliminate the process of design altogether" (1988–1989, p. 316). Data indicate that this happened. Partisan and reelection politics influenced the design process, specifically the policy option that was chosen (the NINR proposal). That policy option moved quickly to the formal agenda, where it then moved forward in the legislative process. The politics of that option kept other alternative solutions from being seriously considered. Thus, the politics of this situation influenced the design process and the selection of the policy option and constrained the availability of other policy alternatives.

Schneider and Ingram Model

In addition to the political context emphasis, Schneider and Ingram (1991, 1993a, 1993b) specifically push for empirical research that studies the social construction of target populations (those groups affected by the policy). They propose that one can best understand agenda setting, alternative formulation, and implementation by knowing how elected officials perceive different target populations; in other words, by knowing the "social construction"—images, symbols, and traits—of such populations.

In their beginning work in this area, Schneider and Ingram proposed a theory in which there is a continuum of target populations categorized as the advantaged, contenders, dependents, and deviants. Their model suggests that there are pressures to initiate beneficial policy that help those groups that are seen positively, while groups that are seen negatively will receive punitive policy. They argue that groups that are viewed positively are the "advantaged" and the "dependents," while the negatively perceived groups are the "contenders" and the "deviants." This is a beginning categorization, and they call for empirical research in this area. They admit that their theory needs three items:

1. A definition of target populations and of social constructions.
2. An explanation of how social constructions influence public officials in choosing agendas and designs of policy.
3. An explanation of how policy agendas and designs influence the political orientations and participation patterns of target populations.

The Schneider and Ingram theory, together with Kingdon's research, provide the best explanation for understanding the process of the NCNR legislation. Schneider and Ingram (1991, 1993a, 1993b) say that one can best understand agenda setting, alternative formulation, and implementation by knowing how elected officials see different target populations and by knowing the social construction, or images, symbols, and traits, of such populations. The data consistently revealed that this NCNR policy was initiated by Rep. Madigan because of the social construction of this target population. Proposing public policy for this target population would help him pass his substitute NIH legislation. Nurses, as a target population, would be on the continuum of positively viewed groups. Although Schneider and Ingram acknowledge that theirs is an emerging model that needs empirical testing to refine and define several of its phenomena, this author found it to be of explanatory value and extreme importance.

Mueller (1988) wrote: "Politicians must be convinced that they will gain from new policies—either through political success or through program effectiveness" (p. 443). The selection of nurses as a target population when Congress members, especially Republicans, needed the female vote contributed to a convincing argument for potential political success for them.

CONCLUSION

"No data are ever in themselves decisive. Factors beyond only the data help decide which policy is formulated or adopted by the people empowered to make the decision to form policy" (James, 1991, p. 14). James is referring to data in a problem stream as described by Kingdon. The accuracy of this quote was seen in this research because the Schneider and Ingram theory of the "social construction of target populations," together with the Kingdon model and the contextual dimension, explained the policy process.

The contextual dimension influenced all aspects of the policy, from agenda setting in 1983 through policy redesign in 1991, with passage of the amended legislation in 1993 that accomplished the original 1983 goal. The importance of studying the political context was demonstrated by the 17 contextual dimensions that influenced this legislative policy process.

Of particular explanatory value in the early agenda-setting and policy-alternative formulation of this legislation were the Schneider and Ingram model and the Kingdon model. The particular amendment was pursued because of application of the "social construction of target populations;" that is, the target population of nurses was chosen because they would help Rep. Madigan's and other Congress members' chances for reelection. With this model, the Kingdon theory adds to the further understanding of this legislation. Within Kingdon's model, neither the problem stream nor the policy stream was decisive for the process of this legislation; rather, it was the political stream. The factors of the political stream (reelection chances for Rep. Madigan and other congresspeople, partisan ideology in Congress, the public mood about gender issues, and turf concerns between government agencies) all strongly influenced the setting of this issue on the agenda. The hypotheses supported by this empirical research include: that policy is more likely to be initiated for those target populations who are positively viewed by members of Congress; issues are more likely to reach the formal agenda when the political stream factors are related to positively viewed target populations; and policy process is best understood in a contextual perspective.

For APN scholars, these case studies contribute to an understanding of agenda setting and policy design by having evaluated the importance of the Schneider and Ingram model, the Kingdon model, policy design, and the contextual dimension to policy initiation, development, implementation, and policy redesign in the creation of the National Institute for Nursing Research and in a state issue relating to prenatal care policy for pregnant women who are not documented.

DISCUSSION POINTS AND ACTIVITIES

1. How did the Kingdon model explain the NCNR getting on the political agenda?
2. How can APNs become aware of factors in the problem stream to which Kingdon alluded?
3. What are examples of policy streams that APNs could be advancing relative to their practice?
4. How can APNs be involved in the political stream?
5. How can APNs anticipate windows of opportunity?

6. According to Schneider and Ingram, to which of the four target populations do nurses belong? Discuss the relevance to agenda setting.
7. What are ways that APNs can network with congressional members and their staffers?
8. How can APNs promote unity among themselves and with other nurses?
9. What current contextual dimensions can promote APN practice?
10. How can APNs use the Kingdon model and the Schneider and Ingram model?

For a full suite of assignments and additional learning activities, use the access code located in the front of your book to visit this exclusive website: http://go.jblearning.com/milstead. If you do not have an access code, you can obtain one at the site.

REFERENCES

Baumgartner, F. R., & Jones, B. D. (1993). *Agendas and instability in American politics.* Chicago: University of Chicago Press.

Bobrow, D. B., & Dryzek, J. S. (1987). *Policy analysis by design.* Pittsburgh, PA: University of Pittsburgh Press.

Bosso, C. J. (1992). Designing environmental policy. *Policy Currents, 2*(4), 1, 4–6.

Cantelon, P. (2010). *National Institute of Nursing Research history book.* Washington, DC: NIH Publishers.

Cobb, R. W., & Elder, C. D. (1983). *Participation in America: The dynamics of agenda-building* (2nd ed.). Baltimore: Johns Hopkins University Press.

Congressional Quarterly (1985, July 27), p. 1493. Washington, DC: U.S. Printing Office.

DeBack, V. (1990). Public policy—nursing needs health policy leaders. *Journal of Professional Nursing, 6*(2), 69.

deLeon, P. (1988–1989). The contextual burdens of policy design. *Policy Studies Journal, 17*(2), 297–309.

Dohler, M. (1991). Policy networks, opportunity structures, and neo-conservative reform strategies in health policy. In B. Main and R. Mayntz (Eds.), *Policy networks: Empirical evidence and theoretical considerations* (pp. 235–296). Frankfurt am Main: Campus Verlag.

Dryzek, J. S. (1983). Don't toss coins in garbage cans: A prologue to policy design. *Journal of Public Policy, 3*(4), 345–368.

Edmunds, M. (2003). Advocating for NPs: Go and do likewise. *The Nurse Practitioner, 28*(2), 56.

Hedge, D. M., & Mok, J. W. (1987). The nature of policy studies: A content analysis of policy journal articles. *Policy Studies Journal, 16*(1), 49–62.

Ingraham, P. W. (1987). Toward more systematic consideration of policy design. *Policy Studies Journal, 15*(4), 611–628.

Ingraham, P. W., & White, J. (1988–1989). The design of civil service reform: Lessons in politics and rationality. *Policy Studies Journal, 17*(2), 315–330.

James, P. (1991). Bravo to the nursing emphasis on policy research. *Reflections, 17*(1), 14–15.

Kingdon, J. W. (1995). *Agendas, alternatives, and public policies.* New York: Harper Collins College Publishers.

Laumann, E. O., Heinz, J. P., Nelson, R., & Salisbury, R. (1991). Organizations in political action: Representing interests in national policy making. In B. Marin and R. Mayntz (Eds.), *Policy networks: Empirical evidence and theoretical considerations,* (pp. 63–96). Frankfurt am Main: Campus Verlag.

Lowi, T. J. (1992). The state in political science: How we become what we study. *American Political Science Review, 86*(1), 1.

Lowney, C. (2009). *Heroic living.* Chicago: Loyola Press.

Makinson, L. (1992). Political contributions from the health and insurance industries. *Health Affairs, 11*(4), 120–134.

May, P. J. (1991). Reconsidering policy design: Policies and publics. *Journal of Public Policy, 11*(2), 187–206.

Mueller, K. J. (1988). Federal programs to expire: The case of health planning. *Public Administration Review, 48*(3), 719–725.

Nagelkerk, J. M., & Henry, B. (1991). Leadership through policy research. *Journal of Nursing Administration, 21*(5), 20–24.

Raudonis, B. M., & Griffith, H. (1991). A model for integrating health services, research, and health care policy formation. *Nursing & Health Care, 12*(1), 32–36.

Schneider, A., & Ingram, H. (1991). The Social Construction of target populations: Implications for citizenship and democracy. Paper presented at the annual meeting of the American Political Science Association in Washington, DC.

Schneider, A. L., & Ingram, H. (1993a). How the social construction of target populations contributes to problems in policy design. *Policy Currents, 3*(1), 1–4.

Schneider, A. & Ingram, H. (1993b). Social construction of target populations: Implications for politics and policy. *American Political Science Review, 87*(2), 334–347.

Stoddard, M. (December 29, 2010). Vigil blames fund loss in infant deaths. *Omaha World Herald,* 2B.

Warner, J. R. (2003). A phenomenological approach to political competence: Stories of nurse activists. *Policy, Politics, and Nursing Practice, 4*(2), 135–143.

CHAPTER 3

Government Response: Legislation

Politics: Playing the Game

Janice Kay Lanier

"Politics is the art of problem solving."

—JONAH GOLDBERG, EDITOR-AT-LARGE, *NATIONAL REVIEW ONLINE*

KEY TERMS

Constituents: Residents of a geographic area who can vote for a candidate and whom the elected official represents.

Interest group: An organized group with a common cause that works to influence the outcome of laws, regulations, or programs.

Lobbyist: An individual who works to influence legislators and other governmental decision makers.

Political action committee (PAC): A formal organization that exists to engage in a process through which candidates for political office are endorsed and otherwise supported. It must adhere to state and/or federal laws in carrying out its activities.

INTRODUCTION

For many nurses, "politics" is a dirty word; it is the seamy side of the policymaking process that they prefer to ignore. Unfortunately, participating in the political aspects of policymaking is not an optional exercise. In many respects, such participation is key to ensuring nurses have a place at the policy table. Before one can influence policy, one has to be in the room where policy is being debated and developed—policy is made by those who show up, not necessarily by people with special expertise, and the usual way into the room is through the door labeled "political participation and savvy." Even nurses who do see the need for political participation are somewhat naïve as to exactly what that participation entails and how to do it effectively. In part, it means playing the political game by the rules—even distasteful rules—at least until nurses have sufficient presence and clout to be able to affect the rules themselves. This chapter is intended to provide insight into the subtle rules governing political participation and set out the options available to nurses for finding their way through the political maze.

POLITICAL INVOLVEMENT: OPTION VERSUS OBLIGATION

"If you're not at the table, you're on the menu."

—SUSAN CLARK, RN, LOBBYIST (PATTERSON, 2011, P. 1)

Nurses are part of a regulated profession in a regulated industry. One cannot become a nurse without meeting the requirements set forth in state laws. These laws contain the statutory definition of nursing practice; licensure requirements and exceptions to those requirements; grounds for discipline and penalties for violating the law; and numerous other provisions. Once one meets the requirements to be called a registered nurse or advanced practice nurse, the law (both state and federal) goes on to define payment mechanisms, establish staffing expectations, identify acceptable professional relationships, etc. These laws, which permeate the practice of nursing and health care in general, are made in political arenas in Washington, D.C., and in state legislatures across the country.

Despite the key role of the political process in their professional lives, most nurses characterize political activism as something for others to do. Politics somehow seems far removed from their everyday reality or experience and is seen as something that interferes with what is really important—caring for patients safely and effectively. Although many nurses decry political involvement, in reality, it is not an option, but a professional obligation. In other words, some level of political participation and political savvy are just as crucial to a nurse's practice as knowledge of pharmacology, physiology, and psychology.

Not surprisingly, nurses' attitudes with respect to political participation have hampered the profession's ability to be viewed by key policymakers as a powerful political force, even in matters dealing with healthcare reform. "Nurses don't show up" is the phrase used by many legislators to describe nurses' participation in the legislative process. Interestingly, the general public believes that nurses and nursing's interests were underrepresented when healthcare reform was debated in Washington in 2009. Nurses no doubt agree with the public's assertion; however, agreeing alone does not ensure a greater role for nurses in future debates. To secure a meaningful place at the policy table, nurses will have to embrace their profession's political side and make the politically-savvy nurse the rule rather than the exception.

Documents setting out professional obligations and expectations for nurses unequivocally agree on the importance of political participation. *Nursing's Social Policy Statement* includes in the elements of the profession's social contract the following statements:

- Public policy and the health care delivery system influence the health and well-being of society and professional nursing.
- Individual responsibility and inter-professional involvement are essential (American Nurses Association, 2010, p. 7).

The statement identifies one of the essential features of professional nursing as the "influence on social and public policy to promote social justice" (p. 9). The *Code of Ethics for Nurses* (American Nurses Association, 2010) alludes throughout to the role nurses play in promoting, advocating, and striving to protect the health, safety, and rights of the patient. This responsibility is not limited to the immediate surroundings in which nursing care is provided, but extends to statehouses, boardrooms, and other arenas in which this advocacy can affect public policy relative to health care and, ultimately, patient outcomes.

Finally, the *Future of Nursing* report issued by the Institute of Medicine in 2010 states that "nurses should be full partners with physicians and other healthcare professionals, in redesigning health care in the United States" (p. S-3). This role will be played out, in part, in the health policy context where nurses should participate in, and sometimes lead, decision-making and be engaged in healthcare reform-related implementation efforts. To be ready to assume this responsibility, nurse education programs should include course content addressing leadership-related competencies for all nurses. These competencies include a firm grounding in politics and policy-making processes.

POLITICS—WHAT IS IT REALLY?

"Politics in a real sense is the people who take the time to participate."

—SEN. DANIEL INOUYE (D-HI)

What is politics? "Politics is a process that includes not only that which is typically associated with political functions (e.g., government, police, workers' unions), but also that which is involved in the regulation, structure, and action of all individuals' behavior" (O'Bryne & Holmes, 2009, p. 155). As political scientists have noted, politics underlies the process through which groups of people make decisions. It is the basis for the authoritative allocation of value. When someone or something has the power to hand out things that are desirable, who gets what, when, and how is determined by politics. In order to be a beneficiary of this largess, people must successfully jump into the political fray.

Although politics is generally associated with behaviors and interactions within civil governments, the essence of politics is applicable to other group relationships— social relations involving authority and power, or methods and tactics used to formulate and apply policy. As long-time U.S. Senator Daniel Inouye (D-HI) acknowledged, "Politics . . . is the people who take time to participate" (Lanier, 1985, p. 166). When one "plays politics," one is considered to be shrewd or prudent in practical matters, tactful, and diplomatic; playing politics is also seen as being contrived in a shrewd and practical way, or being expedient.

There is nothing particularly sinister about these descriptions; however, when one probes current popular electronic sources, the less positive aspects of the political process surface. Linking words such as "intrigue" and "control" to "political power" and governmental functions subtly sends a message that there is something unsavory about politics. When one plays politics, one engages in political intrigue to take advantage of a situation or issue; exploits an option or relationship; and/or deals with people in an opportunistic, manipulative, or devious way. These latter perceptions are what cause politics to be seen as one of the less savory societal activities that many people (especially nurses) go out of their way to avoid.

Nursing practice itself has many tasks or activities associated with it that are seen as distasteful by the general public. Once nurses accept the premise that political participation is as integral to everyday practice as other nursing-related tasks, they should simply don their protective gear and wade in! Before doing so, however, a bit of preparation is warranted.

Putting Politics in Perspective

Although the number of men in nursing has increased over the years (comprising approximately 6–7% of the total number of registered nurses [American Association of Colleges of Nursing, 2011]), the vast majority of nurses continue to be women. Women's struggle to achieve a place at the policymaking table has evolved and parallels the societal changes affecting women as a whole. Going from a largely subordinate role in a patriarchal society to prominent leadership roles in boardrooms (Lanier, 1985), women are now faced with more career choices than ever before. With that transition has come increased opportunities to fill power positions in the workplace and a more powerful presence overall. The suffrage movement in the 20th century gave women the right to vote, and a certain amount of attendant power outside of the workplace came along with that right. Whether women have made the most of that power over the years is debatable; however, political parties recently have become very aware of the importance of the women's vote and are making concerted efforts to win it. Because nursing remains largely a woman's profession, the forces affecting women are the same ones that affect how nurses will be received (and succeed) in the political arena.

With the economic down turn of the early 21st century, health care became one of the few growth industries in the bleak economy. Health care also re-emerged as the focus for one of the most significant policy debates facing the United States. Because of the financial stake state and federal governments have in health care, and the vast investment special interest groups have in the healthcare system, the reform efforts and attendant policymaking took on political overtones from the outset.

Politics and power go hand-in-hand. It's all about power relationships. Interestingly, the concept of "power" is changing as technology has flattened the world and lessened the importance of the traditional trappings of power—money, name, and job title. Despite these changes, power and the perceptions associated with it control political processes and outcomes. While the source of that power may vary, its essence does not.

Power does not exist in a vacuum. Every aspect of power implies a relationship between two or more people. There are varying degrees of power. Simply because someone is powerful in one situation does not mean that power translates to a different venue. Power takes on several forms—coercion, persuasion, and manipulation. Coercion depends on force for its effectiveness, persuasion involves the acceptance of positions put forth by one person without threats, and manipulation is the con man form of power. One can have power because of the position held or because of a special expertise that is needed in a particular situation. The amount or type of resources at one's disposal can determine how much power can be exerted and how that power will affect the relevant political relationships

Nurses most often use persuasion (or perhaps manipulation) rather than coercion to achieve their desired goals. To be an effective persuader, a certain amount of expertise is required not only with respect to the complex issues at hand, but also with respect to the processes and dynamics—the politics—that are at play. In the traditional context in which playing politics is seen as a means to manipulate governmental decisions, a fundamental understanding of the legislative process is important in order to wield or grasp a modicum of power. In other words, there is no substitute for expertise.

Passage of the Affordable Care Act in 2010 was only the beginning of what promises to be an ongoing debate that will affect the future of the nursing profession, as well as health care itself, in the years ahead. Who actually benefits is also the root of healthcare reform debates. Logically, nurses, by virtue of their numbers alone (making up the largest segment of the healthcare workforce), should have the potential to influence the far-reaching policy changes affecting health care; however, the extent of that influence has yet to be measured, and it will happen only if nurses are genuine payers in the political game. The public is certainly supportive of an increased role for nurses in these discussions and debates, thus giving nurses a power base from which to build. However, nurses, especially advanced practice nurses, must first seize the moment and take advantage of the unprecedented opportunities open to them.

Wading In: What Does It Look Like?

"There are two things one should never watch being made—sausage and laws."

—Anonymous

The tools of the legislative process include know-how, networks, and money. Know-how means one must be familiar with both the political processes and the people who are the actors on the political stage, but sadly, the majority of people cannot identify their federal, state, or local elected officials. While many can name the President of the United States, few will be able to say with assurance who represents them in the halls of Congress and fewer still can name their state senators or representatives. Effectiveness in the world of politics is not possible unless one knows who is in the game. Technology has made it easy to learn the identity of lawmakers at every level by simply going to federal or state websites and entering zip code data. These sites also provide brief biographical information, photos, and other pertinent and helpful background material.

Why is this important? Politics is at heart a people process and, like other people-centered endeavors, the relationships among and between people determine outcomes. Nurses are well aware of how important communication and personal connections are in the care-giving context, and those same principles also affect the world of politics. Knowing a state representative and being able to recognize him or her on sight, while also knowing something about the issues, are fundamental to producing solid relationships. Just as nurses realize the importance of establishing good rapport with clients, that same principle applies when establishing the connections needed to influence lawmakers.

In addition to knowing the people, one must also know the process—how laws are made. Most nurses complete a government course in high school and promptly disregard most of the subject matter because it holds little relevance for them at the time. While diagrams depicting "How a Bill Becomes a Law" are important, they are also very rudimentary (see **Figure 3-1**). There is much more to the process than can be neatly depicted on a chart.

Anatomy of Congress: There are 535 members: 100 senators (two from each state) and 435 House members. The party in control of the majority of seats holds considerable power:

- Setting legislative agenda
- Chairing all committees
- Identifying problems
- Identifying possible solutions that are more likely to be enacted

Each state will follow a similar pattern—two chambers, a senate, and a house (except in Nebraska where there is a unicameral system).

Bills are ideas that legislators have determined need to be ratified into law. The ideas can come from many sources: the legislator's own experiences, the issues brought forward by **constituents**, or by special **interest groups**. Once the idea is drafted into the proper bill format, it is introduced into the House or Senate, depending on the chamber to which the bill's chief sponsor belongs. (All budget bills are initiated in the House, as it was designed to be most representative of the average citizens' interests. Because of the importance of budgeting in regards to policymaking, it was given a primary role in the budget process.)

Once introduced, a bill is then referred to a standing committee for further consideration. These standing committees are generally subject-matter focused, so bills

Figure 3-1   How a bill passes through Congress.

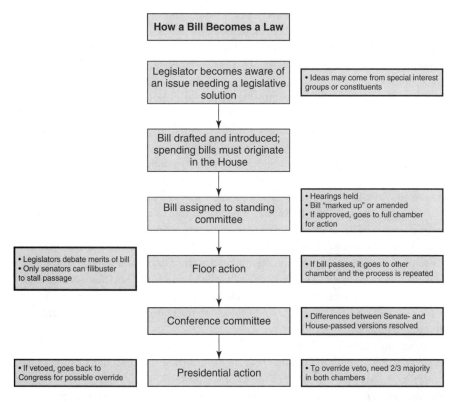

related to health care go to a health committee, finance issues to a banking committee, farm-related matters to the agriculture committee, and so on. Standing committees can be configured differently over time and subcommittees may be named to consider particular bills in greater detail. Committee hearings are important, but they often appear to be more chaotic than productive. Much of the real business of law making is conducted behind the scenes, but one must also participate in the defined processes to earn a place at the more informal behind-the-scenes-tables.

Committee chairs are extremely influential, particularly with respect to the subject matter areas that are the focus of the committee's work. Chairs determine what bills will be heard and when, and they establish the procedural framework under which the committee operates. The chair's position on an issue can determine its fate from the outset. Because of the extent of their power and influence, committee chairs are able to raise large sums of money from special interest groups to support their re-election, and re-election is always an important consideration for lawmakers. House and Senate leadership (elected by their colleagues) determine who will be named as committee chairs. Certain committees are seen as more prestigious than others, so being named the chair of one of those committees is even more important to an ambitious legislator. Not surprisingly, political considerations play a role in this entire process. Being aware of the dynamics that are the foundation of the overall committee process helps ensure more effective representation by those who want to influence the outcome of the committee's work.

If a bill is able to garner committee approval, it goes to the full chamber for a vote. The timing for scheduling a vote, as well as various attempts to amend the bill or delay the vote, are all integral parts of the lawmaking process. Much maneuvering occurs backstage and the ability to influence these less public interactions is as important as the words or concepts being debated. Again, peoples' relationships and politics determine the ultimate results. To be able to be effective in one's efforts to influence outcomes, one must be aware of these relationships and take them into account. Once a bill is approved in either the House or Senate, it must begin the process again in the other chamber. The chief executive (president or governor) must sign the bill before it can become law and all of this must happen within a single legislative cycle—two years. It is not surprising that it often takes several years for a particular legislative issue to finally become law, especially when the issue is not one that garners a lot of public interest or attention. The state and federal processes each have special nuances, but the overall process is similar for both, as are the people dynamics that affect each step of the process.

Given all the hidden factors that affect success on Capitol Hill or in state legislatures, how can an individual nurse hope to have sufficient knowledge or time to make a difference in the policymaking aspects of the profession? Fortunately, the American Nurses Association (ANA) and its state constituent associations, as well as specialty nursing groups, can provide their members with the tools they need to be successful. The success of these organizations' efforts in the legislative arena depends in large part on their members' involvement with and understanding the importance of an effective legislative presence on behalf of the profession in Washington, D.C., and in statehouses across the country. An individual nurse need only become a member of his/her professional association and then take advantage of the resources provided by these organizations to be part of the cadre of politically-active nurses who are taking seriously the obligations set forth in the profession's social policy statement and its code of ethics. These organizations keep nurses informed about what, why, and how things are happening, as well as help develop succinct messages to be conveyed to key lawmakers.

EFFECTIVE LOBBYING: A THREE-LEGGED STOOL

In addition to knowing the procedural aspects of lawmaking, nurses can also benefit from understanding the lesser known but equally important relational aspects of the process: the connections not depicted on any chart purporting to show how a bill becomes a law. Success in the legislative arena is much like a three-legged stool, with each leg essential to the sturdiness of the stool as a whole. The first leg is the formal lobbying effort provided by independent paid individuals, many of whom have close ties with elected and appointed officials. Leg number two is the grassroots leg, and the third leg is the political leg—the one that actively tries to influence the outcome of elections.

Leg One: Professional Lobbyists

No bill becomes law without lobbyists' input. Lobbying is the act of influencing—the art of persuading—a governmental entity to achieve a specific legislative or regulatory outcome. While anyone can lobby, **lobbyists** are most often individuals who represent special interest groups and are looked to as the experts by lawmakers who need information and rationale for supporting or not supporting a particular issue. The role of lobbyists has become even more critical as the complexity of legislation has increased; for example, the 1914 law creating the Federal Trade Commission was a total of eight pages, the Social Security Act of 1935 totaled 28 pages, and the Financial Reform bill (conference version) of 2010 contained 2,319 pages (Brill, 2010). Legislators, often pressed for time, rely on lobbyists' expertise to help them understand what they are voting for or against.

> *On September 18, 1793, President George Washington laid the cornerstone for the U.S. Capitol. While the shovel, trowel, and marble gavel used for the ceremony are still displayed, repeated efforts to locate the cornerstone itself have been unsuccessful.*
>
> *At times, policymaking seems as shrouded in mystery as the location of the Capitol's cornerstone. That's why you need an experienced partner (a.k.a. lobbyist) to help you unravel the mystery.*
>
> —A pitch for Capitol Tax Partners, a lobbying firm

According to the Center for Responsive Politics, there were 10,404 federal lobbyists in 1998; in 2010, there were 12,488. While this number represents a decrease from a high of 14,869 in 2007, the number of lobbyists has significantly increased over the years. In 1998, $1.44 billion was spent on lobbying; in 2010, the total was $2.61 billion, again down from $3.49 billion spent in 2009. Nevertheless, this represents a general increase overall. The American Nurses Association reported spending $1,197,342 on its lobbying efforts, utilizing the services of six lobbyists. The American Hospital Association, on the other hand, spent $13,585,000 and employed 72 lobbyists, many of whom were categorized as "revolving door" lobbyists, or individuals who left positions in the legislative or regulatory arenas for typically more lucrative private sector employment. (The revolving door provides an entry and connections that are invaluable to a lobbyist and the special interests he/she represents. The more revolving door lobbyists an organization employs, the better connected it is to the inner workings of Capitol Hill.)

The willingness of entities to invest the level of resources associated with lobbying efforts is indicative of how important the connections forged by lobbyists are to the reputations of the interest groups, and to their ability to get the job done. Members of special interest groups expect legislative success, and that success comes with a price. Tellingly, it is a price many nurses are reluctant to embrace. Nurses must be more aware of the key role that lobbyists play and be willing to support the lobbying efforts of professional associations by becoming members of these organizations. Success in the halls of Congress and at statehouses is integral to the advancement of the profession itself and its societal values. Nurses want their legislative agenda advanced successfully, and that expectation comes with a price tag that only nurses can pay.

Leg Two: Grassroots Lobbyists

While the paid lobbyists are the ones who most commonly come to mind when thinking of lobbying efforts, the so-called grassroots lobbying can be more effective if appropriately organized and informed. Grassroots lobbyists are constituents who have the power to elect officials through their vote. When constituents have expertise and knowledge about a particular issue (such as nurses in the healthcare reform debates), they are especially valuable resources for their elected officials. While issues debated in Washington, D.C., are national in scope, members of Congress are still concerned about how the issue is perceived back home. The connections established by a nurse constituent with his/her lawmakers at the federal, state, and local levels may provide timely access and a listening ear at key points during the policymaking process. To be effective, grassroots lobbyists must recognize that getting a law passed can take many years and entails compromise and commitment, along with an understanding of the political forces at work. In addition to employing paid lobbyists, professional nurse organizations have become increasingly aware of the strength of grassroots lobbying—seen by some as the most effective of all lobbying efforts (deVries & Vanderbilt, 1992).

Many state-level associations have established legislative liaison programs that match legislators with a nurse constituent from their districts, then provide nurses the tools needed to become an effective resource for the legislator. The American Nurses Association has also initiated similar efforts, as have other specialty nursing organizations at the federal level. These kinds of relationships take time to develop, but they provide both tangible and intangible benefits if diligently nurtured. An individual nurse who is willing to serve in a liaison capacity can markedly increase a legislator's understanding of nursing and the role nurses play in health care. With increased understanding, the legislator is more apt to be supportive of the profession's legislative agenda.

Before embarking on a lobbying effort, it is important to be aware of ethics laws as they relate to lobbying. Most states have strict reporting requirements, along with restrictions that apply to the use of funds and gifts to influence legislators. These laws generally are targeted at the paid lobbyists rather than grassroots efforts, but because each state defines "lobbying" differently when determining when the ethics laws apply, it is important to review the relevant statutes so as to avoid unwanted surprises later. State nurses associations can provide guidance on this matter.

There is no substitute for visibility in the legislative arena. Showing up is what political activism is all about, and showing up is the essence of lobbying. Building trusting relationships, demonstrating interest and concern for the public good, and providing information on issues important to the nursing profession are all things that can be done through regular participation in all aspects of the legislative process. Grassroots lobbying has been described by some as a "contact sport" (Patterson, 2011, p. 1), with the contacts taking various forms, such as in-person visits (the most effective), personally written letters, fax messages, phone calls, and emails.

Grassroots initiatives can put additional pressure on lawmakers if done well; however, it is not without its risks. Promising to unleash a firestorm of support or opposition to a measure is only effective if the people making up the grassroots actually respond. Promising and not delivering a grassroots campaign affects credibility and actually weakens the interest group's overall influence. When the grassroots response is a message that is repeated verbatim (as with form letters or computerized email messages), it becomes clear that the effort is not a spontaneous outpouring of individuals' sentiments and, therefore, is not the most effective approach. Volume does matter—legislators will ask how many letters or phone calls have been received either supporting or opposing the particular issue—but the best communication includes at least something about the writer's personal experiences with the matter being legislated.

Effective communication tips:

Written:

- Communication should be typed, no longer than two pages and addressing no more than two issues.
- State the purpose of the communication at the beginning.
- Present clear, compelling rationale for the position(s) being advocated.

- When expressing disappointment about a past vote or position, do so respectfully.

Verbal:

- Identify up front the amount of time allocated for the meeting.
- Avoid too much small talk that eats up the allotted time, but take advantage of any shared connections or experiences that might enhance rapport.
- Time should be structured so that the issue can be presented succinctly.
- Do not assume the legislator or aide has the same amount of expertise as you do on the subject, and do not get too complex in your explanations.
- Provide a one-page summary at the end that highlights key points.
- Always send a follow-up note or letter after a meeting, thanking the legislator and/or aide for speaking with you. Always reiterate the points you made during the discussion.

While most people think of lawmaking when considering how policy is made, regulation and rule making are equally important to nursing's agenda. Regulations are made by executive branch agencies in accordance with the somewhat complex administrative procedures acts passed by lawmakers. While the processes vary from state to state, the relationship considerations apply equally to the enactment of laws and the adoption of regulations. One must know the process and the people and establish a reputation as a trustworthy, reliable resource in order to be an effective voice for the profession.

The relationships at issue are not limited to elected officials. Rather, a savvy lobbyist—whether professional or grassroots—knows the value of establishing connections with staff members and legislative aides working for lawmakers, as well as with other lobbyists from various special interest groups. These latter relationships frequently can be more important than direct contact with the legislators themselves. Timing is often the key to success, and having a timely "heads-up" about what is transpiring behind the scenes can mean the difference between success and failure. The connections with staff and other lobbyists are frequently the source for the kinds of tips and gossip that define and redefine strategies for advancing one's agenda.

No lawmaker can be an expert on every issue; therefore, they have grown increasingly reliant on professional staff members to serve as their eyes, ears, and often spokespersons. This is true for state legislators as well. Staff members frequently have political/constituent ties to the legislator.

Congressional staff members include:

- Chief of staff or administrative assistant with oversight responsibilities
- Legislative directors responsible for day-to-day legislative activities
- Press secretary
- Legislative assistants (LAs) who are responsible for specific legislative issues. For example, the health LA may also work on education and Social Security issues. LAs are very influential because of the role they play in the lawmaker's daily activities. The LA may "staff" the congressperson at committee hearings and prepare the member's statements and questions for witnesses. They accompany the legislator to meetings with lobbyists and constituents and are often the gatekeepers who funnel information and opinions. The LA also works with the office called the Legislative Council to draft bill language that includes the policy concepts identified by the lawmaker. The LA is someone a nurse should cultivate and work through.

Committee staff: These individuals support the work of congressional committees. Separate staff members are allocated to the majority and minority parties, with a larger number serving the majority party. Committee staff members have a narrower focus than the legislator's personal staff and are typically older and more experienced. Their duties include:

- Planning committee agendas
- Coordinating hearing schedules and witnesses
- Preparing legislation for committee and floor action
- Gathering and analyzing data
- Drafting committee reports
- Working cooperatively with their counterparts in the other chamber

It is best not to wait until there is an important bill pending to begin developing relationships. Regular contact with legislator offices and staff members to convey interest in the activities and issues they are dealing with and volunteering to serve on committees and task forces can help to develop name recognition, credibility, and trust.

A successful lobbying initiative depends on several additional relational components that are particularly relevant to nurses:

- *Unity:* Divisiveness within the profession is a certain road to defeat and fuels the opposition's fire. Opponents are well aware of the potential impact a united nursing profession could have on health policy decisions and other important issues. Nurse's numbers alone are formidable. For that reason, competing interests subtly and purposefully poke at the hot spots that typically divide nurses (e.g., educational preparation; union vs. non-union). Nurses often align themselves within specialty practice groups and are willing to lobby only when an issue relevant to that particular group is being considered. Ideally, all nurses should have a basic understanding or awareness of the legislative initiatives of specialty groups. They should actively support the initiatives of their colleagues, or, at a minimum, refrain from opposing the cause publicly; instead, concerns should be shared privately in hopes of working towards a compromise position.

- *Outreach:* Nurses have often been too insular in devising legislative strategies. Instead they should seek and define bases of support external to the profession. Identify groups and individuals who have something to gain if the cause is successful or something to lose if it is not. Groups may include consumers, other licensed professionals, and special interest groups such as AARP.

- *Timing:* There are windows of opportunity for a political agenda to move forward. Sometimes it is important to wait for the right climate or the right moment to proceed. Nurses often become impatient when their well-meaning advocacy, which often is intended to improve the public's health, seems to fall on deaf ears. Patience and timing are essential to success. Because of the critical nature of timing, it is often important to be ready to respond at a moment's notice. It is also important to be aware of the general environment in which an issue is being considered. For example, when a state is facing significant budget shortfalls or the nation is headed towards unfathomable deficits, it would not be a good time to try to move a costly program forward without identifying a credible, sustainable funding stream. During periods of reform, there is a stronger likelihood that change can be made.

The legislative process is an evolving one, founded on compromise. Settling for part of an initiative may be the best way to eventually achieve the entire goal. Willingness to persevere and keep returning to the legislature year after year, if necessary, is essential. New faces are chosen at each election and the volatility of the entire political arena can result in major philosophical changes in a relatively short time.

Leg Three: The Role of Money

The final leg of the stool is the one that causes much discomfort and concern to nurses and others: money. Politics in its most primitive form is on display when considering how money influences who wins or loses an election. The amount of money that flows to and through the legislative process has raised serious questions as to whether the whole process is "For Sale" to whoever has the deepest pockets. Unfortunately, winning an election or re-election, even at the local level, can be a very expensive proposition costing millions of dollars. The total spending by political parties, candidates, and issue groups for the mid-term elections in 2010 is estimated to have exceeded $4 billion—a trend that is likely to continue in light of the recent United States Supreme Court decision in *Citizens United v. Federal Election Commission* (2010).

Not only has the amount of money flowing to campaigns increased dramatically, the source of those dollars (who has the deep pockets) has also changed and is expected to change even more in the future. For example, American Crossroads GPS (the brainchild of Republican strategists Karl Rove and Ed Gillespie, both of whom held influential staff positions under former President George W. Bush), American Action Network, Republican Governors Association, and the Chamber of Commerce are groups based in Washington, D.C., that financed state races across the country on behalf of Republican interests in 2010. On the Democratic side, organized labor, EMILY's List, and the League of Conservation Voters continue to contribute millions to fund campaign messages (Crowley, 2010). While these groups may appear to operate independently of each other, in actuality "coordination is as easy as walking across the hall" of their shared office space (p. 31). How this evolving dynamic will affect future elections and alliances remains to be seen, but its existence cannot be ignored or under estimated.

> The Court in its *Citizens United* ruling struck down the 2002 federal campaign finance law prohibiting unions and corporations from spending money directly advocating for or against candidates. The First Amendment was the basis for the Court's decision. The League of Women Voters has voiced its support of legislation that would require disclosure of the sources of the spending that is now legal and basically unlimited as long as the efforts are not coordinated with an individual's campaign.

The need to raise the kind of money in question often discourages potential candidates and gives greater influence to special interest groups that are able to generate large sums of money from members and supporters. Re-election is essential to maintaining incumbency and the opportunity to continue to affect policymaking; therefore, re-election considerations become important almost as soon as the oath of office is administered. Raising money is a year-round expectation, with political party leaders putting pressure on their ranks to meet ambitious fundraising goals. Success in these endeavors often determines who will be elected to leadership positions in the House and Senate and appointed as committee chairs. Incumbents have a significant edge in the fundraising race, which further disadvantages newcomers and ultimately affects election results. For example, in the 2008 election, the odds of a challenger beating an incumbent if the challenger spent under $1 million were 302:1. If the challenger were able to spend $2 million or more the odds changed to 14:9. Contrast that to the 1998 election cycle, when a non-incumbent who spent $500,000 or more had an even chance of victory (Center for Responsive Politics, 2010).

While the convergence of politics and money is not always pretty, ignoring the importance of financial contributions to moving ones' legislative agenda forward is naïve at best and will ultimately undermine efforts to advance the positive aspects of the nursing profession's agenda. Nurses, like all other citizens, need to know at least the basics of what is happening in the political arena with respect to funding political campaigns. Because of the importance of political contributions, nurses should also provide financial support to those entities that are able to make strategic political contributions on their behalf. Unfortunately, when accounting for political contributions to federal candidates in 2010, contributions from nursing-focused groups ranked far below those of other healthcare-related interest groups. For example, according to information compiled by the Center for Responsive Politics, based on reports from the Federal Elections Commission as of April 25, 2011, the highest amount contributed to federal candidates in 2010 by a healthcare PAC (the National Association of Community Pharmacists) was $1,719,403. The American Nurses Association's contributions totaled only $582,911 during that same time frame (Center for Responsive Politics, 2011). It should therefore come as no surprise that organized nursing interests are at a disadvantage when trying to gain the ear of legislative decision-makers. Were it not for other sources of power—numbers and the general trusted reputation of the nursing profession—trying to gain a seat at the policy table would be an elusive aspiration at best.

Despite the need to know, following the money can be a difficult task: however, thanks to technology, it is not an impossible undertaking. State/county governmental websites include the campaign finance reports filed by political parties and candidates on the local level, and the Center for Responsive Politics (http://www.opensecrets.org) is a good resource for federal election funds. The first step is simply to gain an understanding of the critical role money plays in the process. While it may seem to undermine the integrity of policymaking, ignoring this reality will ensure frustration and likely failure.

Along with the money component of this leg of the stool, special interest groups also affect election outcomes by endorsing candidates running for office. Candidates who want to demonstrate their appeal to the overall electorate prize these endorsements; this is particularly true for endorsements issued by nurse organizations such as the

American Nurses Association on the federal level and state constituent associations of ANA on the state level. This level of political activity occurs through the associations' **political action committees (PACs)**. Federal and state election laws contain many requirements and restrictions a PAC must follow. For example, in order to participate in federal candidate advocacy, a federal PAC must be established and reporting requirements and contribution levels set forth in federal law adhered to. Similarly, if an organization wishes to endorse candidates seeking state office, it must set up a state PAC and follow state election laws. Generally, a federal PAC endorses candidates seeking a federal office such as the presidency or a congressional office, while state PACs focus on candidates running for state-wide offices such as governor, attorney general, secretary of state, and state legislative bodies. An endorsement may include monetary support for the campaign, or simply a publicized communication of support. According to Gallup's annual Honesty and Ethics survey released in December 2010, nurses continued to be recognized as the most trusted profession by the general public (Gallup, 2010); therefore, an endorsement from a nursing organization has value that transcends money.

Typically, organizations issuing endorsements have a process for doing so that can be fairly complex and usually involves a screening component. Decisions are based on criteria that take into consideration the political climate, the political index (the ratio of Republicans to Democrats to Independents in the district), the voting record of incumbents, and other intangible factors. While candidate endorsements can enhance an organization's perceived power, the decisions are not without risks both internally and externally. Externally, endorsing the "wrong" candidate—the loser—can have repercussions when trying to gain support for a legislative initiative from the elected official—the unendorsed winner—once the election is over. Internally, members of endorsing organizations who are unhappy about an endorsement decision may cancel their membership as a sign of protest, thus weakening the power in numbers that is especially important for nursing organizations.

Elections are inherently a partisan process where political party labels do matter. Nurses are not all Republicans or all Democrats, and the partisan nature of candidate endorsements is often distasteful and misunderstood. Endorsements, regardless of the political party of the candidate, are useful tools on several levels, however. First, exposing candidates to issues important to the nursing profession during the endorsement screening process is a way to educate potential lawmakers about these issues. Candidates are introduced to nurses who may be looked to as resources in the future when healthcare issues arise. Additionally, candidates who may not be particularly well versed about the complexities of the healthcare system receive information from a nursing perspective that they may not get elsewhere. Finally, an endorsement is not a directive to vote for a particular candidate, but serves as one more tool voters can use when making their own decisions. For nurses, an endorsement sends a signal that the candidate has participated in the screening process and appears to be someone nurses should seriously consider. Before reacting negatively to an endorsement decision made by a nursing organization, nurses should contact the organization to obtain more information as to why the decision was made. Voicing concerns to the decision-makers is productive, while cancelling membership serves only to undermine the profession's power base.

In addition to being aware of the inter-relational aspects of the legislative and political processes, it is also important to understand some of the labels attached to those who are players on the political stage. It is especially important when the labels mean different things to different people. For example, "One of the most incendiary words in today's political lexicon is *progressive*" (Moser, 2010, p. A-11). Members of the liberal wing of the Democratic Party use this term proudly, while conservatives use it as a term of reproach. For liberals, the word means "a set of policies (that) were attempts to address real problems that emerged in the development of an urban, industrial society. These policies have brought about immense tangible improvements in the lives of ordinary Americans" (Moser, p. A-11). Conservatives believe progressivism is an ideology that ignores the principles of limited government, separation of powers, and even unalienable individual rights that are the principles underlying the foundation of the United States. "The complexities of day-to-day operations of government make it necessary to take the operations out of the hands of the people themselves and entrust it instead to trained experts" (Moser, p. A-11) is a belief attributed to Liberals that Conservatives liken to fascism. According to Moser, "The problem is both sides are right, but neither seems willing to consider the other's definition" (p. A-11). Whether we can have a real national conversation or will simply continue to engage in the shouting match is unclear; however, some of the trends that are evolving make it more important than ever for all participants to speak the same language.

TRENDS AND TOOLS

Trends

I had endured plenty of rough politics in Texas. I had seen Dad and Bill Clinton derided by their opponents and the media. Abraham Lincoln was compared to a baboon. Even George Washington became so unpopular that political cartoons showed the hero of the American Revolution being marched to a guillotine. Yet the death spiral of decency during my time in office, exacerbated by the advent of twenty-four hour cable news and hyper-partisan political blogs, was deeply disappointing. The toxic atmosphere in American politics discourages good people from running for office. (Bush, 2010, p. 120)

Whether today's political climate is really nastier than in the past is debatable. "Perhaps the 19th-century political cartoons and stump speeches were uglier than anything seen today" ("In Search of Civility," 2010, p. A10), but today's technology enables these attacks to be more powerful because they spread "farther, faster, and linger longer" (p. A10). In addition to fueling what can be characterized as bully-like behavior, the power of technology gives more opportunity for citizen groups to develop, grow, and spread their message. The Tea Party movement is one such group, but others such as the "no labels" group are springing up. The trend of more citizen action is likely to continue, with its actual impact yet to be determined.

The Tea Party is characterized as a "conservative revolt" that is shaking up the Republican Party; however, the Democratic Party is not immune from the forces of unrest and frustration that gave rise to the movement. Generally, "Tea Partiers favor traditionally smaller government, unfettered financial markets, defanged regulation, and shrinking federal entitlements" (Scherer, 2010, p. 28). Whether Tea Partiers are the extremists they are portrayed to be, or whether their goals appeal to more main-stream Americans, remains to be seen. Thus far, there is no organizational structure for the Tea Party that parallels what is in place for the established Republican and Democratic parties; rather, it is a movement or loose aggregation of ideologues whose influence is fueled by evolving social media technology and a few dynamic individuals. The movement has generated enthusiasm, however. What also remains unclear is how much long-term impact it will have over the Republican Party and, ultimately, election outcomes. Candidates running for the U.S. Senate in seven states (Nevada, Colorado, Utah, Alaska, Kentucky, Delaware, and Florida) who were singled out for support by avowed Tea Partiers were victorious in the 2010 primary elections. They defeated Republican mainstream rivals, many of whom were handpicked by party leaders in Washington, D.C. Of the seven, four were successful in the general election.

Taking the stage after the 2010 election was a movement called the "no labels" group that purports to put aside traditional party labels in favor of a more centrist approach that espouses "doing what is best for America." "Political outliers—not quite Republican, not quite Democrat—are forming new alliances in a communal search for 'home'" (Parker, 2010, p. A13). The group thus far does not offer policy solutions to America's challenges; rather, it promotes civil behavior in public discourse. Its founders are high-ranking political operatives from both political parties, as well as candidates who lost an election because their positions were not liberal or conservative enough for the more extreme wings of their parties. Corporate backers include Andrew Tisch, co-chairman of Loews Corp.; Ron Shaich, founder of Panera Bread; and Dave Morin, ex-Facebook executive. The group kicked off its efforts in December 2010, so the extent of its impact remains unclear.

While the impact of technology and the fate of these emerging political groups are unclear, what is clear is the trend toward more dissatisfaction with the traditional two-party system that has controlled the political process. The ability of rogue groups fueled by the power of the Internet and other technology to form and send a widespread message will have an impact on election outcomes and campaign strategies in years ahead. The 2010 uprisings in Egypt and other Middle-Eastern countries are further evidence of the power that can be unleashed through electronic social networks. Nurses and nursing organizations should be aware of the potential of technology and use it to their advantage. Technology levels the power playing field and provides a cost-effective, far-reaching mechanism to leverage power that heretofore was available only to those with extensive resources at their disposal.

Tools

Although the political process itself may seem formidable, there are tools nurses can use to make participation feasible. Technology provides the information one needs to be an informed voter; however, it is often difficult to wade through the political rhetoric or to know who or what is the source for the information. Technology, although potentially useful, can be so overwhelming that its usefulness is lost in the clutter. Information from non-partisan sources can be especially useful in sorting out the kind of information being provided; the League of Women Voters and the Center for Responsive Politics are examples of two such sources. In addition, websites of professional nurse organizations often include governmental affairs links and background information that is available to members and, on a limited basis, to non-members.

Other tools:

- *EMILY's List:* Founded in 1985 by 25 women who understood the importance of money to the political process. EMILY—Early Money Is Like Yeast—raised $1 million by 1988 and over $10 million by 1992 in support of pro-choice Democratic women candidates. It issued its first presidential endorsement in 2007, supporting the candidacy of Hillary Clinton. While clearly targeted at Democratic women candidates, the organization has become a formidable political force whose interests often parallel those of nurses. EMILY's List is a network designed to provide its members with information about candidates and encourages them to write checks directly to the candidates. Its membership had grown to 600,000 by 2010 and, in addition to being a national PAC, it also provides training opportunities for potential women candidates running for state and local offices, prepares women to work in political campaigns, and has undertaken get-out-the-vote initiatives in targeted states. EMILY's List is credited with helping to elect 80 House members, 15 senators, and 9 governors.
- *WISH List (Women in the Senate and House):* Formed in 1992 to support pro-choice Republican women, it has contributed $3.5 million to its candidates since its inception, while also offering candidates advice and training opportunities.
- *The Susan B. Anthony List:* Formed in 1992 to support pro-life candidates and advance the pro-life agenda.

Federal and state government websites can be ready sources of information about the status of legislative initiatives, the individuals serving in elective offices, and the legislative process in general. These sites have links to all three branches of government (executive, legislative, and judicial) and can provide historical perspectives about past legislative sessions, as well as information on current ones. Federal legislative information is available through the Library of Congress at http://thomas.gov. You may also sign up for email alerts by contacting the offices of committee chairs and asking to be placed on their email lists.

When trying to decide which candidates to support in a particular election, candidates' nights can be especially useful, particularly those sponsored by nursing or healthcare-related organizations where the focus is often on healthcare issues. Audience members have a chance to see each candidate respond to questions and often can have an opportunity to talk to them one-on-one. While the candidates' answers to difficult questions may not be as responsive as one might wish, it could be instructive to see them in action.

What other tools can a nurse use to influence decisions around issues of importance, both professionally and more generally?

- First and foremost, vote. Voting records are readily available and people can easily check to see whether someone regularly exercises his/her right to vote. Being able to say "I am a voter in your district" with authority can make a difference in how the rest of the message is received.
- Be an informed voter. Do not rely on media messages; check out websites, attend candidates' nights, watch debates, and contact candidates directly through their campaigns to learn more about their philosophy and priorities.
- Volunteer to help during a campaign if a candidate seems especially knowledgeable/supportive of the nursing profession's issues. This can be as simple as addressing postcards or putting up a campaign sign to making phone calls or going door-to-door. Candidates remember those who help them, and doing so also provides an opportunity to get to know the candidate's staff and family members, many of whom are likely to have a strong influence over candidate perceptions and positions once the election ends.
- Contribute to a campaign and let the candidate know that the contribution comes from a nurse. Offer to hold a fundraiser or house party for the candidate. This level of assistence is very much appreciated by the candidate and can help gain access once the election is over.
- Letters to the editor provide an opportunity to express an opinion about a candidate or issue to a ready audience. Elected officials and candidates regularly monitor these communications, as do other readers.
- Write letters, call, or send email messages to elected officials to let them know how you feel about a particular issue. These messages, especially if not part of a mass mail/call initiative, can be very influential.

- Take advantage of resources provided by nursing organizations to keep informed about what is happening in a timely manner.
- Join a professional nurse organization and volunteer to be part of its political action arm. Let the organization know of your particular concerns and offer to testify should a legislative initiative arise that is within your areas of concern or expertise.
- Consider becoming part of organized political efforts in your county or voting district, such as county political parties or other efforts that will inevitably spring up through social media opportunities.
- Volunteer for committees (e.g. school districts, city council) doing foundational work that could become the basis for local policies.
- Join organizations such as the League of Women Voters to forge connections and gain a broader awareness of the political dynamics affecting decision-making.
- Run for office, locally, statewide, or nationally.

CONCLUSION

Then-State Representative Kevin DeWine (R-Fairborn), speaking at a Nurses' Day event at the Statehouse in Ohio, noted that the job of nurses and others is to make his life miserable. He then went on to rhetorically ask who wouldn't want a job that essentially offers a 2-year minimum contract for basically part-time work, and where no one pays attention to how you are doing the job. He concluded, "That is what you do if you don't hold me accountable for the decisions I make on a regular basis, not just on Election Day" (DeWine, personal communication, March 2005).

Holding elected officials accountable for their decisions means one must pay attention to what is happening in Washington and at statehouses on a regular basis. While politics may not be pretty, it is an integral part of how things get done. The decisions made by elected officials affect nursing practice and nurses' professional lives each and every day. To ensure a positive future for the nursing profession, as well as a healthcare system that reflects nurses' perspectives, nurses are required to engage in the political side of their profession. It need not be time-consuming, but it must become a more common occurrence that all nurses accept as essential to their professional practice.

RUNNING FOR ELECTIVE OFFICE—ONE NURSE'S EXPERIENCE

In 2008, after over 25 years of working in the state legislative arena as a lobbyist for nursing's interests, I became a candidate for the state House of Representatives. I had worked as a nurse in the clinical arena for many years and, after earning my Juris Doctor (JD), had practiced law as a healthcare attorney. I frequently spoke with nurses and nursing students about the importance of getting involved in the political process and often was asked why I didn't run myself. Heretofore, I had always managed to dismiss that possibility as far-fetched. Now healthcare reform was a major issue, along with education reform and the economy, and I soon became convinced that my background would appeal to voters who wanted change. Before proceeding, I had to make certain my family was on board, my employer would be supportive, and that I could put together a solid campaign team. If all those elements fell into place, I determined I would enter the race.

By the late fall of 2007, I had negotiated a satisfactory arrangement with my employer and was assured by my family that they were on board as well. In addition, I found campaign managers who were excited to take on the Lanier campaign to put a nurse in the statehouse! Although the incumbent was not eligible for re-election due to term limits, the race was not going to be easy. I was running as a Democrat in a very Republican district, and I faced a challenge in the primary election, which meant the campaign needed to get busy fast for the early March vote.

A March election meant campaigning during the cruel winter months. Climbing over snowdrifts to get signatures on candidate petitions, hammering campaign signs into frozen ground, and going door-to-door to meet voters in temperatures that would put Alaska to shame became routine. Was it fun? Not necessarily. But it was part of the job I signed on for when I said I wanted to be the candidate, so I did it almost without giving it a second thought.

In addition to the physical side, I also had to raise money to buy the signs, establish a credible web presence, and print the campaign literature being distributed on my behalf. That meant making phone calls and sending what I called my "begging letter" to everyone I could think of who might support the effort financially. There was no how-to book that really addressed all the aspects of campaigning, so I was learning on the job each day, every day.

Nurses were my best supporters and no one worked harder on our weekend "Nurses Make House Calls" initiatives. On the rainy, frigid-cold Election Day, nurses stood outside polling places with "Lanier" signs as one last reminder of who to look for on the ballot. That night, as the election results came trickling in, we soon learned that we had been successful, so there were a few moments of celebration with friends, family, and supporters. What a fun night! Winning made it all worthwhile. The next day, however, the campaign for the general election started its 8-month marathon.

This time, the snow had turned to warm/hot days with more time for meeting voters and raising those elusive funds. By the time the November election day arrived, I had knocked on over 10,000 doors personally, and the total neared 16,000 when the efforts of volunteers were included. We had participated in numerous local parades and attended candidates' nights, festivals, and fundraisers. Many special interest groups had issued valued endorsements of my candidacy, while others disappointingly endorsed my opponent. I had answered countless questionnaires about my position on every issue imaginable. We had designed a series of direct mail pieces and other materials to give voters a reason to vote for me. I survived some hurtful negative encounters with people who were convinced that my party affiliation meant I was un-American, and I learned to ignore cruel blog comments that were focused on the superficial, rather than genuine issues. I shared a stage with presidential candidate Barack Obama and was introduced by then-Senator Hillary Clinton at a local rally. I attended a VIP briefing with a United States senator and was treated to some remarkably frank discussions about how to address some of the serious problems affecting the state and the nation.

Throughout the process, I learned how many people were struggling with the challenges posed by job losses and foreclosures. I talked with people who could not get the health care they needed because they had lost or never had adequate health insurance coverage. I watched as volunteers set up a health clinic designed to serve economically disadvantaged people, many of whom were working in minimum wage jobs. I visited local farms, preschools, and a school for children with autism.

Despite all the efforts by so many, I did not win the seat in the House I worked so hard to attain. [Editor's note: Ms. Lanier won nearly 40% of the total vote, a remarkable feat as a Democrat in a highly Republican district. She is to be celebrated for this effort.] Winning is lots more fun than losing, so the November election night party was subdued at best. In the end, all agreed that we ran a good campaign and had no regrets or what ifs to carry around. Although the loss was incredibly disappointing, I have no second thoughts about taking the chance. I have a whole new understanding of and appreciation for the political process and politics in general. I met people I would never have met otherwise, and my life is richer for having done it. My family, particularly my grandchildren, got to experience a political campaign first hand. They know what it feels like to distribute candy during a parade and to do a "lit drop" through many neighborhoods.

So what is it like to be a candidate for an elective position that was not featured in the local media, one that was more people-focused than media driven?

- First and foremost, I found it to be one of the loneliest experiences of my life. Although I was constantly around people, I was really always on my own. Knocking on doors and never knowing what might be on the other side was disconcerting, but my nursing experience prepared me well to deal with whatever arose. I probably had more information about people's health status than the local health department!
- It was a very humbling experience with a huge learning curve. I learned how much I didn't know about the many issues facing people each day. I came to appreciate the unrealistic expectations we have for our elected officials. We elect people to state and federal legislatures expecting them to find solutions to all of the varied problems that challenge our cities, states, businesses, schools, industries, environment, and economy, and then do not give them the tools or time they need to be successful.

- I realized once I received my first campaign contribution that it was no longer about my own personal ambitions, but it was bigger than that. I now owed something to others; my best effort was put forth to ensure their trust in me was not misplaced. When I got tired or discouraged, I thought about the $5 contributions I received from retired nurses who wanted to help me in some way, and that kept me moving ahead. I also learned, sadly, how those big contributions really do have an impact. Because a campaign, even so-called down ticket races, are expensive and few people (especially a nonincumbent) can raise the dollars needed or expected to be a credible candidate, when someone or some group hands you a check with multiple zeros in the amount, it has an impact. That's a fact, like it or not.
- You cannot do it alone. A good team is essential—campaign manager, treasurer, volunteer coordinator, media/public relations/web specialist, and a constituency willing to work for you. Being a candidate is a full-time job. It was a year out of my life in which I had to be on my best behavior at all times because you never know who may be watching. My family members were also affected and had to be careful of what they said and did.
- Hard work alone will not result in a victory. Timing and location (district demographics—the political index) are critical factors as well. No candidate should run unopposed, however, so candidates should be encouraged to come forward. Voters should always have a genuine choice on Election Day. Sadly, the rigors of campaigning, including the personal scrutiny, discourage rather than encourage broad participation.
- People actually thanked me for running, which really surprised me.

Government is only as good as the people who hold elective office. Cynicism and a lack of participation will eventually doom our form of government. Partisanship needs to take a backseat to collaboration in order to solve the very serious problems facing all of us. Nurses can be candidates or part of a campaign team or simply a volunteer, but regardless of what they do, they should do something!

DISCUSSION POINTS AND ACTIVITIES

- Watch the HBO movie *Iron Jawed Angels*. What political considerations were at play in efforts to win voting rights for women? Have women today become complacent with respect to the importance of voting? Is the fight waged by suffragettes similar to the one nurses have waged to gain recognition of advanced practice? Describe. How does complacency imperil future professional advances for nursing?
- There are many metaphors for the future role of advanced practice nurses in the healthcare system. Select one of the metaphors below and describe the political considerations that come into play with respect to the selected metaphor.

1. The future role of advanced practice nurses is like a great roller coaster on a moonless night. It exists, twisting ahead of us in the dark, but we can only see the track that is just ahead. We are locked in our seats, and nothing we may know or do will change the course that is laid out for us; in other words, the future role is outside of our control.

2. The future role of advanced practice nurses is a huge game of dice. It is entirely random and subject only to chance. Since everything is chance, all we can do is play the game, pray to the gods of fortune, and enjoy what luck comes our way; in other words, the future is totally random and we do not know how or if our actions make a difference.

3. The future role of advanced practice nurses is like a great ship on the ocean. We can travel freely upon it and there are many possible routes and destinations. There will always be some outside forces, such as currents, storms, and reefs, to be dealt with, but we still have the choice to sail our ship where we want it to go; in other words, we can choose whatever future we want if we are willing to work with a purpose and within the knowledge and constraints of outside forces.

4. The future of advanced practice nurses is a blank sheet of paper. It is there for us to fill in with our actions and decisions in the present. If we choose the future we want and spend time within our professional lives trying to make it happen, it will probably materialize. If we leave it to the powers that be to decide upon and plan the future, we will have a very different kind of future—one dominated by traditional powerful forces. In other words, we have control over our future if we choose to act upon it.

Source: Adapted from Facing the Future, 2006.

For a full suite of assignments and additional learning activities, use the access code located in the front of your book to visit this exclusive website: http://go.jblearning.com/milstead. If you do not have an access code, you can obtain one at the site.

REFERENCES

American Association of Colleges of Nursing. (2011). Enhancing diversity in the nursing workforce. Retrieved from http://www.aacn.nche.edu/media/factsheets/diversity.htm

American Nurses Association. (2010). *Code of ethics for nurses.* Washington, DC: Author.

American Nurses Association. (2010). *Nursing's social policy statement.* Washington, DC: Author.

Brill, S. (2010, July 12). On sale: Your government. *Time, 176*(2), 28–33.

Bush, G. W. (2010). *Decision points.* New York, NY: Crown Publishers.

Center for Responsive Politics. (2010). The dollars and cents of incumbency. Retrieved from http://www.opensecrets.org/bigpicture/cost.php

Center for Responsive Politics. (2011). Health professionals. Retrieved from http://www.opensecrets.org/pacs/industry.php:txt=H01&cycle=2010

Citizens United v. Federal Elections Commission (2010). 130 S. Ct. 876.

Crowley, M. (2010, September 27). The new GOP money stampede. *Time, 176*(13), 30–35.

deVries, C. M., & Vanderbilt, M. (1992). *The grassroots lobbying handbook*. Washington, DC: American Nurses Association.

Facing the Future. (2006). Lesson 38: Metaphors for the future. Retrieved from http://www.facingthefuture.org/Curriculum/DownloadFreeCurriculum/tabid/114/Default.aspx

Gallup. (2010). Nurses top honesty and ethics list for 11th year. Retrieved from http://www.gallup.com/poll/145043/nurses-top-honesty-ethics-list-11-year.aspx

In search of civility [editorial]. (2010, December 21). *Columbus Dispatch*, p. A10.

Institute of Medicine. (2010). *Future of nursing report*. Washington, DC: The National Academies Press.

Lanier, J. (1985). *Power, politics, and the nurse*. In L. DeYoung (Ed.), *Dynamics of Nursing* (5th ed., pp. 166–178). St. Louis, MO: C.V. Mosby Company.

Moser, J. (2010, November 9). "Progressive" means different things to different people. *Columbus Dispatch*, p. A11.

O'Bryne, P., & Holmes, D. (2009). The politics of nursing care. *Policy, Politics, and Nursing Practice, 10*(2), 153–157.

Parker, K. (2010, November 30). Moderates are looking for a new home. *Washington Post/Columbus Dispatch*, A13.

Patterson, K. (2011). Top bill: How to influence lawmakers. *Nursing Spectrum/Nurse Week*. Retrieved from http://news.nurse.com/article/20110124/national01/101240027/-1/frontpage

Scherer, M. (2010, September 27). It's tea time. *Time, 176*(13), 26–29.

CHAPTER 4

Government Regulation: Parallel and Powerful

Jacqueline M. Loversidge

KEY TERMS

Board of nursing: A state government administrative agency charged with the power and duty to enforce the laws and regulations governing the practice of nursing in the interest of public protection.

Certification: A form of voluntary credentialing that denotes validation of competency in a specialty area, with permission to use a title.

Federal Register: A daily publication of the federal government that contains current executive orders, presidential proclamations, rules and regulations, proposed rules, notices, and sunshine act meetings.

Interstate compact: The legal agreement between states to recognize the license of another state to allow for practice between states. The compact must be passed by the state legislature and implemented by the board of nursing.

Licensure: A form of credentialing whereby permission is granted by a legal authority to do an act that would, without such permission, be illegal, a trespass, a tort, or otherwise not allowable.

Multistate regulation: The provision that allows a profession to be practiced in more than one state based on a single license.

Mutual recognition: A method of multistate regulation in which boards of nursing voluntarily agree to enter into an interstate compact allowing the state to recognize and honor the license issued by the other state.

Prescriptive authority: Legal authority to prescribe drugs and therapeutic devices, usually within a practice-specific formulary.

Professional self-regulation: Voluntary process of compliance to a set of moral, ethical, and professional standards agreed to by a profession.

Public hearings: Meetings held by state or federal administrative agencies for the purpose of receiving testimony from witnesses who support or oppose regulations, or to receive expert testimony.

Recognition (official recognition): A form of credentialing that denotes a government authority has ratified or confirmed credentials of an individual.

Registration: A form of credentialing that denotes enrolling or recording the name of a qualified individual on an official roster by an agency of government.

Regulation: Governing or directing according to a rule, or bringing under the control of a constituted authority, such as the state or federal government.

Rules/regulations: Orders that outline methods of procedure issued by government to operationalize a law.

INTRODUCTION

Regulation of the U.S. healthcare delivery system and the healthcare providers who practice within the system is complex. Much of the complexity is attributable to the vastness of the industry, the manner of financing health care, and the proliferation of laws and regulations that govern practice and reimbursement in the interest of public welfare.

This chapter focuses on the major concepts of the regulation of health professionals with emphasis on advanced practice nurses (APNs). Understanding the process of **licensure** and credentialing and its impact on the practice of advanced practice nursing is fundamental to being a competent practitioner. Understanding the regulation of the healthcare system empowers the APN to advocate on behalf of the profession and consumers of health care.

REGULATION VERSUS LEGISLATION

The legislative process is one approach to governance. A parallel, yet equally powerful, approach is the regulatory process. Together, laws and regulations shape the way public policy is implemented. It is important for the APN to understand both processes and know how to influence each process. Major differences between the two processes are described here.

Laws are promulgated and passed by the legislative branch of government (Congress at the federal level or the state legislature for state laws) and establish the framework and authority base for the regulatory process. Once passed, laws must be implemented by administrative agencies (the executive branch) of government. Laws are written using broad language to provide for flexibility and adaptability in application of the law over time. The administrative agency charged with implementing the law adds **regulations** and/or **rules** (terms used interchangeably with the same meaning) that amplify the law and describe how the administrative agency will put the law into practice.

> EXAMPLE: One provision in the nurse practice act provides that a duty of the **board of nursing** is to examine, license, and renew the license of duly-qualified individuals. The regulations amplifying that provision of law specify the criteria for eligibility, application procedures, and how and when examinations are conducted.

It is important to note that regulations may never exceed the parameters of the statute they intend to amplify; however, both statute and regulation have the force and effect of law.

The first step in establishing a new law or revising an existing law begins with the introduction of a bill by a legislator or group of legislators (sponsors) during a legislative session. The sponsor may introduce legislation to address an issue or concern of his or her constituents, or an administrative agency may seek a legislative sponsor to modify its practice act for a variety of reasons. The bill must be passed during the legislative session in which it is introduced or it "dies" and must then be reintroduced in a subsequent session.

Legislators may amend bills at any time during the legislative process. Amendments may be made to a bill during several points of review, for example during a subcommittee hearing, a full committee hearing, on the floor of the House or Senate, or in a conference committee. Amendments may be favorable to the sponsor and constituency, or they may be unfavorable as a result of political maneuvering. Some amendments may change the intent of the original bill, and so there is always risk involved when bills are up for discussion and debate. For example, provisions in nurse practice acts may be changed through passage of a bill that affects another healthcare law or a statewide budget bill. It is important for the APN to monitor a bill throughout the legislative process and exert influence for positive outcomes. It is equally important for the APN to be aware of any legislation that may influence practice and the interests of healthcare consumers.

Regulations, on the other hand, can be promulgated at any time during the year by an administrative agency. Some states require periodic review of regulations by the agency responsible for administering those rules in an effort to assure that rules reflect changes in the environment. The time frame for implementation of the regulation varies according to the Administrative Procedures Act (APA) of the state, but generally the regulation becomes effective within 30 to 90 days of publication of the final regulation. Regulations may be amended by the issuing agency based on public input prior to the publication of the final regulation. The administrative agency working on the regulation has discretion in determining what amendments, if any, are made; however, public comment may be very influential in determining the final outcome.

HEALTH PROFESSIONS REGULATION AND LICENSING

Definitions and Purpose of Regulation

Regulation, as defined in *Black's Law Dictionary*, means "the act or process of controlling by rule or restriction" (Garner, 2009, p. 1398). Health professions regulation provides for ongoing monitoring and maintenance of an acceptable standard of practice for the professions in the interest of public welfare.

Regulation is needed to protect the public because of the technical complexity of the healthcare system. Diversity in educational credentialing, proliferation of types of providers, lack of public information about competency of healthcare providers, and the bundling of healthcare services make it difficult for the public to understand and evaluate options. The public trusts that every healthcare provider is competent to perform the duties assigned, particularly those who are licensed or registered by a state authority. Because the secondary harm that can come to an individual by an incompetent provider may be life threatening, a major role of the regulatory agency is to ensure the public safety. In addition, the regulatory process provides the public a forum to resolve complaints against healthcare providers (Sheets, 1996).

The laws (statutes) that credential and govern a profession are called *practice acts*. The practice act generally includes sections governing practice, education and credentialing, licensure and certification, disciplinary action, continuing education, the composition and scope of authority of its governing board, and its rule-making authority. Accompanying regulations (rules) specify the details related to initial licensing requirements, standards for acceptable practice, disciplinary procedures, and standards for continuing education. Some states regulate both continuing education and competence; because continuing competence is difficult to measure, however, many states focus on the more measurable outcome of continuing education.

The regulatory process clarifies and amplifies enabling statutes and defines the methods that the governing authority will use to enforce an existing law. Regulations cannot be instituted by an administrative agency without the expressed intent of a law. Silence of the law on an issue cannot be presumed to be the will of the legislature. When there is no prior statutory authority or legislative precedent to address an issue, the legislative process must be initiated.

EXAMPLE: An APN petitions the board of nursing to clarify whether **prescriptive authority** is within the scope of practice for the APN. The board's staff refers the APN to a provision in the statute that allows the APN to "diagnose and treat" common, well-defined health problems under approved written protocols. The staff conclude that "treatment" may include prescriptive authority as an "additional act" if permitted in the approved written protocols of the nurse and physician preceptor. No specific language is found in the statute that authorizes writing prescriptions by the APN. When the medical board receives the board of nursing's opinion, an attorney general's opinion is requested. The attorney general concludes that the board of nursing may not extend the scope of practice of the APN through regulation. The expressed will of the legislature in regard to the scope of practice for the APN must be sought using the legislative process. Note that not all state boards of nursing are granted statutory authority to express formal opinions and some must rely on the express language in the practice act and regulations, the attorney general's office, or the courts.

History of Health Professions Regulation

At the end of the 19th century, physicians were the first healthcare providers to gain legislative **recognition** for their practice. The definitions of the practice of medicine are all-encompassing and include any act to diagnose or treat, or attempt to diagnose or treat, any individual with a physical injury or deformity. Herein lies the problem faced by APNs and other healthcare providers who are not physicians: how to define a scope of practice that does not overlap with this broad definition. The history of nursing regulation is characterized by efforts to accommodate this medical preemption (Safriet, 1992).

The early regulation of nurses was permissive (voluntary), providing for nurses to register with the governing board, hence the title "registered nurse." In some states, nurses were registered by the medical board prior to the establishment of a separate board of nursing. During this period, there was no competency assessment. Nurses seeking registration provided evidence of graduation from an approved nursing education program, and "good moral character" was evaluated by requiring references or endorsements from nurses registered by the board. The first board of nursing and nurse practice acts were passed in 1903 by North Carolina, followed by New York, New Jersey, and Virginia (Sheets, 1996). Boards of nursing began to establish written and practice examinations to measure competency; however, the practice acts were still permissive. Graduates of nursing-education programs not registered with the board were still permitted to practice nursing, but they were not permitted to use the title "RN." The first mandatory licensure law was enacted by New York in 1938 (Weisenbeck & Calico, 1995), and by the 1950s, mandatory licensure laws for the practice of nursing became widespread, requiring anyone who practiced nursing to be licensed by the state board of nursing. These mandatory licensure laws protected not only the title but also the scope of practice for nurses, resulting in greater public protection.

History of Advanced Practice Nursing Regulation

The 1960s set the stage for the expansion of nursing practice, as well as the practice and regulation of APNs. The birth of the federal entitlement programs, Medicare and Medicaid, increased the number of individuals with access to government-subsidized health care. With a predicted shortage of primary care physicians, the first formal nurse practitioner programs were opened (Safriet, 1992).

In 1971, Idaho became the first state to legally recognize diagnosis and treatment as part of the scope of practice for the advanced practice nurse. The regulation of APNs was accomplished through joint agreement of the state board of nursing and the state board of medicine for each permissible act of diagnosis and treatment. The model of regulation established in Idaho set a precedent for subsequent models for the regulation of APNs: that is, some form of joint regulation by the board of nursing and board of medicine. The joint regulation was designed to compensate for the broad definition of the practice of medicine and is based on the determination that advanced practice nursing was a "delegated medical practice" requiring some oversight by physicians. Today, the struggle continues between nursing and medicine to define the scope of practice of the APN and to determine which regulatory board should maintain oversight.

Since 1971, virtually every state has developed some form of legal recognition of the APN. Both the American Nurses Association (ANA) and the National Council of State Boards of Nursing (NCSBN) have proposed model rules and regulations for the governing of advanced practice nursing. However, because the battles for regulation of APNs are fought in highly political state-by-state environments, there is a plethora of titles, definitions, criteria for practice, scopes of practice, reimbursement policies, and models of regulation that is difficult for policymakers to navigate and understand in today's rapidly changing healthcare delivery system.

Since 1988, *The Nurse Practitioner: The American Journal of Primary Health Care* has provided an annual survey of each state's board of nursing and nursing organizations to gather information on the legislative status of advanced practice nursing. Significant strides have been made by many states in regard to APNs gaining sole authority for scope of practice with no requirements for direct physician supervision. As of 2010, 24 states reported that APN scope of practice is regulated solely by the board of nursing, with no statutory or regulatory requirements for physician direction, supervision, or collaboration. In 20 states, the board of nursing has sole authority for the scope of practice of APNs, but there is a requirement for physician collaboration. APNs can prescribe, including controlled substances, independent of physician involvement in 14 states, and in 35 states APNs can prescribe, including controlled substances, with some degree of physician involvement (Phillips, 2010). All states now allow some form of prescriptive authority (Pearson, 2002).

Methods of Professional Credentialing

Regulation of the health professions is achieved through various methods of credentialing. The method selected is determined by the state government and is based on at least two variables: 1) the potential for harm to the public if safe and acceptable standards of practice are not met, and 2) the degree of autonomy and accountability for decision-making by the professional. The least restrictive form of regulation to accomplish the goal of public protection should be selected (Gross, 1984; Pew Health Professions Commission, 1994).

The term *restrictive*, as used in this context, means the degree to which the model restricts an individual who has not met the prescribed criteria in the law and received the explicit authority of the administrative agency from practicing within the scope of practice of the profession. Four methods of credentialing are used in the United States. Each of the methods is based on the regulation of the individual provider. The methods are described separately, moving from the most restrictive to the least restrictive method of credentialing.

Licensure

A *license* is "a permission, . . . revocable, to commit some act that would otherwise be unlawful" (Garner, 2009, p. 1002). The licentiate is "one who has obtained a license or authoritative permission to exercise some function, esp. to practice a profession" (Garner, 2009, p. 1005). Licensure is the most restrictive method of credentialing and requires anyone who practices within the defined scope of practice to obtain the legal authority to do so from the appropriate administrative agency of the state.

Licensure implies competency assessment of the professional at the point of entry into the profession. A licensing examination is administered and ongoing continuing education or competency assessment by the legal authority is conducted to provide some assurance that acceptable standards of practice are met. Licensure offers the public the greatest level of protection by restricting use of the title and the scope of practice to the licensed professional who has met these rigorous criteria. Unlicensed persons cannot call themselves by the title identified in the law, and they cannot lawfully practice any portion of the scope of practice.

The administrative agency holds the licensee accountable for practicing according to the legal, ethical, and professional standards of care defined for the profession to the extent to which the laws and rules require. Disciplinary action, through an administrative disciplinary procedure that assures due process, may be taken against licensees who have violated provisions of statute or regulation. Most of the health professions are regulated by licensure because of the high degree of potential for harm to the public by individuals who are not qualified to practice the profession.

Registration

Registration is the "act of recording or enrolling" (Garner, 2009, p. 1397). Registration provides for a review of credentials to determine compliance with the criteria for entry to the profession and permits the individual to use the title "registered." Registration serves as title protection, but does not preclude individuals who are not registered from practicing within the scope of practice, as long as they do not use the title.

Registration does not necessarily imply that any competency assessment has been conducted prior to the registration. Some state laws may have provisions for removing incompetent or unethical providers from the registry or marking the registry when a complaint is lodged against a provider, but removing the person from the registry may not necessarily provide public protection because the individual may continue to practice as long as the title is not used. Some types of practitioners engage in a practice, never having been placed on a registry; an example is the lay midwife who never implies to the public that he or she is a registered nurse midwife and who does not use the title "nurse" midwife. States are required to maintain a registry of unlicensed assistive personnel who practice in long-term care facilities as a result of the Omnibus Budget Reconciliation Act of 1987.

The title "registered nurse" was formulated in the early days of nursing regulation, when the state boards registered nurses. Though nurses have been subject to licensure requirements for many years, the term *registered* has historical significance and has never been changed.

Certification

A *certificate* is "a document certifying the bearer's status or authorization to act in a specified way" (Garner, 2009, p. 255). As applied to nursing regulation, certification is a voluntary process that may involve completion of required requisite education or competency assessment, usually conducted by proprietary professional or specialty nursing organizations, denoting that the individual has achieved a level of competence in nursing practice beyond the entry-level competence measured by licensure.

Certification, like registration, is a means of title protection. *Certification* is a term that may be used by both governmental agencies and proprietary organizations. When certification is awarded by proprietary organizations, it does not have the force and effect of law. However, in some states, certification is a regulated credential; states may offer a "certificate of authority" to practice within a prescribed scope or may offer certification to assistive personnel, such as dialysis technicians. When choosing a provider, astute consumers may inquire as to whether a provider is certified as a means of assuring a level of preparedness to practice. Employers also use certification as a means of determining eligibility for certain jobs or as a requirement for promotions within the agency. Some states have enacted regulations that require an APN to be certified by a specialty nursing organization to be eligible to practice in the advanced role.

Recognition

Recognition is "confirmation that an act done by another person was authorized . . . the formal admission that a person, entity, or thing has a particular status" (Garner, 2009, p. 1385). As applied to nursing regulation, **official recognition** is a method of regulating APNs used by several boards of nursing that implies the board has validated and accepted credentials for the specialty area of practice. Criteria for recognition are defined in the practice act and may include requirements for certification.

Professional Self-Regulation

Self-regulation occurs within a profession through the desire of members of the profession to set standards, values, ethical frameworks, and safe-practice guidelines beyond the minimum standards defined by law. This voluntary process plays an equally significant role in the regulation of the profession, as does legal regulation. The definition of professional standards of practice and the code of ethics for the profession are examples of **professional self-regulation**. The members of national professional organizations set standards of practice for specialty practice and determine who can use selected titles by administering certification examinations. Continuing education requirements, as well as documentation of practice competency, are often required for periodic recertification. The standards are periodically reviewed and revised to reflect current practice. Legal regulation recognizes professional standards as the acceptable standard of practice when making decisions regarding what constitutes safe and competent care.

Even though professional organizations can develop standards, they have no legal authority to ensure compliance with said standards, as only legal regulation provides a mechanism for monitoring and enforcing compliance with standards of practice. Legal regulation and professional regulation are two sides of the same coin, working together to fulfill the profession's contract with society.

REGULATION OF ADVANCED PRACTICE NURSES

Advanced practice nursing regulation has been the focus of the Advanced Practice Task Force/Advisory Committee of the National Council of State Boards of Nursing (NCSBN) for two decades. The evolution of APN practice across the United States has resulted in a patchwork of titles, scopes of practice, and regulatory methods. To bring some uniformity to the regulation of APNs and advanced practice registered nurses (APRNs), the NCSBN convened the Advanced Practice Task Force. Through the years, the task force has developed position papers for consideration by state boards of nursing in a quest for greater standardization and to strengthen the public protection mandate held by boards. The culmination of this work is found in the *Consensus Model for APRN Regulation: Licensure, Accreditation, Certification, & Education.* This report is the outcome of the work of the APRN Consensus Work Group and the National Council of State Boards of Nursing APRN Advisory Committee. It defines APRN practice, describes the APRN regulatory model, identifies the use of titles, defines specialties, describes new APRN roles and population foci, and offers strategies for implementation (APRN Joint Dialogue Group, 2008).

National nursing certifying agencies play an important role in the professional regulation of APNs. Specialty nursing organizations develop verification examinations to measure the competency of nurses in an area of clinical expertise. Most boards of nursing require the APN to be certified in the clinical specialty area appropriate to the educational preparation to legally practice in the role. The regulatory body has the authority to accept certification examinations if the examination meets the criteria predetermined by the board. The board may not "surrender regulatory authority by passive acceptance without evaluation of the examination content, procedures and scoring process" (National Council of State Boards of Nursing, 2002). To be legally defensible for licensure purposes, the certification examination must meet certain psychometric standards. The foundational basis for regulatory sufficiency is the examination's ability to measure entry-level practice; that it is based on a job analysis that defines job-related knowledge, skills, and abilities; and that it is developed on psychometrically sound principles of test development.

The NCSBN and the national nursing specialty organizations collaborated to establish criteria that boards of nursing could use in the evaluation of certification examinations (Canavan, 1996). The Requirements for Accrediting Agencies and Criteria for APRN Certification Programs were developed in 1995 and updated in 2002 (National Council of State Boards of Nursing, 2002). The criteria can be located on the NCSBN website at http://www.ncsbn.org.

The national organizations that prepare certification examinations for APNs include the following:

- American Academy of Nurse Practitioners
- American Association of Nurse Anesthetists Council on Certification
- American College of Nurse–Midwives Certification Council
- American Nurses Credentialing Center
- National Certification Board of Pediatric Nurse Practitioners
- National Certification Corporation for the Obstetric, Gynecologic, and Neonatal Nursing Specialties

The NCSBN Advanced Practice Nursing Task Force has also sought to bring greater standardization to APN regulation in an effort to increase the mobility of APNs. In 2000, the NCSBN Delegate Assembly passed the Uniform Advanced Practice Registered Nurse Licensure/Authority to Practice Requirements. These requirements include: 1) an unencumbered RN license; 2) graduation from a graduate-level advanced practice program that is certified by a national accrediting body; 3) current certification by a national certifying body in the advanced practice specialty appropriate to educational preparation; and 4) maintenance of certification or evidence of maintenance of competence (National Council of State Boards of Nursing, 2002). Adoption of these uniform requirements by boards of nursing will facilitate the ease with which APNs can become a part of the multistate regulation model. The NCSBN Model Act/Rules and Regulations were updated in August 2008 and parallel the *Consensus Model for APRN Regulation* (National Council of State Boards of Nursing, 2008).

The State Regulatory Process

The 10th Amendment of the U.S. Constitution reserves all powers not specifically vested in the federal government for the states. One of these is the duty to protect its citizens (police powers), and the power to regulate the professions is one way the state exercises its responsibility to protect the health, safety, and welfare of its citizens. State law provides for administrative agencies to assume the responsibility for regulation of the professions. These agencies have administrative, legislative, and judicial powers to make and enforce the laws.

Administrative agencies have sometimes been called the fourth branch of government because of their significant power in the daily execution and enforcement of the law. They are given referent authority by state and federal governments to promulgate rules and regulations, develop policies and procedures, and interpret laws to implement the agency mission.

Boards of Nursing

Each state legislature designates a board or similar authority to administer the practice act for the profession. The board's powers, duties, and composition are defined by the law. Traditionally, there are three major duties for licensing boards: 1) control entry into the profession through examination and licensure; 2) monitor and discipline licensees who violate the scope and standards of practice; and 3) monitor continuing education and/or competency of licensees to protect the public from unsafe or poor quality practice. In most states, boards of nursing have the additional duty to establish criteria for review and approval of nursing education programs that lead to licensure as a registered nurse (RN) or licensed practical nurse or licensed vocational nurse (LPN/LVN), and to set criteria for recognition of and prescriptive powers for APNs.

There are 60 boards of nursing in the United States and its territories. Each board of nursing is a member of the National Council of State Boards of Nursing. Some states have separate boards for licensing RNs and LPNs. As members of the NCSBN, the boards have the privilege of using the national licensure examination and meeting together to discuss matters of common interest (National Council of State Boards of Nursing, 2008).

Composition of the Board of Nursing

Generally, boards are composed of licensed nurses and consumer members. In most states, the governor appoints the members, athough in at least one state, North Carolina, elections are conducted for the board vacancies. Nurses who are interested in serving as board members often gain appointment to those positions through the helpful endorsements of their professional associations, as well as the support of their district legislators.

Some state laws designate that nurses from specific educational and practice settings, as well as APNs, must be represented on the board of nursing. In other states, the criteria for appointment only require licensure in the profession and a residency requirement. Information on vacancies on the board of nursing can be obtained from the board office or the governor's office. Knowing the composition of the board and when vacancies occur is important to allow the profession to exercise political influence in gaining the desired representation on the board. Information related to serving on boards and commissions is found later in this chapter.

Board Meetings

All state government agencies function within open meeting or "sunshine" laws that permit the public to observe or participate in the discussions of the board, though boards may go into closed "executive session" when necessary; rules for executive sessions are specified in the APA and must be adhered to by the agency. The board may meet in executive session for certain reasons, including discussion of personnel matters, obtaining legal advice, contract negotiation, and disciplinary matters. Boards usually "report out" of executive session when public session resumes. All voting is a matter of public record and occurs only in open public session.

Board meetings may vary in the degree of formality. Most states' APA requires the board to post notice of meetings and the agenda in a public place, usually 30 days prior to the meeting. Sometimes the notice of meeting is published in major state newspapers. The agenda is public and available on request from the board office or from its website.

Participants in the board meeting include the board members, the board staff, and legal counsel for the board. Legal counsel advises the board in matters of law and jurisdiction. Some boards may have "staff" counsel, but many states receive advice from their representative in the state attorney general's office, known as an "assistant attorney general," or AAG. Staff or other invited guests may present reports during the meeting. Individuals may provide testimony to the board on matters of interest.

In making decisions, board members must consider several factors, including implications for the public welfare, national standards of care, impact of the decision on the state as a whole, and the legal defensibility of the decision. First and foremost, the board must act only within its legal jurisdiction. All actions of the board are a matter of public record. Most boards of nursing publish newsletters that summarize the major actions of the board during each meeting. Licensees may request to be placed on the mailing list for the newsletter if one is not automatically received.

Monitoring Competency of Nurses: Mandatory Reporting

The most critical role of the board of nursing is assuring public safety. Most nurse practice acts (NPAs) have mandatory reporting provisions that require employers to report violations of the NPA. Licensed nurses also have a moral and ethical duty to report unsafe and incompetent practice to the board of nursing. The NPA defines those acts that are considered misconduct and provides for a system of due process to investigate complaints against licensees. Procedures for filing complaints, conducting investigations, and issuing sanctions for violations are enumerated in rules and regulations of the NPA.

The licensed nurse is accountable for knowing the laws and regulations that govern the practice of nursing in the state of licensure and adhering to the legal, ethical, and professional standards of care. Some NPAs include standards of practice in the regulations. Other states may refer to professional or ethical standards established by professional associations. The employing agency also defines standards of practice through policy and procedures that must be followed by each nurse employee.

A nurse who holds a multistate license (one license that permits a nurse to practice in more than one state as long as the state is entered into a multistate compact) is held accountable for knowing and abiding by the laws of the state in which the practice occurs in addition to the home state of licensure. Multistate regulation is discussed in more detail later in this chapter. Ignorance of the law is not an excuse for misconduct.

Most boards of nursing now have the complete NPA online on their websites, as does the National Council of State Boards of Nursing (see http://www.ncsbn.org).

Instituting State Regulations

Government agencies have the authority and duty to promulgate regulations to amplify its statute. As discussed earlier in this chapter, a law may provide overarching parameters, but the details of the processes required to implement the law are written into the regulations. The APA of each state specifies the process for ratifying regulations, including how the public is notified of proposed regulations and its opportunity for public comment. It is important that the APN becomes familiar with the APA to know when and how to provide comment. State processes differ; some states have designated commissions or committees responsible for review and approval of regulations, while other states submit regulations to the general assembly or to committees of the legislature. Certain elements are common to the promulgation of regulations. These include 1) public notice that a new regulation has been proposed, or of a proposal to modify an existing regulation; 2) opportunity to submit written comment or testimony, and in addition the opportunity to present oral testimony at a rules hearing; and 3) publication of the final regulation in a register or state bulletin.

In some states, a fiscal impact statement is required. This statement estimates the cost of compliance with the regulation. Also, in some states, the rule promulgation process requires oversight by a commission of legislators whose role it is to ensure that the regulatory agency instituting the rules does in fact have the authority to do so, does not exceed the scope of its rule-making authority, and does not draft rules that would conflict with its own statute or that of any related discipline. For example, in the case of nursing, legislative commissions would cross-check the statutes and rules regulating other health professions.

Monitoring State Regulations

Administrative agencies promulgate hundreds of regulations each year. Regulations that affect advanced nursing practice could be put into effect by a variety of agencies. Knowing which agencies are most likely to have the authority to put forth regulations that affect health care and professional practice, as well as monitoring the legislation and regulations proposed by those agencies, is important to protect the scope of practice of APNs.

The most obvious agencies the APN should consider tracking are the licensing boards of other health professions, such as medicine, pharmacy, counselors and therapists, and other health professionals. In this rapidly changing healthcare environment, numerous conflicts occur over scope of practice issues, definitions of practice, right to reimbursement, and requirements for supervision and collaboration.

When reviewing regulations, there are several points that are important to consider. **Exhibit 4–1** provides some key questions to consider when analyzing a regulation for its impact on nursing practice.

Exhibit 4-1 Questions to Ask When Analyzing Regulations

1. Which agency promulgated the regulation?
2. What is the source of authority (the statute that provides authority for the regulation to be promulgated)?
3. What is the intent or rationale of the regulation? Is it clearly stated by the promulgating agency?
4. Is the language in the regulation clear or ambiguous? Can the regulation be interpreted in different ways by different individuals? Discuss advantages of language that is clear versus ambiguous.
5. Are there definitions to clarify terms?
6. Are there important points that are not addressed? That is, are there omissions?
7. How does the regulation affect the practice of nursing? Does it constrain or limit the practice of nursing in any way?
8. Is there sufficient lead time to comply with the regulation?
9. What is the fiscal impact of the regulation?

Consider the following situation and how the proposed regulations would affect the practice of the APN.

EXAMPLE: Assume the board of pharmacy has drafted the following definition of the practice of pharmacy: The practice of pharmacy includes, but is not limited to, the interpretation, evaluation, and implementation of medical orders; the dispensing of prescription drug orders; initiating or modifying the drug therapy in accordance with written guidelines or protocols previously established and approved by a practitioner authorized to independently prescribe drugs; and the provision of patient counseling as a primary healthcare provider of pharmacy care.

If this definition was included in the pharmacy practice act requiring that anyone who "initiated or modified a drug therapy in accordance with written guidelines or protocols" must be licensed as a pharmacist by the board of pharmacy, how would this affect the practice of nursing and, especially, the APN? This is but one example of numerous definitions of scope of practice that have significant overlap with the advanced practice of nursing. A solution to this dilemma would be to negotiate for the addition of an exemption for APNs in the pharmacy practice act.

In a growing managed care market, it is also critical for APNs to be aware of regulations that mandate benefits or reimbursement policies and to lobby for inclusion of APNs. Several states have instituted open-panel legislation, known as "any willing provider" and "freedom of choice" laws. These bills mandate that any provider who is authorized to provide the services covered in an insurance plan must be recognized and reimbursed by the plan. Insurance company lobbyists, as well as business lobbyists, oppose this type of legislation. As managed care contracts are negotiated, APNs must ensure that services of the APN are given fair and equitable consideration. Other important areas include workers' compensation participation and reimbursement provisions and liability insurance laws.

APNs achieved landmark success in 1997, with grassroots lobbying efforts, to gain Medicare reimbursement for all nurse practitioners, regardless of location of practice. Prior to 1997, Medicare reimbursement for nurse practitioners was restricted to those nurse practitioners who provided services in specific geographic locations and who practiced with physician supervision.

In summary, state agencies that govern licensing and certification of healthcare facilities, administer public health services (e.g., public health, mental health, alcohol and drug abuse), govern reimbursement, as well as the health professions licensing boards, are all agencies that could promulgate regulations that would have implications for the practice of the APN.

Serving on Boards and Commissions

One way to participate actively in the regulatory process is to seek an appointment to the state board of nursing or other board or commission that affects health policy. Active participation in the political process, especially during times of rapid change and reform, will ensure the voice of APNs is heard in setting the public policy agenda.

When seeking appointments to boards and commissions, select an agency whose mission and purposes are consistent with your interest and expertise. Because most board appointments are gubernatorial or political appointments, it is important for the APN to obtain endorsements from legislators, influential community leaders, and their professional associations.

Letters of support should document the APN's contributions to employment and community service. Delineate involvement in local, state, and national organizations. The letter from the employer should indicate a willingness to provide the time to fulfill the responsibilities of the position during the term of office. In addition, a personal letter from the APN who is seeking appointment to the governor that expresses interest in serving on the board should be offered, including the rationale for volunteering for service on the particular board or commission, evidence of a good match between one's expertise and the role of that board or commission, and expression of a clear interest in serving the public. A résumé or curriculum vitae should be attached. Letters should emphasize desire to serve over self-interest; appointment decisions should be based on how much the individual can offer the board or commission in serving the public good. This kind of public service requires a substantial time commitment; it is wise to speak to other members of the board or call the executive director or administrator of the agency to determine the extent of that commitment.

The Federal Regulatory Process

Many forces have contributed to the federal government becoming a more central figure in the regulation of the health professions. The most significant factor is the advent of the Medicare and Medicaid programs. The federal initiatives that have grown out of these programs are largely focused on cost containment (prospective payment) and consumer protection (combating fraud and abuse) (Jost, 1997; Roberts & Clyde, 1993).

With the "graying" of Americans, the cost of administering the Medicare program is skyrocketing, with predictions of bankruptcy if substantive changes are not made in either the criteria for eligibility or the methods of reimbursement. Numerous changes to the system are expected in the coming years.

One of the most significant changes occurred in July 2001 when the Centers for Medicare and Medicaid Services (CMS) was created to replace the former Health Care Financing Administration (HCFA). The reformed agency provides an increased emphasis on responsiveness to beneficiaries and providers and quality improvement. Three new business centers have been established as part of the reform: Center for Beneficiary Choices, Center for Medicare Management, and Center for Medicaid and State Operations (Centers for Medicare and Medicaid Services, 2001).

The practice of APNs has also been influenced by changes in the Medicare reimbursement policy. In 1997, legislation was passed in Congress calling for Medicare reimbursement of APNs regardless of setting and went into effect in January 1998. These regulations provide direct reimbursement to APNs for providing Medicare Part B services that would normally be provided by a physician. These services are not restricted by site of geographic location as services have been in the past. Under this legislation, APNs can see both new and continuing patients without restriction. Reimbursement rates are set at 80% of the lesser of the actual charge or 85% of the fee schedule amount for the physician (American Academy of Nurse Practitioners, 2003). APNs must secure a Medicare provider number to be eligible for reimbursement.

The evolution of government has changed the relationship between the state and federal regulatory systems. Responsibilities once assumed by the federal government have been shifted down to the state level, such as administration of the Medicaid programs and management of the welfare program. The impetus guiding this change is that states are better equipped to make decisions about how best to assist their citizens and the sentiment against creating federal bureaucracy and increasing the tax burden. Even though states have primary authority over regulation of the health professions, federal policies also have an enormous effect on healthcare workforce regulation. All the policies related to reimbursement and quality control over the Medicare and Medicaid programs are promulgated by the U.S. Department of Health and Human Services and are administered through its financing agency, the CMS. Other federal statutes that have a regulatory impact on healthcare providers and that the APN should be familiar with include the following:

- Clinical Laboratory Improvement Amendments of 1988 (CLIA 88)
- Occupational Safety and Health Act of 1970 (OSHA)
- Mammography Quality Standards Act of 1987 and 1992 (MQSA 87 and 92)
- Omnibus Budget Reconciliation Act of 1987 and 1990 (OBRA 87 and 90)
- Americans with Disabilities Act of 1990 (ADA)
- North American Free Trade Agreement of 1993 (NAFTA, effective date January 1, 1994)
- Telecommunications Act of 1996
- Health Insurance Portability and Accountability Act of 1996 (HIPAA)
- Patient Protection and Affordable Care Act, Public Law 111-148 (PPACA, effective date March 23, 2010)

The Veterans Administration hospitals and the Indian Health Services both are regulated by the federal government, as are the uniformed armed services. Individuals who are employed in these services must be licensed in at least one state and are subject to the laws of the state in which they are licensed and the standards of care and policies established in the federal system. The Supremacy Clause of the U.S. Constitution gives legal superiority to federal laws (Braunstein, 1995). When a federal law or regulation is enacted, it takes precedence over any state law. State laws in conflict with federal laws cannot be enforced. At times, the courts may be asked to determine the constitutionality of a law or regulation to resolve jurisdictional disputes.

The Commerce Clause of the U.S. Constitution limits the ability of states to erect barriers to interstate trade (Gobis, 1997). Courts have found that the provision of health care is interstate trade under antitrust laws, and this finding sets the stage for the federal government to preempt state licensing laws in the practice of professions across state boundaries, if it chooses to do so.

The impact of technology on the delivery of health care, such as "telehealthcare" or "telecare," allows providers to care for patients in remote environments and across the geopolitical boundaries defined by traditional state-by-state licensure. This raises the question as to whether the federal government will intercede in standardizing licensing requirements across state lines to facilitate interstate commerce, usurping the state's authority. Licensing boards are beginning to identify ways to facilitate the practice of telehealthcare, while at the same time preserving the power and right of the state to protect its citizens by regulating the professions at the state level. One innovative approach to nursing regulation, **multistate regulation**, is discussed later in this chapter.

The most recent of these federal initiatives is the Patient Protection and Affordable Care Act. The passing of this law in 2010 represented a national movement toward comprehensive and far-reaching national healthcare system reform. It represents the broadest revamping of health care since the Medicare and Medicaid programs were created in 1965. The provisions of the law are slated to be enacted over a 5-year period, and include requirements for consumer protection, improvement of the quality of health care, lowering of healthcare costs, increasing access to affordable care, and holding insurance companies more accountable (HealthCare.gov, 2010).

The Patient Protection and Affordable Care Act includes a number of provisions related to nursing, many of which are applicable or specific to the APN. Among these related to nursing are increased funding for a primary care workforce, grants for funding nurse-managed health centers through the Department of Health and Human Services (HHS), clarification of the funding of advanced nursing education to include accredited midwifery education, expansion of the Nurse Loan Repayment and Scholarship Programs (NLRP) to provide loan repayment for students who serve in faculty positions in accredited nursing programs for at least 2 years, and increases in the Nurse Faculty Loan Program.

Even more specifically applicable to APNs are provisions related to the inclusion of nurse practitioners and clinical nurse specialists as ACO (accountable care organization) professionals. ACOs are legally formed structures, comprised of a group of providers and suppliers, to manage and coordinate care for Medicare fee-for-service beneficiaries. The law also authorizes HHS to establish a grant program for states or designated entities to establish community-based interprofessional teams to support primary care practices, increases Medicare payments for primary care practitioners, and increases reimbursement rates for certified nurse–midwives. A graduate nurse education provision would appropriate monies to establish graduate nurse education demonstration programs in Medicare. There are numerous other provisions in this law as enacted; a complete list of key provisions related to nursing may be found on the American Nurses Association website (http://www.nursingworld.org).

However, the success of this historic legislation is threatened and the final outcome is in question.

Promulgating Federal Regulations

The federal regulatory process is a two-step process established by the federal Administrative Procedures Act. A notice of proposed rule-making (NPR) is published in the proposed rule section of the *Federal Register*, which informs the public of the substance of the intended regulation and provides information on how the public may participate in providing comment, attending meetings, or otherwise participating in the regulatory process. The second step involves careful consideration of public comment by the agency and amendment to the regulation, if warranted. The final regulations are issued by the agency through publication in the rules and regulations section of the *Federal Register* and become effective 30 days after publication (see **Exhibit 4-2**).

Exhibit 4-2 The Federal Rule-Making Process

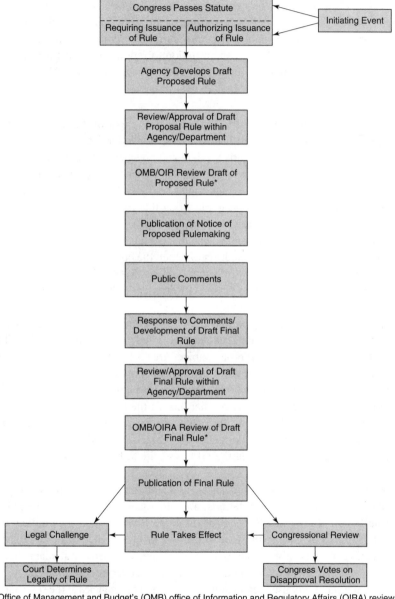

* The Office of Management and Budget's (OMB) office of Information and Regulatory Affairs (OIRA) reviews only significant rules, and does not review any rules submitted by independent regulatory agencies

Source: Copeland, C. W. (2008, August 28). The federal rulemaking process: An overview. Congressional Research Service Report RL32240. Retrieved from http://openregs.com/docs/copeland-rulemaking-process.pdf

Emergency Regulations

Provisions for promulgating emergency regulations are defined at both the state and federal levels. Emergency regulations are enacted if an agency determines that the public welfare is immediately adversely affected. Emergency regulations may take effect immediately upon publication, are generally temporary, are effective for a limited time (usually 90 days, with an option to renew), and must be followed with permanent regulations that are instituted in accordance with the APA process.

Locating Information

The *Federal Register* is the bulletin board or newspaper of the federal government. It is published Monday through Friday, except for federal holidays, and is updated daily by 6 a.m. It contains executive orders and presidential proclamations, rules and regulations, proposed rules, notices of federal agencies and organizations, sunshine act meetings, and corrections to previous copies of the Federal Register. Each document in the *Federal Register* begins with a heading that includes the name of the issuing agency, the Code of Federal Regulations title, and a brief synopsis of the contents. After the heading, a preamble is published that contains the type of action, summary of action, deadline for comments, address to which the comments may be sent, a contact person, and other supplementary information (Goehlert & Martin, 1989). The *Federal Register* may be accessed online via the Governmental Printing Office (GPO) website at http://www.gpoaccess.gov/fr/index.html.

The Code of Federal Regulations (CFR) is a compilation of all final regulations issued by the executive branch agencies of the federal government. The CFR consists of 50 titles that represent broad subject areas. The CFR is updated annually in sections; each quarter, one section of the CFR is updated according to a schedule that includes all regulations that have been passed since the prior printing. Consequently, there is never a publication that has all the regulations passed in it for the year. An index that helps in locating rules by agency name and subject headings is published and revised semiannually (Goehlert & Martin, 1989). The Code of Federal Regulations is online at the GPO website at http://www.gpoaccess.gov/cfr/index.html.

Each state government publishes similar documents that identify the proposed regulations, notices, final regulations, and emergency regulations. The publication is usually called the State Register or the State Bulletin, and the publication cycle can be obtained by calling the state legislative printing office or the state legislative information system office. Copies of these documents are usually available in the local libraries and may be available online on the state's governmental website.

The myriad of proposed regulations promulgated by agencies at the state and federal levels is so expansive that it is to the APN's advantage to belong to the appropriate professional organizations, most of which employ lobbyists whose business it is to track legislation. Specialty organization newsletters and journals, legislative subscription and monitoring services, and bulletins that summarize proposed regulations may be used to monitor these processes. Subscription services track legislation for an agency or organization and provide an abstract, including the substance of bills and regulations and the progress through the legislative or regulatory process. Both free and subscription legislative information services are available online. Examples of online services include the following:

- State Net: Information and intelligence for the 50 states and Congress, located at http://www.statenet.com
- Thomas Legislative Information: Sponsored by the U.S. Library of Congress, located at http://thomas.loc.gov
- GPO Access: Located at http://www.gpoaccess.gov
- Federal Legislative Branch: Located at http://www.USA.gov. This is the U.S. government's official web portal.

In addition, numerous private services are available and can be found by searching the Internet. Several nursing and healthcare associations also feature relevant updates and information on current legislative and public policy issues (see **Exhibit 4-3**).

Exhibit 4-3 Selected Websites of Interest

---

http://www.statenet.com Legislative and regulatory reporting services from all 50 states and Congress. A subscription service that provides comprehensive and timely information on legislation.

http://thomas.loc.gov Thomas Legislative Information System. Sponsored by the U.S. Library of Congress. Summarizes bills, provides full text of bills and the Congressional Record, information on the legislative process, and U.S. government Internet resources.

http://www.ahrq.gov Agency for Healthcare Research and Quality. Provides Information on healthcare research, evidence reports, clinical practice guidelines, consumer health information; hyperlinked to U.S. Department of Health and Human Services.

http://www.ctel.org Center for Telemedicine Law. Information on the latest findings in the regulation of telemedicine, proceedings of national telemedicine task force, state-by-state updates on telemedicine legislation.

http://www.nursingworld.org American Nurses Association. Access to all ANA services; access to *Online Journal of Issues in Nursing*; jointly prepared with Kent State University.

http://www.ncsbn.org National Council of State Boards of Nursing. Information on all National Council services and committee activities, access to state nurse practice acts, information on progress of multistate regulation.

http://www.hhs.gov U.S. Department of Health and Human Services. Access to all agencies within the department—that is, ACHPR, CDC, CMS, HRSA, NIH, and so forth. Includes consumer information and policy information.

http://www.hschange.com The Center for Studying Health Systems Change. A Washington, D.C.–based research organization dedicated to studying the nation's healthcare systems and the impact on the public.

http://www.nurse.org State-by-state display of advanced practice nursing organizations, links to related sites that contain legislative and regulatory information, NP Central (a comprehensive site for APN CE offerings, salary information, job opportunities).

http://www.nursingethicsnetwork.org Nursing Ethics Network. A nonprofit-organization committed to the advancement of nursing ethics. Site contains ethics research findings and online inquiry.

http://www.acnpweb.org American College of Nurse Practitioners. Comprehensive site featuring latest trends and issues affecting APN practice and regulation.

http://www.aanp.org American Academy of Nurse Practitioners. Comprehensive site featuring latest trends and issues affecting APN practice and regulation.

http://www.cms.hhs.gov/hipaa Centers for Medicare and Medicaid Services. Provides latest legislative and regulatory information on reimbursement, HIPAA implementation.

http://www.hhs.gov/ocr/hipaa Office of Civil Rights. Fact sheets, sample forms, FAQs on HIPAA implementation, along with related links and educational materials.

http://www.iom.edu Institute of Medicine. Provides objective information to further science and health policy. A leading and respected authority on health issues. Access to published reports.

Providing Public Comment

There is a small window of opportunity for public input into the development of regulations. Most comment periods are a minimum of 30 days from the date of the publication of the proposed rule, although sometimes an NPR will provide for a longer period of time to submit comments if the agency anticipates the issue will be one of strong public interest or will be controversial in nature. It is very important that the APN is vigilant in tracking when the comment periods are set.

Public hearings may be held by an agency on a proposed rule, but are not required unless the APA establishes criteria for when a public hearing must be held by the agency. Generally, the agency is required to hold a hearing when a request is made by a specified number of individuals or agencies. Written comments received by the agency are made a part of the permanent record and must be considered by the agency's board or commission members prior to the publication of the final rule. A final rule can be challenged in the courts if the judge determines that the agency did not comply with the APA or ignored public comments.

The *Federal Register* names the individual in the agency who can be contacted to submit comments. It is best to place the comments in writing to ensure inclusion in the public record, though it is permissible to call the agency and provide comments orally if time is of the essence. Faxing comments or providing an electronic copy may also be an option if the comment period is near expiration. It is of utmost importance that the deadline posted in the *Federal Register* is met because agencies can rightfully disregard comments received after the deadline.

When providing public comment in writing, or testimony at a hearing, it is important for the APN to:

- Be specific regarding whether the regulation is supported or opposed. Give examples using brief scenarios or experiences when possible.
- Have credible data to back the position, such as statistics. Use research findings that can be explained in common language; avoid medical jargon.
- Know what the opposition is saying and respond to these concerns.
- Convey a willingness to negotiate or compromise toward mutually-acceptable resolutions.
- Demonstrate concern for the public good, rather than self-interest.
- Be brief and succinct. Limit remarks to one or two pages or 5 minutes for oral testimony.

Regulatory agencies charged with public protection are more likely to address concerns that are focused on how the public may be harmed or benefited rather than concerns that seem like turf protection and professional jealousy. Demonstrate support for your position by having colleagues who represent a variety of organizations and interests submit comments. This is a powerful method to employ; it is important to demonstrate the degree of concern because the number of comments received is one way the agency measures support or nonsupport for the regulation.

Strengths and Weaknesses of the Regulatory Process

The regulatory process is much more ordered than the legislative process, in that the administrative procedures act in each state and at the federal level directs the process that must be undertaken. There is guaranteed opportunity for comment and public input, as the regulatory process has built-in delays and time constraints that slow down action. On the other hand, the regulatory process also is much more controlled by administrative agencies and can often become tedious and complex in detail of implementation. Regulations may not always be written by individuals who are knowledgeable about the substance or impact of new or revised rules, making the public input process especially important.

One power that may be provided to administrative agencies is to interpret regulations. It is especially important to be aware that existing regulations may be misinterpreted by the staff or board of an agency, resulting in a new meaning being imposed rather than the original intent of the regulation.

New interpretations to existing statutes and regulations may occur over time. For this reason, it is especially important to review opinions and/or declaratory rulings of the board, attorney general opinions, and opinions of the court. Official opinions carry the force and effect of law even though they are not promulgated according to the APA. There is a fine line between the duty to interpret existing laws and regulations and establishing new laws or standards without complying with the APA. The courts have revoked several board rulings, requiring boards to institute new regulations according to the APA. In some states, such as Ohio, official opinions interpreting statute or regulation are only generated by the attorney general's office or the courts. However, regulatory boards may offer interpretive guidelines or other documents to facilitate public understanding and compliance.

CURRENT ISSUES IN REGULATION AND LICENSURE

Regulation in a Transforming Healthcare Delivery System

The current system of regulation of healthcare professionals is based on the regulation of the individual provider and the employment setting. Questions have been raised as to whether this system is the best means of public protection, or whether the system has become a means of protecting the profession and creating monopolies for services (Gross, 1984; Pew Health Professions Commission, 1994). As new healthcare occupations and professions have emerged, there has been increasing professional debate about which tasks can be accomplished by which professions. Overlapping scopes of practice have naturally emerged among nursing, medicine, pharmacy, social work, physical therapy, occupational therapy, and other licensed health professions. Overlapping scopes of practice are appropriate when competency and education to perform the acts are substantially equivalent, but restrictive practice acts have made overlapping scopes of practice a battlefield for debate, a debate with which APNs are very familiar.

The Pew Health Professions Commission (1995) published a sweeping report that began to change thinking about the existing regulatory systems. The report suggested that the current century-old regulatory system is out of sync with the nation's healthcare delivery and financing structures and in need of major reform. The web of laws and regulations created by bureaus, agencies, boards, and legal departments makes it difficult for the public and those regulated to participate in what Dower and Finocchio (1995) call an "exclusionary scheme" (p. 2). The Pew Health Professions Commission suggested that states review the regulatory process in light of the following criteria:

- Does regulation promote effective health outcomes and protect the public from harm?
- Are regulatory bodies truly accountable to the public?
- Does regulation respect consumers' rights to choose their own healthcare providers from a range of safe options?
- Does regulation encourage a flexible, rational, and cost-effective healthcare system?
- Does regulation allow effective working relationships among healthcare providers?

- Does regulation promote equity among providers of equal skill?
- Does regulation facilitate professional and geographic mobility of competent providers? (Dower & Finocchio, 1995, p. 1)

Workforce regulation has a tremendous impact on the cost and accessibility of health care. Restrictive scopes of practice limit the ability of comparably-prepared providers to provide care, while employers have expanded the use of unlicensed assistive personnel (UAP) who infringe on the scope of practice defined for the licensed nurse. Boundary disputes within and across disciplines flourish—between nursing and allied health providers, allied health providers and medicine, nursing and medicine, dental hygienists and dentists, and nurses and UAPs.

The Pew Task Force on Health Care Workforce Regulation challenged the state and federal government to respond to the complex issues regarding the education and regulation of the health professions. The task force offered 10 recommendations to make the state regulatory system more responsive to the evolving healthcare system, calling for attention to standardized and understandable language, standardization of entry-to-practice requirements, assurance of initial and continuing competence of healthcare practitioners, and the redesign of professional boards, including the creation of super boards with a majority of consumer representatives. The report also called for better methods of assessing the achievement of objectives and disciplinary processes (Pew Health Professions Commission, 1995). Since then, the Institute of Medicine has issued a number of reports related to safety in healthcare systems. A part of that focus has called for licensing and certification bodies to pay greater attention to safety-related performance standards and expectations for health professionals (Kohn, Corrigan, & Donaldson, 2000).

A consensus report issued by the Robert Wood Johnson Foundation (RWJF) and the Institute of Medicine (IOM) on the future of nursing was released in October 2010. The report, *The Future of Nursing: Leading Change, Advancing Health*, provides four key messages to guide changes and remove barriers that prevent nurses from being able to function effectively in a rapidly evolving healthcare system. These messages are that nurses should be enabled to practice to the full extent of their education and training, should be able to access higher levels of education and training in an improved education system that allows for academic progression; should be full partners in the interprofessional redesign of the U.S. healthcare system; and finally that effective workforce planning and policymaking needs better data collection and information infrastructures. Eight recommendations for fundamental changes are found in the report, along with related actions for Congress, state legislatures, the Centers for Medicare and Medicaid Services, the Office of Personnel Management, and the Federal Trade Commission and Antitrust Division of the Department of Justice. The eight recommendations are: 1) remove scope-of-practice barriers; 2) expand opportunities for nurses to lead and diffuse collaborative improvement efforts; 3) implement nurse residency programs; 4) increase the proportion of nurses with a baccalaureate degree to 80 percent by 2020; 5) double the number of nurses with a doctorate by 2020; 6) ensure that nurses engage in lifelong learning; 7) prepare and enable nurses to lead change to advance health; and 8) build an infrastructure for the collection and analysis of interprofessional healthcare workforce data (Institute of Medicine, 2010).

There is a window of opportunity to achieve significant reform in the regulation of the health professions in the 21st century. Advanced practice nurses must be open to the concept of new regulatory models that may emerge. Regulation will determine who will have access to the patient, who will serve as the gatekeeper in a managed care environment, who will be reimbursed, and who will have autonomy to practice. APNs must be visible participants throughout the political process to shape a dynamic and evolving system that is responsive to the healthcare environment and ensures consumer choice and protection.

Multistate Regulation

Technology has transformed the healthcare delivery system and is challenging the state-by-state regulatory and licensing system. Mergers, acquisitions, and buyouts of healthcare systems have produced giant conglomerates that operate across state lines, with care being coordinated by case managers who may be located in distant states. The Internet and e-mail afford patients access to hundreds of disease specialty home pages on the World Wide Web sponsored by institutions and voluntary associations. Over the past decade, a variety of telemedicine services have emerged, serving both patients and healthcare providers. United HealthCare's website, called OptumHealth (http://www.optumhealth.com) offers nursing online services. Individuals submit questions and nurses research answers and provide personalized information within 48 to 72 hours (Gobis, 1997).

Although states have done much over the years to facilitate the interstate mobility of nurses, there are still cumbersome licensure processes that make seamless transitions across geopolitical boundaries difficult or impossible. The confusion is especially prominent in the regulation of APNs. Not only are there a variety of methods used to regulate APNs, ranging from second licensure to official recognition, titles vary from state to state, as do the scopes of practice and even the jurisdiction for regulation (i.e., nursing, medical, or joint boards). The NCSBN definition of Uniform Advanced Practice Registered Nurse Licensure/Authority to Practice Requirements will promote standardization of APN regulation to allow APNs to participate in multistate regulation as well as compete in a global market. Moving to a multistate regulatory system has advantages for the profession and must be carefully executed state by state to ensure that the mission of the boards to protect the public is achieved.

To that end, the NCSBN delegate assembly adopted the **mutual recognition** model of multistate regulation in 1997. Mutual recognition is a method of licensure in which boards voluntarily enter into an **interstate compact** to legally recognize the policies and processes of a licensee's home state to permit practice in the remote state without obtaining an additional license. If a violation of law occurs, the state in which the violation occurs is responsible for disciplinary action (National Council of State Boards of Nursing, 1998).

To implement the mutual recognition model of nursing regulation, each state legislature must sign the interstate compact into law. Advanced practice nurses initially were not a part of the interstate compact agreement, but with the move toward adoption of the Uniform Requirements for Licensure/Authority to Practice, APNs will be able to participate in the multistate regulation process. The APN must reside in a state that has already joined the interstate compact and subscribed to the uniform requirements. The multistate license does not, however, include prescriptive authority, which must be sought independently in the state of practice.

Given the climate in the federal government related to the business of health care and the concept that this business is interstate commerce, a number of states have quickly moved to preserve state regulation of the professions, while facilitating interstate practice. As of June 2010, 24 states are participating as "compact states" (National Council of State Boards of Nursing, 2010).

THE FUTURE OF ADVANCED PRACTICE NURSE REGULATION

Much has been written in this chapter on the problems and issues related to the regulation of APNs. However, not all of the problems associated with the full utilization and practice of the APN are external to the profession; some of the problems have been created within the profession. The proliferation of APN educational programs with numerous specialty areas that have limited scopes of practice has created much of the public confusion regarding the role and scope of practice of the APN. Multiple educational pathways to achieve APN certification and legal credentialing have complicated the regulatory process further (O'Malley, Cummings, & King, 1996). The numerous titles used for APN practice are confusing not only to the public, but to regulatory agencies such as the Centers for Medicare and Medicaid Services that establish national reimbursement policies. Clear definitions of APN role and title, educational requirements, and scope of practice must become a regulatory priority.

Credentialing APNs has been a major source of debate at the national level. Should this level of provider be licensed rather than officially recognized? Should there be a core competency examination developed at the national level for APN credentialing? Do certification examinations developed by the specialty nursing organizations meet the legal defensibility of an entry-level licensure examination? Who is an APN? Should there be a minimum education requirement for use of the title? These are all questions that continue to be raised in forums between specialty nursing organizations and licensing agencies. Until the role of the APN is clearly understood by consumers and policymakers, APNs will continue to be underutilized and undervalued.

Two important issues related to the future of advanced practice nursing regulation that require monitoring by APNs include the NCSBN initiative to consider state board of nursing regulation of APNs in the future, and the related matter of the direction in which future APN education is moving, the practice doctorate.

The NCSBN 2006 draft Vision Paper, *The Future Regulation of Advanced Practice Nursing,* has been the subject of debate among advanced practice nursing organizations and the American Association of Colleges of Nursing (AACN) (American Association of Colleges of Nursing, 2006; National Council of State Boards of Nursing, 2006). The final report of the APRN Consensus Work Group and the NCSBN APRN Advisory Committee (APRN Joint Dialogue Group, 2008) was a major step in reaching a level of agreement between stakeholders in organized nursing. Major foundational requirements for licensure are described in this document, including a call for boards of nursing to be solely responsible for licensing advanced practice nurses.

Parallel to new directions in regulation of APNs is the new direction in advanced clinical nursing education. In an effort to respond to the changes in national direction for health professions education and credentialing, the AACN Board of Directors endorsed a Position Statement on the Practice Doctorate (DNP) in Nursing (American Association of Colleges of Nursing, 2004), which calls for a move in educational preparation for advanced practice nurses' to the doctorate level from the masters level by the year 2015. The AACN cites the need for change in graduate nursing education as a response to the increasing complexity of the nation's healthcare environment and points to national calls to action from the Institute of Medicine (IOM), the Joint Commission on the Accreditation of Healthcare Organizations (JCAHO), and the 2005 National Institutes of Health (NIH) report calling for the development of nonresearch clinical doctorates in nursing. Two AACN task forces have been initiated to address questions related to nursing education, certification, regulation, and practice that have been raised by the development of DNP programs. As of March 2010, 120 DNP programs are currently enrolling students nationwide, and the AACN reports that 161 others are under development at U.S. nursing schools (American Association of Colleges of Nursing, 2010).

Reimbursement

Significant breakthroughs are being made in reimbursement policy for APNs, largely as a result of the formation of grassroots lobbying efforts and coalitions of APN specialty-nursing organizations. With the passage of federal legislation in 1997 allowing APNs to bill Medicare directly for services, APNs have had the opportunity to increase consumers' access to care. The managed care markets value efficiency and effectiveness in providers, and so APNs are learning how to cost out services in the competitive market to win contracts and demonstrate cost-effective, quality-care outcomes to patients.

In managed care contracts where reimbursement is capitated, the amount of reimbursement is not as important as knowing whether the services can be provided for the capitated fee. Research studies are needed to document the cost of care and demonstrate nursing interventions that reduce the use of costly healthcare services over time. Studies that demonstrate the value-added activities of nursing intervention, cost–benefit analysis of interventions, and patient satisfaction with care are emerging in the literature and can be very useful in negotiating contracts for patient populations. Understanding the business aspects of healthcare financing and creating successful practices are new roles for entrepreneurial APNs who are managing the health care for a group of clients. It is a role in which APNs are gaining more comfort and experience.

Impact of the Nurse Shortage on Regulation and Licensure

Supply and demand projections substantiate that the shortage of nurses and other healthcare providers will continue well into 2015. The factors driving the shortage include a growing aging population who will consume more healthcare services, the aging of the nursing workforce resulting in a large cohort of nurses retiring from the profession, and the inability of nursing to attract men, minorities, and young people into the profession. Even though there have been numerous initiatives at the state and federal levels to reverse this trend, the nurse shortage continues to fuel policy on work environment issues across the nation.

Several issues bear monitoring during this period of a declining nursing workforce. They include the following:

1. *Delegation and supervision of unlicensed assistive personnel (UAP).* Practices for UAPs will continue to be debated and expanded as the shortage of licensed staff make it difficult to meet all the care demands of the public. Providing safe and effective care while delegating care to UAPs will place additional responsibilities on the licensed nurse.

2. *Mandatory overtime legislation.* Research has shown that fatigue affects the mental acuity of an individual, leading to more errors in judgment and in medical errors that could result in harm to the patient. The Institute of Medicine has published findings that link medical errors to the number and educational level of nurses employed as well as to fatigue of the staff (Institute of Medicine, 1999). Employers have used the concept of patient abandonment to force employees to remain on duty against their will, threatening staff who leave the employment setting with patient abandonment that would result in a report to the licensing board. Laws have been passed in several states that preclude an employer from requiring staff to work beyond their scheduled assignment against their will.

3. *Staffing ratios.* In some states, the nurses have organized to pass legislation to implement staffing ratios that guarantee a nurse-to-patient ratio dependent on the acuity of the patient. Staffing ratios have both positive and negative implications. Although the regulations for staffing ratios may require a set number of nurses to be employed, the minimum ratios imposed by law may be seen by

the employer as the maximum number that must be employed, thereby placing a cap on hiring and negatively affecting the quality of care.

4. *Foreign nurse recruitment.* There is often an attempt to increase the recruitment of foreign-educated nurses when there is an acute nurse shortage in the United States. Legislation is often introduced during these periods of time to relax the standards for licensure and to accept competency examinations that are not equivalent to the National Council Licensure Examination (NCLEX). The nursing community must be vigilant to these attempts to lower the standards for licensure and thus prevent discrimination against U.S.-educated graduates.

5. *Proliferation of new nursing education programs.* Nationally, colleges, universities, and other accredited and legitimate public and private educational institutions are finding that the business of nursing education is becoming more attractive, and there are more qualified applicants for nursing programs then there are seats. However, proprietary organizations are also seeing nursing education as an opportunity for profit, without consideration of the infrastructure and support systems necessary to carry out a quality program. State Boards of Nursing are being challenged to strike a balance between an open marketplace and a desire to protect the stretched interests of existing programs that are struggling to maintain a cadre of qualified faculty and ensure clinical placements for their students.

Other trends and issues will surface over the next several years that may affect the regulation of nurses and APNs. It will be increasingly important to stay abreast of legislative and regulatory initiatives and to affiliate with professional organizations to preserve and protect professional standards.

CONCLUSION

Today is an era of rapid transformation in almost every aspect of life. Change is constant, and it rapidly forces adaptability and flexibility on the part of all individuals. Changes in the delivery of health care are transforming the practice and regulation of the APN. Today, the APN must develop skills to capitalize on the chaos in the healthcare system and create opportunities for the advantage of the profession rather than fear the future. One way to capitalize on the times is to become politically astute and learn to shape public policy through working with coalitions of nurses, other providers, and consumers to advocate for quality health care at an affordable cost.

Knowing how to navigate the regulatory process will give the APN the tools needed to become a confident spokesperson. Seeking and finding information on the status of issues critical to the APN, such as reimbursement, scopes of practice, and licensure issues, keeps the APN knowledgeable about how best to influence outcomes.

Participating in professional nursing organizations provides a forum for building strong coalitions and gaining power in the political process. Each APN has the ability to make a difference.

DISCUSSION POINTS AND ACTIVITIES

1. Contrast the major differences in the legislative and regulatory processes.
2. Describe the major methods of credentialing. List the benefits and weaknesses of each method from the standpoint of public protection and protection of the professional scope of practice.
3. Discuss the role of professional organizations in regulating professional practice.
4. Describe an ethical dilemma that you have recently experienced. What principles were in conflict with each other? Which principle ruled in your decision? Why?
5. Obtain a copy of a proposed or recently promulgated regulation. Using Exhibit 4-1, analyze the regulation for its impact on nursing practice.
6. Assume the board of nursing has promulgated a regulation requiring all APNs to have 20 contact hours of continuing-education credit in pharmacotherapeutics each year to maintain prescriptive authority. Write a brief (no more than two pages) testimony supporting or opposing this proposed regulation.
7. Describe the federal government's role in the regulation of health professions. Do you believe the role will increase or decrease over time? Explain your rationale.
8. Discuss the pros and cons of multistate regulation. Based on your analysis, defend a position either for or against multistate regulation.
9. Prepare written testimony for a public hearing defending or opposing the need for a second license for APNs.
10. Contrast the board of nursing and the national or state nurses association vis-à-vis mission, membership, authority, functions, and source of funding.
11. Identify a proposed regulation. Discuss the current phase of the process, identify methods of offering comments, and submit written comments to the administrative agency.
12. Download at least one resource from one of the websites listed in Exhibit 4-3 and evaluate it according to reliability of the author, last update, and appropriateness of data. Share the resources with colleagues.
13. Evaluate the board of nursing in your state using the criteria for review of regulatory agencies developed by the Pew Health Professions Commission (1995).
14. Identify the states that have implemented nurse-staffing ratios. List some of the obstacles the state has encountered in the implementation phase.

CASE STUDY 1: Regulation of Pronouncement of Death in Ohio

The profession vested with the responsibility and legal authority to pronounce death varies from state to state. In Ohio, the statutory responsibility for pronouncement of death is prescribed in Chapter 2105 of the Ohio Revised Code. This section of state law is titled "Descent and Distribution," and includes the definitions of living and death, the determination of next of kin, and the disposition of personal estates. Section 2105.34 is subtitled "Determination and Evidence of Death." This section designates the physician as the licensee who may determine death and establishes that the criteria for the determination of death must be in accordance with section 2108.40 of the Revised Code. Death is defined in that section of state law as "either irreversible cessation of circulatory and respiratory functions *or* irreversible cessation of all functions of the brain, including the brain stem, as determined in accordance with acceptable medical standards" (emphasis added). Mention of immunity from civil liability and criminal prosecution relative to pronouncement of death is also addressed in this section. It should be noted that this section of statute is separate from both the medical practice act and the nurse practice act.

The role of the physician in the pronouncement of death is further prescribed in Rule 4731-14-01 of the Ohio Administrative Code. This rule amplifies the Medical Practice Act and specifies that only a currently certificated physician may pronounce a person dead, though the physician may do so without personally examining the body of the deceased if a competent observer has "recited the facts of the deceased's present medical condition to the physician and the physician is satisfied that death has occurred." In this rule, licensed registered nurses and licensed practical nurses are listed, among others, as possible competent observers. As a part of a policy course, master's level students in a nurse practitioner track were given the option of engaging in a field experience to meet part of the requirements for the degree. Relevant criteria for the substance of the field experience included the following: a: 1) a researchable topic; 2) use of a scholarly approach (i.e., must use a theory or model as a foundation or framework); and 3) amenable to written and oral presentation. Several students were enthusiastic about such an opportunity and approached the course faculty, who in turn contacted her state representative. The representative encouraged this approach to learning about public policy, and willingly met with the students and two faculty members (both faculty were teaching the policy course). He brought the state nurse's association's legislative agenda with him to aid in the discussion, the goal of which was to identify a legislative issue that would be substantively useful to nurses in Ohio. The students, faculty, and legislator jointly decided that the restrictions requiring that the pronouncement of death by a physician was a timely issue. In most cases, the registered nurse is with the patient at the time of death. The requirement of physician pronouncement of death poses hardships on not only nurses who are attending to the deceased patient, but also on distraught family members who must await arrival of the physician. In many facilities, the attending physician may be the one required to make the decision; in facilities such as long-term care, there may be a substantial delay between the actual time of death and the arrival of the physician. Modification of the statute to permit registered nurses to pronounce death would be of great benefit to Ohio nurses, their clients, families, and significant others.

Once the legislative issue was identified, the students proceeded to the research phase of the project. The legislator and faculty members served as resources and guides, suggesting that students first determine whether this change had been made in other states. Students found that nurses had been granted authority to pronounce death in 22 other states, and from that list, they conducted a telephone survey of nurses who had been intimately involved in the legislative change in 5 of those 22 states. The telephone interviews revealed that the bulk of the opposition experienced during the process came from organized medicine (e.g., state medical associations).

The next step was to work with stakeholders to identify major issues. The majority of stakeholders was supportive, and included the state nurse's association and organizations representing hospice and long-term care. The state medical association indicated that they would not oppose language permitting nurses to pronounce death, though they did indicate they would not support language allowing nurses to sign the death certificate. Nurses who researched this issue were told by those who worked on legislation in other states that physicians were reimbursed for signing a death certificate but not for pronouncing death. A bill was drafted and introduced into the Ohio House of Representatives by the faculty members' representative. The state medical association remained neutral during introduction. The bill was assigned to the House Health Committee. While in Committee, the state medical association sought to amend the bill by eliminating the nurses' authority to pronounce death in acute care facilities, by adding language describing requirements for documentation of death and for defining what it would mean to notify the physician of death in a "timely manner." The bill spent the better part of the General Assembly in Committee, but passed out of Committee. At this time, other politically-charged advanced nurse practice issues were pressing in the legislature, such as removing barriers to prescribing schedule II drugs. Whether those issues were a distraction from this bill or whether the bill garnered support from more legislators, the bill moved successfully out of the House. The bill than became stuck in a "lame duck" session, meaning that November elections had occurred and the political party of the governor's office and the General Assembly changed; the current legislators would no longer hold a majority and the probability of many bills awaiting passage was unlikely. The current legislative leadership announced that there would be no lame duck session and the prouncement bill died in session without ever getting to the Senate.

The bill's sponsor left the legislature to take a position in his home district. The House bill lost momentum without his influence in the Senate when the new Senate leadership did not seem interested in picking up the bill.

Whether or not nurses will eventually be given legislative authority to pronounce death will be dependent on whether a sponsor can be found and is willing to reintroduce the issue in the next General Assembly, the level of energy organized nursing is willing to spend on this particular issue, and the positions of various stakeholders relative to the bill's support or opposition. At this juncture, registered nurses in Ohio continue to be limited to the same role they have always played in the pronouncement of death, that of a competent observer.

DISCUSSION POINTS AND ACTIVITIES

1. Identify ways to increase the likelihood for the legislation to pass in this General Assembly or the next.
2. Determine a complete list of possible stakeholders. What groups may be interested in this change in regulation besides the state nurse's association, state medical association, hospice association, hospital association, and long-term care?
3. Discuss the notion of "incremental legislation," noting the changes that were made to the language while the bill was in the House Health Committee.
4. Who do you think could carry on the work started by students after they graduate? What do you think students learned from this field experience?
5. Whom would you choose to spearhead this bill? For what reasons?

CASE STUDY 2: Changes in Regulations

Advanced practice nurses may find themselves in teaching roles. Schools of nursing often employ APNs to teach advanced practice students, or may be asked to teach assessment skills at the undergraduate level. APNs engaged in teaching roles must have an understanding of the regulations affecting nursing education in addition to those affecting general and advanced nursing practice. The following case focuses on changes in education rules in one state, though the process could easily be applied to changes in any regulations affecting nursing.

In most states, education regulations devote a section to the supervision of nurse students by qualified faculty and instructional personnel, and also speak to the leadership of the nursing program by qualified administrators (e.g., chairs, deans, or directors). In one state, a long-standing regulation accounted for the occasional absence of the program administrator in the case of illness or other personal reason. The regulation read that if the program administrator was absent for a period of 30 or more business days, a qualified interim administrator would need to be named, and the board of nursing notified. This regulation, in effect, protected the integrity of the nursing programs by assuring continuity of program leadership.

During a revision of all of the education regulation, which, in that state, is required every five years, the rule was redrafted so that the period of time was extended to 90 days from 30 days, and it is believed that this was an effort to make the rule more "generous." However, additional language in the same regulation was added so that the scope of the rule expanded from the coverage of short absences, lasting a month or more, to include the vacating of the position by the administrator, that is, resignation. In addition, the word "interim" was deleted. In effect, a nursing program would have to replace the administrator within a 90 day period. In most cases, this time frame is inadequate to conduct a search and hire a qualified person to fill the position. It is not uncommon for chair or dean searches to take up to a year in most colleges and universities.

A group of nursing education program leaders in the state discussed the impact of the regulation change as it was stated in draft form. The board of nursing held an open public hearing as a part of the rulemaking process; the group sent a representative to give both oral and written testimony. The board of nursing heard the testimony, and as a result had a more complete understanding of the meaning of the rule change to nursing education programs. The board of nursing redrafted the regulation; the revised draft still included both absences and vacancies, but also included language that required the designation of a qualified registered nurse to replace the program administrator *or* to serve as an interim program administrator.

DISCUSSION POINTS AND ACTIVITIES

Keeping in mind that it is imperative for nursing programs to comply with all board of nursing rules to maintain their approval status, consider the following questions:

1. If the draft language had not been changed, what would have been the effect on nursing programs if an administrator resigned unexpectedly?
2. What is the impact of the word "or" in the revised language?
3. Identify ways that APNs can stay abreast of potential changes in relevant nursing or related regulations.
4. Discuss the value of involvement with nursing organizations as a means to have an impact on changes in regulations; that is, how might a regulatory agency weigh the testimony of an individual versus the testimony of an organization representative?

For a full suite of assignments and additional learning activities, use the access code located in the front of your book to visit this exclusive website: http://go.jblearning.com/milstead. If you do not have an access code, you can obtain one at the site.

REFERENCES

American Academy of Nurse Practitioners. (2003). Medicare reimbursement fact sheet. Retrieved from http://www.aanp.org/NR/rdonlyres/D498CAF2-7BE6-4D89-A588-9DBC9CBD901A/0/MedicareReimbursementFactsheet.pdf

American Association of Colleges of Nursing. (2004). AACN position statement on the practice doctorate in nursing. Retrieved from http://www.aacn.nche.edu/DNP/DNPPositionStatement.htm

American Association of Colleges of Nursing. (2006). Nursing organizations respond to NCSBN's draft 2006 APRN vision paper. Retrieved from http://www.aacn.nche.edu/Education/ncsbnvision.htm

American Association of Colleges of Nursing. (2010). Doctor of nursing practice (DNP). Retrieved from http://www.aacn.nche.edu/Media/FactSheets/dnp.htm

APRN Joint Dialogue Group. (2008). Consensus model for APRN regulation: Licensure, accreditation, certification & education. Retrieved from https://www.ncsbn.org/170.htm

Braunstein, M. (1995). Homecare in cyberspace. *Computer Talk for Homecare Providers*, 5–12.

Canavan, K. (1996). Credentialing agencies agree on outside review. *American Nurse, 28*(5), 6.

Centers for Medicare and Medicaid Services. (2001, June 14). Fact sheet: The new Centers for Medicare and Medicaid services. Retrieved from http://www.hhs.gov/news/press/2001pres/20010614a.html

Copeland, C. W. (2008, August 28). The federal rulemaking process: An overview. Congressional Research Service Report RL32240. Retrieved from http://openregs.com/docs/copeland-rulemaking-process.pdf

Dower, C., & Finocchio, L. (1995). Health care workforce regulation: Making the necessary changes for a transforming health care system. *State Health Workforce Reforms, 4*, 1–2.

Garner, B. A. (2009). *Black's law dictionary* (9th ed.). St Paul, MN: West.

Gobis, L. J. (1997). Licensing and liability: Crossing the borders with telemedicine. *Caring, 16*(7), 18–24.

Goehlert, R. U., & Martin, F. S. (1989). *Federal administrative law. Congress and law making: Researching the legislative process* (2nd ed.). Santa Barbara, CA: ABC-CLIO.

Gross, S. (1984). *Of foxes and hen houses*. Westport, CT: Quorum.

HealthCare.gov. (2010). About the law: Patient Protection and Affordable Healthcare Act. Retrieved from http://www.healthcare.gov/law/about/Index.htm

Institute of Medicine. (1999). To err is human: Building a safer health system. (Report of the IOM). Retrieved from http://www.iom.edu /CMS/8089/5575.aspx

Institute of Medicine. (2010). The future of nursing: Leading change, advancing health. Retrieved from http://www.iom.edu/~/media/Files/Report%20Files/2010/The-Future-of-Nursing/Future%20of%20Nursing%202010%20Recommendations.pdf

Jost, T. S. (1997). *Regulation of the health professions*. Chicago: Health Administration Press.

Kohn, L. T., Corrigan, J. M., & Donaldson, M. S. (Eds). (2000). *To err is human: Building a safer health care system*. Institute of Medicine of the National Academies. Washington, DC: National Academies Press.

National Council of State Boards of Nursing. (1998, April). *Multi state regulation task force communiqué.* Chicago: Author.

National Council of State Boards of Nursing. (2002). Regulation of advanced nursing practice position paper. Retrieved from https://www.ncsbn.org/1993_Position_Paper_on_the_Regulation_of_Advanced_Nursing_Practice.pdf

National Council of State Boards of Nursing. (2006). Draft—Vision paper: The future regulation of advanced practice nursing. Retrieved from https://www.ncsbn.org/Draft_APRN_Vision_Paper.pdf

National Council of State Boards of Nursing. (2008). APRN model act/rules and regulations. Retrieved from https://www.ncsbn.org/170.htm

National Council of State Boards of Nursing. (2008). Contact a board of nursing. Retrieved from https://www.ncsbn.org/515.htm

National Council of State Boards of Nursing. (2010). Map of NLC states. Retrieved from http://www.ncsbn.org/nlc

O'Malley, J., Cummings, S., & King, C. S. (1996). The politics of advanced practice. *Nursing Administration Quarterly, 20*(3), 62–69.

Pearson, L. J. (2002). Fourteenth annual legislative update. *Nurse Practitioner, 27*(1), 10–52.

Pew Health Professions Commission. (1994). *State strategies for health care workforce reform.* San Francisco: UCSF Center for the Health Professions.

Pew Health Professions Commission. (1995). *Report of task force on health care workforce regulation* (executive summary). San Francisco: UCSF Center for the Health Professions.

Phillips, S. J. (2010). 22nd annual legislative update. *Nurse Practitioner, 35*(1), 24–47.

Roberts, M. J., & Clyde, A. T. (1993). *Your money or your life: The health care crisis explained.* New York: Doubleday.

Safriet, B. J. (1992). Health care dollars and regulatory sense: The role of advanced practice nursing. *Yale Journal of Regulation, 9*, 2.

Sheets, V. (1996). *Public protection or professional self-preservation.* NCSBN Monograph, 3.

Weisenbeck, S. M., & Calico, P. A. (1995). *Issues and trends in nursing* (2nd ed.). St. Louis, MO: Mosby.

CHAPTER 5

Policy Design

Patricia Smart

KEY TERMS

Fire alarms: Signals built into a policy that alerts policymakers that the design, implementation, or evaluation phase is in danger of failing.

Participation: Extent to which individuals in the target population join in government programs.

Policy link: Connection between policy ideas and their implementation.

INTRODUCTION

The purpose of this chapter is to examine the component of the policy process that involves the "tools" that government uses to get people to do what they might not ordinarily do. The scope of government's involvement in social issues in the United States has increased rapidly during the last 90 years. Federally funded healthcare programs such as Medicare and Medicaid have made a major impact on how health care is implemented by providers and perceived by the public. As noted by Comer (2002), government involvement in health care has occurred at the state and local levels through program administration, educational preparation, licensing, and regulation of practice.

Health care is fraught with a multitude of factors that are difficult to identify and control, and the issue of healthcare reform has polarized the country. As noted by Eileen T. O'Grady (2010), there is massive misinformation and confusion about the many aspects of this bill: "It is like a giant root ball that cannot be understood without untangling and pulling apart each root" (p. 8). The intractability of most factors that lie within the healthcare field prevents uncomplicated, comprehensive, easily understandable solutions. One of the most elusive factors inhibiting policy success is the ability to predict consumer behavior and participation in a program. The gap in matching desired behavior with appropriate government tools is discussed in this chapter. Advanced practice nurses (APNs) are in a perfect position to help policymakers have a clear understanding of how important target population participation can be maximized by choosing the appropriate tool.

The United States has one of the most sophisticated healthcare systems (although challengers call it a "sick care system") in the world in terms of technology and preparation of healthcare professionals. Yet in many of the health indices designed to evaluate the overall health of a country, the United States rates comparatively low. For example, the average life expectancy for females in the United States is 80.9 years, while in many other developed countries such as Japan, Canada, and the Netherlands, a female's life expectancy is 86.1, 82.9, and 81.9 years, respectively (Central Intelligence Agency, 2009b). Infant mortality also is an important measure of a nation's health. In 2009, the United States ranked 33rd (6.3/1000 live births under one year) among industrialized countries in infant mortality (Central Intelligence Agency, 2009a). New cases of low birth weight and very low birth weight, both of which contribute to infant mortality, have increased in the United States (U.S. Department of Health and Human Services, 2002). The system is broken. It suffers from unwarranted variations in performance, effectiveness, and efficiency.

Efforts have been made by previous administrations to address the issues of cost, access, and quality, and those efforts were a reflection of the current political philosophies and ideologies. For example, the government programs in the 1960s reflected a democratic ideology where there was less concern with outcome-based planning and more concern with access, while in the 1980s under a Republican administration, regulatory efforts attempted to reduce costs through outcome-based choices, individual responsibility for cost, and less expansion.

Policies are usually designed to influence behavior and, as noted earlier, get people to do what they ordinarily might not do. As noted by Longest (2002), health policies address health concerns through laws, regulations, or programs that focus on health determinants including behavioral choices, the physical environment in which people live and work, and social factors. Although many studies regarding the policy process have been conducted, few have examined the process of policy design in issues of health care. The focus of most policy studies has been on the implementation of effective programs, and data have been gathered on statistical outcomes. This author argues that design considerations also should be a component to be considered during all phases of the policy process to promote policy success. For example, in the agenda-setting phase, the social issue must be stated in such a way that it will capture the attention of lawmakers and framed so that government response will be feasible and adaptable. During the implementation phase, the design of the policy provides guidance and also provides an overall picture of the plan by specifying the intended outcomes. During the evaluation phase (this phase should be specified in the design), the program objectives are clearly identified and measurable, or it would be difficult to determine that the focus is on an outcome that addresses the original issue.

THE POLICY PROCESS

Policies reflect public opinion. The policy players are a collection of actors whose task is to find a solution to intractable problems. According to Thompson (1981), the policy process "involves a complicated interaction among government institutions, actors, and the particular characteristics of substantive policy areas" (p. ix). Policies that address social problems in the United States usually are formulated by a combination of leg-islators and aides, the executive branch, courts, and special-interest groups. Profes-sional experts are often asked to serve as panel members or consultants or to serve on committees that provide input to policymakers, and so advanced practice nurses are asked to serve on committees that relate to health care. For example, nurse leaders were invited to sit at the table during the early 1990s when Hillary Clinton was proposing a national plan to change existing healthcare policies.

The proliferation of participants in policy formation makes systematic program design that is focused on outcomes difficult to achieve, which is also complicated by the fact that social problems are usually intractable and difficult to solve. Safriet (2002) reports that most social issues are not brought to the attention of policymakers until there is a crisis with multiple causative factors. Decision-making with regard to relevant factors that relate to or have an impact on perceived social problems often is conducted hastily because of lack of information, constituency impatience, and lack of expertise (Dryzek, 1983).

REVIEW OF POLICY RESEARCH

Other chapters in this text review the research contributions to modern thought regard-ing agenda setting, implementation, and evaluation. Notable work has been conducted and many of the models stemming from this work are in use today in the study of the policy process. For example, Pressman and Wildavsky in 1973 noted the complexity of implementation and the difficulty in achieving policy success when many branches and divisions of government attempt to work together. Bardach (1977), in his classic work, identified certain relationships among policy actors that developed through game play-ing. He identified activities, such as bargaining and negotiating among players, which make a tremendous impact on policy success and failure. Bardach also notes that a good policy must begin with a design that incorporates scenarios that can anticipate games and "**fire alarms**." For example, in some states, APNs have to be willing to allow a representative from the board of pharmacy or the board of medicine to be on the governing board that regulates nursing at the advanced level.

Other notable political scientists who also contributed to the study of the policy process include Kingdon (1995); Cohen, March, and Olsen (1972); and Dryzek (1983). These researchers looked at the way decisions were made (loose coupling, garbage can model) and the complexity of the policy.

Policy Links

During the 1980s, political scientists studied the content of policy with the inten-tion of providing an understanding of the link between policy design and policy out-come (**policy links**). Their efforts hold importance for APNs whose roles often require interpretation and implementation of policies. To improve the likelihood of policy success, APNs must be able to critically analyze policy content: specifically, they must be able to understand what the original intent of the policy is and if the policy is designed in such a way as to assure the intended outcome.

Schneider and Ingram (1990) argued for a closer look at design and proposed a framework to examine behavioral assumptions and attributes of policy content that can be employed by APNs to conduct the work of government. This framework was used by this author and also was used by Roch, Pitts, and Navarro (2010) to examine how racial and ethnic representation influences the tools public officials use in designing policies to address discipline in public schools.

Government policies are subject to a wide scope of interpretation that depends on who brings problems to national attention and which legislative group attaches itself to problems and solutions. Policies are often vague, with unclear mandates. This is intentional, in order to provide more discretion in the implementation of policies. An opportunity exists for APNs who recognize the value of vagueness; rather than waiting for clear directives, the nurse must learn and become comfortable with ambiguity because it allows discretion and flexibility in decision-making and action, thereby enhancing the ability to individualize management.

THE DESIGN ISSUE

Unclear mandates often result in a mismatch between congressional intent and bureaucratic behavior. For example, federal money that is allocated to states for harm-reduction programs, such as smoking cessation during pregnancy, may reach a segment of the target group that may not need it. Many college-educated women will not smoke during pregnancy, yet private healthcare providers have access to as much federal money to develop an antismoking program as their public agency counterparts.

Linder and Peters (1987) report that policy design was a reason for policy failure. Describing some programs as crippled at birth, these scholars note that the best bureaucracies in the world may not be able to achieve desired goals if an excessively ambitious policy is used (i.e., the problem is too complex for a single policy or agency). Also, if there is a misunderstanding of the nature of the problem, inappropriate policies may be formulated. Linder and Peters propose that implementation should be examined, but only as one of the conditions that must be satisfied for successful policymaking. They maintain that by shifting the focus of study to policy design, a more reliable and explicit answer can be found regarding policy success.

Other scholars concur with Linder and Peters. Ingraham (1987) argues that a systematic analysis of program design, rather than analysis using the garbage can model of agenda setting, could enhance policy success by allowing the option of considering alternative strategies and providing causal links, culminating in theory building. She focuses her work on two areas of policy design: the level of design (sophistication of the design) and the location (exclusive to the legislative arena, exclusion of experts).

Upon reviewing the policy literature, it is apparent that the design phase of the policy process continues to be an area where few policy scholars choose to focus their efforts. However, there are a few policy studies that look at design when examining social policy. For example, in a study conducted to examine policy-instrument utilization to promote electricity-efficient household appliances and office equipment, Varone and Aebischer (2001) determined that the political climate in which a policy is implemented is a critical factor to be considered when choosing instruments. In addition, the work of Roch, Pitts, and Navarro (2010), as noted earlier, looked as policy tools. In summary, policy design is an integral component of the policy process. An understanding of policy tools or instruments chosen for policy design and the underlying assumptions of policymakers during the design process is critical to an understanding of the overall policy process.

POLICY INSTRUMENTS

The study of the instruments or tools by which the government achieves desired policy goals has allowed researchers to examine policies in relation to their intent and to begin to infer predictive capabilities of tools. Two scholars proposed a framework for studying policy based on policy tools. Schneider and Ingram (1990) offer a framework to analyze implicit or explicit behavioral theories found in laws, regulations, and programs. Their analysis uses government tools or instruments and underlying behavioral assumptions as variables that guide policy decisions and choices. Their contention is that target group compliance and utilization are important forms of political behavior that should be examined closely. Combined with process variables such as competition, partisanship, and public opinion, Schneider and Ingram argue that the tools approach moves policy beyond considering the standard analysis and improved frameworks. They note that policy tools are substitutable and states often use a variety of tools to address a single problem. To understand which tools are most productive, emphasis should be placed on using them in conjunction with a particular policy design, and APNs can use their knowledge of policy tools to make suggestions and recommendations to government leaders who are designing policies and programs.

Government Tools

Schneider and Ingram (1990) state that public policy almost always attempts to get or enable people to do things they would not have done otherwise, and policy tools are those methods chosen by policymakers to overcome barriers to policy-relevant actions. Large numbers of people in different situations are involved in policymaking. Actions required by these players include compliance with policy rules, utilization of policy opportunities, and self-initiated actions, which promote policy goals. Schneider and Ingram suggest several issues that may affect the failure to take actions needed to ameliorate social, economic, or political problems: 1) lack of incentives or capacity; 2) disagreement with the values implicit in the means or ends; or 3) the existence of high levels of uncertainty about the situation that make it unclear what people should do or how to motivate them. The researchers describe five specific policy tools used by governments in designing policy. In addition, they identify five broad categories of tools, which include authority, incentives, capacity building, symbolic and hortatory, and learning.

Authority Tools

These are used most frequently by governments to guide behavior of agents and officials at lower levels. Authority tools are statements backed by the legitimate power of government that grant permission and prohibit or require action under designated circumstances. An example of an authority tool is a law, regulation, or mandate that requires that women qualify for prenatal services under regulated criteria.

Incentive Tools

These assume individuals are utility maximizers and will not be motivated positively to take action without encouragement or coercion. These tools rely on tangible payoffs (positive or negative) as motivating factors. Incentive policy tools manipulate tangible benefits, costs, and probabilities that policy designers assume are relevant to the situation. Incentives assume individuals have the "opportunity to make choices, recognize the opportunity, and have adequate information and decision-making skills to select from among alternatives that are in their best interests" (Schneider & Ingram, 1990, p. 516). An incentive tool, for example, may be coupons for free public transportation to prenatal clinics to encourage pregnant women to seek care. However, if the APN assumes that lack of transportation is a barrier to access prenatal care (in that transportation options do not exist, regardless of cost), the outcome from an attempt to use this particular incentive may fail.

Capacity-Building Tools

These devices provide information, training, education, and resources to enable individuals, groups, or agencies to make decisions or carry out activities. These tools assume that incentives are not an issue and that target populations will be motivated adequately. For capacity-building tools to work, populations must be aware of the risk factors the tools possess and how these tools can help. Capacity-building tools focus on education. For example, information may point out the risks of smoking and drugs on a fetus, and information on such risk factors is distributed to the target population through brochures, computer disks, or presentations. The underlying assumption is that information about the cessation of smoking is considered valuable, and that pregnant women will stop smoking if they have correct information.

Symbolic and Hortatory Tools

These instruments assume that people are motivated from within and decide whether to take policy-related actions on the basis of their beliefs and values. An example of this type of tool is a poster directed at adolescents that uses an adolescent model to issue advice or a warning. Such tools seek to gain the attention of the target population (adolescents) through use of peer imagery. Slogans also are symbolic and are used so that consumers link a positive or negative outcome to a particular behavior.

Learning Tools

These tools are used when the basis upon which target populations might be moved to take problem-solving action is unknown or uncertain. Policies that use learning tools often are open-ended in purpose and objectives and have broad goals. A needs assessment of the target population may be conducted by a task force, which provides knowledge and insight for policymakers and is an example of a learning tool. For example, if a community program related to addressing childhood obesity is to be proposed, a needs assessment must be conducted to determine what information is going to be needed before a proposal is drawn up for presentation to the county council.

Policy tools are important resources for the APN because they can enhance efforts to provide accurate information so that the patient can make informed decisions. For example, educational pamphlets relating to health promotion behaviors, such as dietary considerations for the diabetic, can be sent home with the patient. This type of tool will reinforce information received from the care provider and help the patient adhere to a fairly complicated change in lifestyle.

Behavioral Dimensions

In addition to understanding the types and the roles of tools in developing policy, the nurse in advanced practice must understand behavioral assumptions and the political context in which tools exist. The political climate in which social problems are addressed often prescribes the choice of tools to be implemented. Various tools are used when addressing similar social problems, and often these tools are interchanged, frequently resulting in differing outcomes when used by different agencies, states, or countries. In the United States, for example, liberal policymakers are inclined to use capacity-building tools when developing policy for poor and minority groups, whereas conservative policymakers might use the same types of tools in developing policy applicable to businesses.

USING TOOLS AS A LOOKING GLASS: TWO CASE STUDIES

Policy design is an integral component of the policy process. The choice of policy tools and the underlying assumptions of policymakers during the design process are critical to the success or failure of a policy. To help advanced practice nurse students wrap their heads around how to analyze the policy process by looking at the tools used to address a policy, it might be useful to briefly discuss a study conducted by a nurse doctoral student studying health policy. The question was: If the United States is supposed to have the best healthcare system in the world, why do we have one of the highest infant mortality rates among developed countries? The research involved analyzing how two different countries address the issue of infant mortality, specifically: what tools did the government in the Netherlands use that had such a different outcome than the United States?

Case Study 1: Comparative Analysis of Pregnancy Outcomes in Two Countries

The study (Smart, 2008) looked at how different governments might approach the issue of infant mortality. South Carolina (U.S.) and the Netherlands were chosen as the foci of study, and the questions related to factors such as political culture, economies, government response, and policy participation. Although the state and national levels of government are different, they are appropriate for comparative analysis because of their bicameral political structures. The most revealing factors regarding the differences in pregnancy outcomes were related to the approaches taken by the two governments to address the issue.

Political Culture

In the area of political culture, differences were evident. Even though South Carolina and the Netherlands are pluralist societies with democratically derived leadership and bicameral legislatures, many factors contribute to very different approaches to policy-making. The Constitution of the United States established a system of checks and balances that has led to a federal legislature that, even when dominated by the same party as the executive branch, has considerable autonomy and may be divided strongly on a given issue. This diffusion of power makes it difficult to enact and implement policies. The structure of federalism (a system of government that allows each state considerable room for decentralized development in terms of adapting to unique human and environmental circumstances) offers opportunities for bolder programs in states than at a national level. In addition, the cleavages and turf issues that exist in the United States present resistance to cooperation. Because of the growth of regulatory activities, policymaking has become more complex, with more interdependency and conflict, while the Dutch government is centralized with little discretion allowed to lower-level administrators in municipalities. This is the result of clear, specifically stated policies that limit administrative and management flexibility.

APNs in the United States often work in settings where even small policy changes involve multiple disciplines or departments and actors. For example, in a primary care setting, such as a family planning center, a policy change relating to Medicaid payment would affect patient recordkeeping for the social worker, dietitian, physician, and business manager, as well as the nurse. The APN must be prepared to assume a leadership role in the collaboration of the various disciplines in providing comprehensive care to the patient.

Economies

The gap between equality and distribution of income is greater in the United States than in the Netherlands. Income in the Netherlands falls within a close range, and so the income gap between the rich and the poor is very narrow; this is as opposed to the United States, where the gap is large and getting larger with the current economic situation and the resulting increased number of unemployed. Sardell (1990) notes that access to health care among the poor and unemployed is a long-standing concern of proponents of maternal and infant care. Despite an unemployment rate that exceeds that of South Carolina, prenatal services are provided to all Dutch women, regardless of income, with minimal financial barriers to care.

Government Response

This research found that governments in both countries used tools similar to those described in Schneider and Ingram's framework (1990), although the policy environments differed a great deal. Policies and initiatives developed and implemented by policymakers were analyzed by applying policy tools used in the conceptualization and implementation of the policy. As noted by Schneider and Ingram, "Policy tools are used to overcome impediments to policy relevant actions" (p. 510). Successful realization of policy goals requires active **participation** by the target population. If policymakers are not cognizant of motivating and deterring factors affecting the decision-making process of the target group, incorrect assumptions regarding participative behavior can result in an ineffective policy.

Although data relating to government responses to the problem of infant mortality revealed that policymakers in both countries were informed regarding beliefs and values of the target population, government-designed policies to address infant mortality in the United States have not been as successful in reducing the rate of infant mortality as in the Netherlands.

The area of family planning reflected the widest gap in the choice of tools. Several initiatives exist in most states, including South Carolina, that address family planning. All initiatives are activated through local and individualized programs, with no single program providing a clear and consistent framework to be followed by others. Although sex education is taught in the state-funded schools, each county may present the package in any form it chooses. Most key policymakers who are informed about the content of the sex-education curriculum practices around the state report that the content is often a very brief (15-minute) discussion each semester that covers broad concepts. In contrast, Dutch schools mandate a comprehensive sex education to all students beginning in the fifth grade. In addition, a government-funded family planning service is available through all general practitioners and midwives. The government is supported in these efforts by the majority of the Dutch citizens and most of the clergy.

Policy Participation

The success of a policy or program is highly dependent upon whether the target population perceives the services provided by the program to be valuable enough to warrant participation. Policy participation in this study revealed that co-production (assumption of the values and involvement of establishment of goals) of a policy is not coordinated in South Carolina, but that Dutch citizens are very involved with policy design and formulation. All Dutch citizens use the same healthcare system and, therefore, have more vested interest. Utilization of services in South Carolina is poor, which informants suggest is the result of very little input regarding policy formulation from the target population. Dutch women fully participate in family planning and prenatal healthcare programs.

Policy–Process Variables

Policy–process variables may make a major impact on the success or failure of a policy or program. Process variables include partisanship, public opinion, interest group strength, homogeneity between policymakers and the target population, and influence of policy analysis. As noted earlier, partisanship is deeply embedded in the United States and it affects decisions on policies addressing maternal and infant health; Democrats are disposed more favorably than Republicans toward capacity-building tools or positive inducements for populations such as the poor. The Netherlands, in contrast, is noted for its ability to provide an overarching relationship among political elites to provide harmony and stability. Lijphart (1977) notes that the Netherlands is "a dramatic example of the survival of a nation state as a stable democracy despite extreme social pluralism" (p. 103).

Public opinion regarding policies that address unwanted pregnancies in the United States is polarized. The divisions between those who favor open, factual, and consistent information regarding sexuality and sex education and those who feel that such an environment would foster more promiscuity and unwanted pregnancies are also reflected in the legislature, while in the Netherlands, public opinion is strongly and cohesively in favor of open communication between adolescents and the community at large regarding unwanted pregnancies. A gap exists in the United States between policymakers and the target population, and most informants state that this gap contributes to the relative lack of public support and the weakness of special-interest groups lobbying for prenatal care. Quite the opposite exists in the Netherlands. Political support is apathetic and inconsistent in South Carolina, yet is supportive, consistent, and proactive in the Netherlands.

CASE STUDY 2: Polypharmacy Problems

Polypharmacy, a common problem in America's geriatric population, increases the risks of drug-to-drug interactions. Advanced practice nurses are committed to providing compassionate, comprehensive, cost-effective health care that focuses on disease prevention, health promotion and patient education, and America's elders need and deserve this quality of care. Some of the factors that exacerbate the problem include: multiple health conditions requiring multiple specialists attending a patient; cost of medications leading to skipped dosing; and use of multiple pharmacies. The use of computer-based recording might help reduce contraindicated drug use, but to date no national or state policies are in place to regulate and reduce the incidence of the practice of writing prescriptions that are inappropriate for use in older adults. Questions that should be addressed when engaged in policymaking include:

1. Identify the goal of a policy written to reduce this practice.
2. What tools might be included in the design phase of the policy process to increase the opportunity of success?
3. How might the chances of success be increased?

BRINGING POLICY TO THE CLASSROOM

It is exciting to watch students as they develop skills relating to policy analysis. It is not uncommon to hear at the beginning of the semester that students don't necessarily like what they are seeing and hearing in the work place, but they feel powerless to do anything about it except on a one-to-one basis with their patients and their families. However, as learners progress through the semester and are required to go through various exercises relating to understanding and developing policy, educators can almost see a change in attitude about what they as APNs can do to become significant actors in the policymaking area. The students are required to take on one health policy issue currently being discussed in their state legislature. They are asked to research the issue and identify what stage the policy is in (agenda setting, design, implementation, etc.), in which committee the issue is currently residing (to determine whether or not it is the right committee to address this issue), determine what and where the resistance is, research the resistance, and propose a solution or counterargument to the resistance. They are then required to visit with their legislator and present their position regarding the issue. These connected exercises help students identify an issue, learn about it to develop a position (and knowledge to support their position), and gain the confidence to articulate their position to a legislator. It is the challenge of meeting a legislator face-to-face that is often overwhelming. A majority of students cite this requirement as one of the most valuable skills they have developed in the program. Students have chosen fascinating topics, such as the affect of street lights on a community, health care for the homeless, and Medicare's donut hole. In addition to studying local government, students are required to form groups and develop presentations related to a country of their choice and, using tools and policy factors, explore how healthcare policies are designed and implemented in other countries. Over the years, students have presented on countries around the globe, looking at wealthy, developed countries such as Canada, France, and Germany, as well as poor countries such as Nicaragua.

CONCLUSION

As a component of advanced practice nursing, active participation in the policy process is essential in the formulation of policies designed to provide quality health care to all individuals. To be effective in the process, APNs must understand how the process works and the points at which the greatest impact might be made. The design phase of the policy process is the point at which the original intent of a solution to a problem is understood and the appropriate tools are employed to achieve policy success. APNs can be extremely effective in this phase as policy tools are considered and selected.

DISCUSSION POINTS AND ACTIVITIES

1. Identify a health policy and the tools used by the institution/agency to implement the policy.
2. Using your understanding of the behavioral assumptions underlying the tools, determine the potential for success or failure of the policy. Identify policy variables that will affect success or failure.
3. Identify a policy (rule/regulation/etc.) that has been in use for several years, yet has had little success. Identify the variables that may be inhibiting success and offer possible solutions. Write or call your legislator to express your concerns (using data) and offer a proposal for revision. Explain why your proposal may increase success of the policy implementation and outcome.
4. How does the political climate affect the choice of policy tools and the behavioral assumptions made by policymakers?
5. Submit an article for publication to a refereed journal about a clinical problem based on the policy design process.

For a full suite of assignments and additional learning activities, use the access code located in the front of your book to visit this exclusive website: http://go.jblearning.com/milstead. If you do not have an access code, you can obtain one at the site.

REFERENCES

Bardach, E. (1977). *The implementation game: What happens after a bill becomes a law.* Cambridge: MA: MIT Press.

Central Intelligence Agency. (2009a). Infant mortality: A comparison. Retrieved from https://www.cia.gov/library/publications/the-world-factbook/index.html

Central Intelligence Agency. (2009b). Life expectancy: A comparison. Retrieved from https://www.cia.gov/library/publications/the-world-factbook/index.html

Cohen, M., March, J. G., & Olsen, J. P. (1972). A garbage can model of organizational choice. *Administrative Science Quarterly, 17,* 1–25.

Comer, M. E. (2002). Factors influencing organized political participation in nursing. *Power, Politics, and Policymaking, 3*(2), 97–107.

Dryzek, J. S. (1983). Don't toss coins in garbage cans: A prologue to policy design. *Journal of Public Policy, 3*(4), 345–368.

Ingraham, P. W. (1987). Toward more systematic consideration of policy design. *Policy Studies Journal, 15*(4), 611–628.

Kingdon, J. W. (1995). Agendas, alternatives, and public policies. Boston, MA: Little, Brown.

Lijphart, A. (1977). *Democracy in plural societies.* New Haven, CT: Yale University Press.

Linder, S. H., & Peters, G. B. (1987). Design perspective on policy implementation: The fallacies of misplaced prescriptions. *Policy Studies Review, 6*(3), 459–475.

Longest, B. B., Jr. (2002). *Health policymaking in the United States* (3rd ed.). Chicago, IL: Health Administration Press.

O'Grady, E. T. (2010). Rolling out reform despite political and legal challenges: The tug of war for public opinion. *Nurse Practitioner World News, 15*(11/12), 8–9.

Pressman, J., & Wildavsky, A. B. (1973). *Implementation: How great expectations in Washington are dashed in Oakland; Or, why it's amazing that federal programs work at all.* Berkeley, CA: University of California Press.

Roch, C. H., Pitts, D. W., & Navaro, I. (2010). Representative bureaucracy and policy tools: Ethnicity, student discipline, and representation in public schools. *Administration & Society, 42*(38), 38–65.

Safriet, B. J. (2002). Closing the gap between can and may in health-care providers' scopes of practice: A primer for policymakers. *Yale Journal on Regulation, 19,* 301–334.

Sardell, A. (1990). *The U.S. experiment in social medicine: The community health center program. 1965–1986.* Pittsburgh: University of Pittsburgh Press.

Schneider, A., & Ingram, H. (1990). Behavioral assumptions of policy tools. *Journal of Politics, 52*(2), 510–529.

Smart, P. A. (2008). Policy design. In J. Milstead (Ed.), *Health policy and politics: A nurse's guide* (3rd ed., pp. 129–155). Sudbury, MA: Jones and Bartlett.

Thompson, F. J. (1981). *Health policy and the bureaucracy: Politics and implementation.* Cambridge, MA: MIT Press.

U.S. Department of Health and Human Services (USDHHS). (2002). *Healthy People 2010.* Washington, DC: National Academies Press.

Varone, F., & Aebischer, B. (2001). Energy efficiency: The challenges of policy design. *Energy Policy, 29,* 615–629.

CHAPTER 6

Implementation

Marlene Wilken

KEY TERMS

Bottom-up perspective: Examines the impact of policy implementation by actions of the individual worker in an organization who interacts with consumers.

Consensus: Collective judgment or belief; solidarity of opinion.

Deflection of goals: A type of maneuver used in policy implementation that creates changes in the original goals.

Dissipation of energies: Actions used by implementation players that can impede, delay, and/or cause the collapse of a program.

Diversion of resources: A type of maneuver used in policy implementation to win favor related to budget decisions.

Implementation of health policy: The process of putting a policy or program into effect.

Top-down model: Examines the actions of administrators and other top-level players and their role in policy implementation.

INTRODUCTION

We have all been involved in situations where policy goals/outcomes were evaluated as successful, partially successful, or not successful. The relative success of a policy or program is heavily dependent upon what happened during the implementation process—that is, how the organization carried out the instructions indicated in the policy/program. As noted in previous chapters, the policymaking process is cyclical, dynamic, and imperfect. The process can be influenced by circumstances, events, and individuals. The preferences and influence of interest groups, political bargaining, and individual and organizational biases play a significant role in the policymaking process, especially during implementation.

Nurses are positioned to play a prominent role in these historic times as healthcare reform is implemented. Health policies reflect the mix of public interest and personal influence and often involve the choice of who will get health care and how, when, and where the health care will be delivered. The implementation process is a participatory endeavor that implies action and has start and end points, and is about who participates, why and how they participate, and with what effect. The success or failure of implementation is judged against the specific policy goals. Hill and Hupe (2002) suggest that implementation should be considered in the context of organizational behavior or management: "Seldom is there a perfect fit between the problem defined by the policymakers, the design of the policy aimed at alleviating the problem, and the implementation delivered by the policy" (p. 5).

Knowing that policy implementation is imperfect and that many things can happen to impede successful implementation helps us appreciate why the American public feels frustrated with government. The frustration is the perceived failure of government to turn promise into performance. Nurses must be engaged in the implementation process, because we all benefit from the nurse's voice; if our voice is missing, the American people lose.

IMPLEMENTATION: THE PROCESS

Players, Control, and Implementation Maneuvers

Implementation of health policy occurs when an individual, group, or community puts policy into use. Polices come in many forms: some are statutory and are the result of legislative enactment or permanent rule; others are nonstatutory in origin, such as procedural manuals and institutional guidelines. Implementation of health policy is an essential part of effective, comprehensive client care for many documentable reasons. Successful implementation depends heavily on the manipulation of many variables. The extent of compliance with a policy is a frequently used measure of the success of the policy's implementation. During implementation, problem identification and problem solving occur in a cyclical pattern with a myriad of variables in play at any one time. The variables include: private agencies and groups that are often contractors for carrying out policies; the target groups themselves; public attitudes, resources, commitment and leadership of officials; and the socioeconomic, cultural, and political conditions in the environment in which polices are supposed to operate (Palumbo & Calista, 1990). The presumption that once regulations and policies are enacted they are largely followed turns out to be unwarranted in many cases. The conscious or unconscious refusal to follow the policy directives can result in noncompliance, making the implementation process far from what the policymakers envisioned.

There are many reasons why policy implementation continues to be a major stumbling block in the policy process. The majority of problems that interfere with policy implementation are people problems, referring to those individuals, referred to as players, who interact with the recipients of the policy or program. People problems are often referred to as political problems. Personal attitudes and perceptions come into play during policy implementation. The **bottom-up perspective** examines the individuals who interact with the consumer; political scientists refer to these players as "street-level" bureaucrats. Nurses are often implementers, and they are faced with many of the dilemmas that can occur when interacting with clients. Implementers practice coping strategies, such as negotiation, and may find themselves in circumstances not foreseen or being confronted with rules that are often vague but within which they are compelled to act. They see themselves required to interpret the policy involved in a creative but justifiable way. Sometimes they are working with scarce resources. How often have you heard someone say, or even think to yourself, "If they would just come down here and see how it is in the real world, they wouldn't make policies that are impossible to carry out!" As a result, implementers may decide to alter the policy/procedure based upon their perception of shortcomings in the policy. These perceptions of policy shortcomings may be based on a desire to enhance their professionalism, strengthen leadership, and perhaps restructure their organization (Hill & Hupe, 2002).

In the **top-down model**, administrators and other top-level players can have a significant impact on policy implementation. Personal attitudes and perceptions come into play during policy implementation. When the results of a policy are determined to be disappointing or worse, administrators are often quick to blame the implementers. When policymakers find out that the policy they wrote yields disappointing results, they may be inclined to take additional measures in hopes of ensuring tighter control of the implementation. Both often add more (internal) rules and regulations. Successful policy also can lead to more of the same policies, with the idea that if a certain policy worked well, adding additional policies may even get better results.

Control is at the core of actions taken by implementers. Control can be exercised in a variety of ways, with the end result being decisions about withholding or delivering elements of the policy. Types of maneuvers that may occur during implementation include: 1) diversion of resources; 2) deflection of goals; and 3) dissipation of energies (Bardach, 1977). The **diversion of resources** manifests itself in several ways. Organizations and individuals who receive government money tend to provide less in the way of exchange for services for that money. Playing the budget game is another diversion. Persons responsible for the budget do what they can to win favor in the eyes of those who have power over their funding. Incentives shaped for implementers by those who control their budgets influence how implementers execute policy mandates.

During the implementation phase, goals often undergo some change, resulting in the second type of maneuver: **deflection of goals**. This change in the goals can be the result of: 1) some feeling that the original goals were too ambiguous; 2) goals that were based on a weak consensus; 3) goals that were not thought out sufficiently; 4) an organization realizing the program will impose a heavy workload; 5) a program that takes the organization into controversy; or 6) required tasks that are too difficult for the workers to perform. The agency will try to shift certain unattractive elements to different agencies, but if nobody wants the responsibility, consumers get the runaround and each agency involved can claim it is not their problem (Bardach, 1977).

The third maneuver—**dissipation of energy**—wastes a great deal of the implementers' time. Dissipation of energy occurs when implementers avoid responsibility, defend themselves against others, and set themselves up for advantageous situations. Some may use their power to slow or stall the progress of the program until one's own terms are met; this action can lead to delay, withdrawal of financial and political support, or the total collapse of a program. There is little in the implementation literature to address how to improve compliance and minimize the types of maneuvers that implementers may use throughout the implementation process. Actions mentioned that may address these issues include building staff capacity to detect and correct noncompliant actions and having staff work with individuals to induce compliance (Deleon & Deleon, 2002).

Gaps

Scholars of policy implementation offer reasons why gaps occur and result in less-than-optimal policy success, while others offer recommendations to policymakers to help ensure policy success. The following list is a summary of the key elements to be considered when making policy and examining policy implementation. Think about a policy or program you have been involved in. Did it turn out the way you thought it would or should? Were there gaps in the implementation process that had an impact on outcomes? Take a look at this list and see if you can identify with any of the reasons for implementation success or failure. Policy:

1. needs to be relevant, feasible, and based on sound theory, with appropriate rationale that will correctly identify the design conditions and desired effect of the target groups;
2. objectives need to be clear and consistent, or, at a minimum, identify criteria for resolving goal conflict;
3. should provide the persons in charge of implementation sufficient jurisdiction and leverage points over the target groups to help reach the desired goals;
4. must maximize the likelihood that the implementing officials and target groups have sufficient resources to comply; and
5. needs to be examined periodically to ensure there is ongoing support from outside and within the agency/organization and that conditions have not changed over time that affect implementation (Mazmanian & Sabatier, cited in Hill & Hupe, 2002).

When policy implementation is examined or evaluated, one question that begs discussion is the notion of what is considered acceptable compliance or adherence? Is

100% compliance or adherence realistic? If not, what measures need to be taken to get closer to an acceptable compliance rate? Does the policy need to be reexamined? What are the implementers doing and reporting? Is this a policy, person, or systems problem? Do the measures of success need to be reconsidered or redefined?

Conclusion

Policy implementation includes the actions and mechanisms whereby policies are brought into practice—that is, where what is written in the legislation or policy document is turned into a reality. In this stage the content of the policy, and its impact on those affected, may be modified substantially, or even negated. In analyzing this stage in the policymaking process, one needs to examine how, when, and where particular policies have been implemented. Problems with policy implementation are widespread. During the implementation process, the various forces of individuals, groups, organizations, and sometimes the governmental bodies are at work. These various forces may be trying to change the policy to meet their own needs and control a part of the implementation process. When the implementers are not working in concert to meet the goals, the recipients lose. Remember, the entire nurse community and other health professionals can affect implementation in both positive and negative ways.

CASE STUDIES: IMPLEMENTATION AND APRNS

Background

Two milestone pieces of health reform legislation were signed into law by President Obama in March 2010: the Patient Protection and Affordable Care Act (P.L. 111-148) and the Health Care Education and Reconciliation Act of 2010 (P.L. 111-152). The new health reform laws provide a complex series of changes in healthcare delivery, payment, coverage, and education. Some of the changes started immediately, while others are to be introduced or phased in over 5 years (American Academy of Nursing, 2010). According to the U.S. Department of Health and Human Services, by 2014 the Affordable Care Act (ACA) will expand coverage to 32 million individuals currently not covered by insurance. Starting in 2011, the law begins to focus on preventive services. Prevention and prevention funding, however, may be pushed into the background as efforts to repeal the Affordable Care Act have been vowed by leaders in the U.S. Congress. Even if repeal efforts fail, lawmakers may hold up funding for portions of the bill. The uncertainty about what Congress will fund and what changes Congress might make to the law means that nurses can impact implementation. Across the country states are pulling together teams, including Medicare and insurance participants, to design plans that put an emphasis on wellness and prevention. What voice will nurses have at the table?

CASE STUDY 1: Direct Physician/Practitioner Supervision of Nursing Interventions and Practices

The American Nurses Association (ANA) and other nurse organizations continue to fight direct physician/practitioner supervision of nursing interventions and practices. In comments submitted to the Centers for Medicare and Medicaid Services (CMS) on August 31, 2010, for the Outpatient Prospective Payment System (OPPS) proposed rule, ANA voiced opposition to the recent Medicare "direct supervision requirements" for outpatient therapy services, particularly for nurse interventions and practices which RNs are uniquely qualified to provide and supervise. Under the 2010 final OPPS rule, a physician or nonphysician practitioner (i.e., nurse practitioners, clinical nurse specialists, and certified nurse–midwives) must be "physically present" and "immediately available" whenever RNs (or others) provide services "incident to" physician services in outpatient settings.

1. Identify those states that still have the physician supervision requirement.
2. Explore what action has been taken by advanced practice registered nurses (APRNs) in these states to remove this requirement.
3. Discuss reasons why physicians would be opposed to removing this supervision requirement.
4. Construct at least two statements that argue for elimination of physician supervision of nursing care.

ANA has reported to CMS on the severe hardship that these supervision requirements can create for nurses and their patients. In rural areas, patients may need to travel long distances because they could not receive sequential outpatient treatments without the onsite presence of a physician or nonphysician provider at a closer facility. The CMS offered to modify this policy somewhat, by applying a two-step/direct-then-general supervision to nonsurgical, strictly monitoring types of services. While a step in the right direction, the ANA indicated that this does not go far enough and called on the agency, in the final OPPS rule, to exempt independent nurse practices, particularly those not subject to supervision in other settings.

1. Write supporting testimony that could be used to persuade lawmakers at the federal level to remove the physician supervision restriction.
2. What sources are available for you to use in providing evidence for removing this requirement?
3. Identify key elements in the testimony that would be the most persuasive for lawmakers.
4. What other organizations could you contact that could support your position?

CASE STUDY 2: Developing and Implementing Innovative
Models of Care

A Center of Medicare and Medicaid Innovation (CMI) has been established within
CMS (Section 3021 of ACA, modified by Section 10306). The purpose is to test
innovative payment and service delivery models to reduce Medicare and Medicaid
program expenditure while enhancing the quality of care. There is sufficient literature to indicate that APRNs have expertise in medicine and healthcare management.

1. Verify that APRNs are serving as consults to CMI.
2. Identify evidence that APRNs can use when serving as consultants to CMI.
3. What steps need to occur to ensure that nurse-led practices, including those
   by APRNs, are eligible and included in the models?

CASE STUDY 3: Medicare Physician Fee Schedule
Proposed Rule

On August 24, 2010, ANA submitted comments to the Centers for Medicare and
Medicaid Reimbursement (CMS) regarding the 2011 Physician Fee Schedule
proposed rule. Under recent legislation, reimbursement to all Medicare Part B providers, including APRNs, has increased by 2.2%. Under the Affordable Care Act
(ACA), Medicare reimbursement for certified nurse–midwives (CNMs) is on par
with that of physicians, just as it is for certified registered nurse anesthetists. Nurse
practitioners and clinical nurse specialists continue to be compensated at 85% of
what physicians receive for providing the same services.

1. Discuss why NPs and CNSs are not reimbursed at 100%.
2. What could be done to change this?
3. What players/stakeholders would you involve in trying to change this?
4. What implementation variables should be addressed?

CASE STUDY 4: Home Health Care and Durable Medical
Equipment (DME)

Currently, under section 6407, subsection (A) of the ACA, a physician must conduct
a face-to-face encounter with the patient prior to certifying the patient for Medicare
and Medicaid home health services. Section 10605 amends this requirement by

allowing a NP or CNS "who is working in collaboration with a physician in accordance with State Law" to conduct a face-to-face encounter on behalf of the physician. This provision does not authorize APRNs or physician assistants (PAs) to certify patients for home health agency services or to order home health services or durable medical equipment (DME). The physician must attest to the fact that the encounter has occurred. In addition, the ACA requirements for physician documentation of a face-to-face encounter by a physician, NP, CNS, or PA prior to ordering DME adds a new and unnecessary restriction to current regulatory practice (American Academy of Nursing, 2010).

1. Find the laws and regulations in your state that address the Medicare and Medicaid Home Health certification process.
2. Identify lawmakers, regulators, and stakeholders who could influence changing this certification process.
3. Create alternate solutions to the certification process (or write language that will amend the certification process) that would expand consumer participation and enhance nurse power.

Case Study 5: Advancing Access to Care Through Full Utilization of APRNs

The evidence is abundant that APRNs provide high-quality care. Nurses can play a crucial role in achieving the goals of access to cost-effective, equitable, and comprehensive health care. Currently, however, these goals are in danger as barriers threaten to impede the full utilization of nurses. The barriers appear in private health plans, federal laws and rules, and state laws.

Consumer access to APRN services has been hindered by private insurers and health plans through discrimination. Such discrimination is evident when private insurers and health plans refuse to recognize APRNs as primary or specialty providers, fail to include APRNs in their provider directory, or pay APRNs at rates lower than physicians.

Section 2706 of the Public Health Service Act addresses "nondiscrimination in health care" and goes into effect in 2014. This provision states that health plans (including group and individual plans) "shall not discriminate with respect to participation under the plan or coverage against any healthcare provider who is acting within the scope of that provider's license or certification under applicable State law" (American Academy of Nursing, 2010, p. 3). APRNs need to assure that the prohibition on discrimination is backed by clear enforcement mechanisms and penalties for noncompliance.

1. What agencies/organizations have an interest in the prohibition of discrimination of APRNs?

2. Discuss the most appropriate way to notify these agencies/organizations that an infringement has occurred.
3. Identify the gaps in implementation that may contribute to this situation.
4. Discuss what actions need to be taken by the players involved to address the compliance charges.
5. Identify mechanisms that need to be in place to prevent discrimination from occurring in the future.

IMPLEMENTATION STRATEGIES FOR THE 2008 *CONSENSUS MODEL FOR APRN REGULATION: LICENSURE, ACCREDITATION, CERTIFICATION, & EDUCATION*

Background

Reaching consensus around a standardized model for all APRN regulation is a significant accomplishment for the APRN community. The process of adopting the 2008 *Consensus Model for APRN Regulation* took four years. In March 2004, the American Association of Colleges of Nursing (AACN) and the National Organization of Nurse Practitioner Faculties (NONPF) submitted a proposal to the Alliance for Nursing Accreditation, now named Alliance for APRN Credentialing, to establish a process to develop a consensus statement on the credentialing of advanced practice registered nurses. Thirty-two organizations responded to an invitation by the Alliance for APRN Credentialing to participate in the APN Consensus Conference in Washington, D.C., in June 2004. After this meeting, the Alliance for APRN Credentialing formed a smaller work group made up of designees from 23 organizations with broad representation of APN certification, licensure, education, accreditation, and practice. The charge to the work group was to develop a statement that addresses the issues delineated during the APN Consensus Conference with the goal of envisioning a future model for APNs. The July 2008 report of the *Consensus Model for APRN Regulation: Licensure, Accreditation, Certification, and Education* was completed through the collaborative work of the APRN Consensus Work Group and National Council of State Boards of Nursing (NCSBN) APRN Advisory Committee, with extensive input from a larger APRN stakeholder community.

The target date for full implementation of the Regulatory Model and all embedded recommendations is the year 2015. The expectation is that the consensus reached on recommendations in the regulatory model will inform decision-makers as the APRN community moves towards full implementation. Stanley, Werner, and Apple (2009) indicated that implementation will occur incrementally or sequentially, but cautioned that there is not time to devote to an education campaign or a discussion regarding how components of the model should be implemented between now and 2015. The APRN community must capitalize on the work done in the 2008 *Consensus Model for APRN Regulation: Licensure, Accreditation, Certification, and Education* as all stakeholders move towards the 2015 target date for full implementation (APRN Consensus Work Group and the National Council of State Boards of Nursing APRN Advisory Committee, 2008).

Building **consensus** among diverse entities or organizations is rarely easy. This laudable goal is particularly challenging within a community that in the past has perceived more advantage to preserving unique differences than moving toward unity. The consensus process requires sustained commitment by all participants and the ability of each participating organization to tolerate the push-and-pull phenomena that occurs during the process. This tenacity, supported by a culture of open communication, is what allowed each participant to state his or her position or understanding and to push an agenda, but ultimately pull back when necessary and appropriate to reach common ground. Finding the balance to accommodate differing viewpoints without missing out on achieving meaningful consensus is essential. At any point, the process can begin to unravel when a party does not believe it has been heard or its perspective recognized in the document.

A separate challenge is overcoming the fear or attitude that the end product is a compromise and therefore not the "best" decision. Because the definition of consensus itself is unclear, some can easily assume that anything less than unanimous consent is compromise. It is critical that participants in the process not adopt this attitude, but instead continue to work through the issues to reach a common agreement that addresses not only the concerns and needs of individual organizations, but is the best decision for the profession. Implementation of the model is the responsibility of each individual organization, but ongoing communication and transparency of actions and decisions are critical. As the implementation of the consensus model for APRN regulation moves forward, only time will tell if the APRN community was successful in reaching true consensus that has a lasting impact on the nurse profession.

Successful implementation of the regulatory model will involve the commitment, coordination, and continued collaboration of all nurse stakeholders, including academic institutions, professional organizations, certification and accreditation bodies, and state boards of nursing. Implementation is the responsibility of each of these entities and has already been put into motion at a variety of levels. Communication is critical to implementation among the academic institutions, professional organizations, certification and accreditation bodies, and state boards of nursing. It is important to develop solutions that include all four types of advanced practice: APRN, CNM, CNS, and CRNA. The LACE communication network will provide a platform for the LACE entities to communicate and continue this collaborative effort. Stakeholder groups have made a long-term commitment to working together to ensure the success of the consensus model. Implementation of the model is the responsibility of each individual organization, but ongoing communication and transparency of actions and decisions are critical. As the APRN stakeholders move forward with implementation of the consensus model for APRN regulation, time will tell if the APRN community was successful in reaching true consensus that has a lasting impact on the nursing profession.

CASE STUDY 6: Restricted Scope of APRN Practice

You are attending a regional/national APRN conference. At lunch, you are seated with APRNs from different states. A conversation ensues and you are educated on the fact that many states have restrictions on the scope of practice for APRNs. One of the keynote speakers addressed how components of the consensus model should be implemented between now and 2015, stressing that the APRN community must capitalize on the work done in the 2008 *Consensus Model for APRN Regulation: Licensure, Accreditation, Certification, and Education.* Your assignment is to work with your colleagues to develop an approach to address the inconsistency among states regarding restrictions on scope of practice.

1. Identify stakeholders in this endeavor.
2. Document the position that each identified stakeholder has in this issue.
3. Address each potential variable in the implementation process that could impact your endeavors related to this issue.
4. Discuss strategies that could be used to address the variables.
5. Where would you find the most current information about individual states and restrictions on scope of practice?
6. Write testimony that you would present to a state legislature to convince them to remove restrictions on scope of practice for APRNs.

Responses to Consider for Case Study 6:
Restricted Scope of Practice

APRN professional organizations need to commit to strategies to override or remove restrictions on nursing practice in state scope of practice laws and regulations. The 41 member organizations of the Nursing Community, a forum for professional nursing and related organizations, produced a document addressing healthcare reform (Nursing Community, n.d.). This consensus document, titled *The Commitment to Quality Health Reform: A Consensus Statement from the Nursing Community,* encourages nurses to be involved in every discussion regarding impending changes in health reform. When addressing scope of practice, nurses are encouraged to use the Institute of Medicine (IOM) definition of primary care, which states "Primary care is the provision of integrated, accessible healthcare services by clinicians who are accountable for addressing a large majority of personal healthcare needs, developing a sustained partnership with patients, and practicing in the context of family and community" (Institute of Medicine, 1994).

For a full suite of assignments and additional learning activities, use the access code located in the front of your book to visit this exclusive website: http://go.jblearning.com/milstead. If you do not have an access code, you can obtain one at the site.

REFERENCES

American Academy of Nursing. (2010). *Implementing health care reform: Issues for nursing.* Retrieved from http://www.aannet.org/files/public/ImplementingHealthCareReform.pdf

APRN Consensus Work Group and the National Council of State Boards of Nursing APRN Advisory Committee. (2008). *Consensus model for APRN regulation: Licensure, accreditation, certification, and education.* Retrieved from http://www.aacn.nche.edu/education/pdf/APRNReport.pdf

Bardach, E. (1977). *The implementation game: What happens after a bill becomes a law.* Cambridge, MA: MIT Press.

Deleon, L., & Deleon, P. (2002). What ever happened to policy implementation? An alternative approach. *Journal of Public Administration Research and Theory, 12*(4), 467–492.

Health Care Education and Reconciliation Act. (2010). Pub. L. No. 111-152, 124 Stat. 1029.

Hill, M. J., & Hupe, P. L. (2002). *Implementing public policy: Governance in theory and practice.* Thousand Oaks, CA: Sage.

Institute of Medicine. (1994). *Defining primary care: An interim report.* Washington, DC: National Academies Press.

Nursing Community. (n.d.). *The commitment to quality health reform: A consensus statement from the nursing community.* Retrieved from http://www.thenursingcommunity.org/#/health-reform/4542347781

Palumbo, D. J., & Calista, D. J. (1990). *Implementation and the policy process: Opening up the black box.* New York: Greenwood Press.

Patient Protection and Affordable Care Act. (2010). Pub. L. No. 111-148, 124 Stat. 119.

Stanley, J., Werner, K., & Apple, K. (2009). Positioning advanced practice registered nurses for healthcare reform: Consensus on APRN regulation. *Journal of Professional Nursing, 25*(6), 340–348.

CHAPTER 7

Program Evaluation

Ardith L. Sudduth

KEY TERMS

Ethical evaluation: An assessment that follows the principles of good conduct and moral behavior.

Evaluation report: A compilation of the findings of a program evaluation study. Reports are presented in a variety of formats depending upon the needs of those requesting the evaluation. Common formats include written reports, electronic transfer, oral presentations with multimedia enhancements, films, and videotapes.

Outcome evaluation: Assesses the extent to which a program achieves its outcome-oriented objectives. It focuses on outputs and outcomes to judge program effectiveness, but may assess a program's process to understand how outcomes are produced.

Policy: A purposeful, general plan of action, which includes authoritative guidelines, that is developed to respond to a problem. The plan directs human behavior toward specific goals.

Program evaluation: Analysis of social programs to gain an understanding of how well the intervention is meeting the objectives and goals set forth in the program's design.

Program evaluation design: The method selected to collect unbiased data for analysis to determine the extent to which a social program is meeting its designated goals, objectives, and outcomes and to assess the social program's merit and worth.

Public policy: A goal-directed plan, developed by a governmental body, that provides a definitive course of action or nonaction.

Qualitative evaluation design: Evaluation methods that assist the evaluator to determine the subjective meaning of a program and its interventions to the individual participants.

Quantitative evaluation design: Methods characterized as the "scientific model" of collecting measurable, objective data, with an emphasis on explanation based upon well-defined expectations and observable events.

Social programs: Solutions developed to help solve an identified problem in society.

Theory: An idea used to design a program and its interventions and to explain and predict broad phenomena observed after data analysis.

INTRODUCTION

Advanced practice nurses (APNs) such as nurse practitioners, school nurses, advanced practice critical care nurses, clinical nurse specialists, and others have become key figures in the provision of health care or in healthcare management of persons enrolled in governmentally funded programs. This involvement will continue to grow as the demand for high-quality care grows in conjunction with the changes occurring in the healthcare system, changing demographics created by the coming of age of the baby boomer generation, changes in the demographics of immigrants, and a growing concern for the rising costs of health care at all levels of government. Nearly all advanced practice nurses are impacted in some way by federal, state, or local health policy as it is interpreted into regulations and/or programs. Advanced practice nurses that are providing care in rural clinics or inner-city clinics usually are part of a program sponsored by the local, state, or federal government. When working with Medicare and Medicaid participants, APNs are participating in governmental programs. Programs funded by governments, nonprofit organizations, and most private foundations require that these programs be evaluated regularly to meet a variety of criteria, including ensuring that the program is being conducted as developed, that there is fiscal responsibility, that goals and objectives are being met, and increasingly, that the outcomes are examined. To assist the APN to meet the frequently mandated requirements for **program evaluation**, this chapter presents some of the components of policy and program evaluation, including conditions of evaluation, ethical considerations, potential design choices, and a few suggestions for reporting the results and recommendations of the evaluation.

Advanced practice nurses are not strangers to evaluation. They have long used evaluation in many clinical settings, including the evaluation of a patient's response to a nursing intervention, use of outcome-based clinical evaluations, evaluation of a management strategy, or a self-evaluation for promotion, and so the transition to using these skills to evaluate a program is a natural evolution of nursing practice. Understanding the process of policy and program evaluation can help the APN contribute to the evaluation of social programs by bringing the unique perspective of nursing practice. The federal government has had a long-standing healthcare **policy** of funding hospitals and health care for the elderly, and policies also have supported funded programs to prepare advanced practice nurses. Healthcare policies are constantly being modified, and changes in healthcare policy continue to be very volatile issues as the public and government have grappled with the multiple issues facing the nation, including access to care, provision of quality care, and the cost to provide care.

To meet the healthcare needs of a population or to help solve a social problem in the community, the APN may decide to seek funding from a governmental agency, foundation, or other resource to develop a new or unique service. Funding resources, including governments and nonprofit companies, demand that the evaluation process be built into the proposal for funding (Fredericks, Carman, & Birkland, 2002; Environmental Protection Agency, 2010). Often, it is the APN who studies the needs for a social program intervention, writes the proposal in collaboration with other interested parties, and works to develop the evaluation process.

POLICY, PUBLIC POLICY, AND SOCIAL PROGRAMS

To start the discussion of the role of the APN in evaluation of a social program, it is helpful to define policy. A policy may be defined as a purposeful plan of action or inaction developed to deal with a problem or a matter of concern in either the public or private sector. A policy includes the authoritative guidelines that direct human behavior toward a set of specific goals and provides the structure to guide action, including the guidelines to levy sanctions that affect the conduct of affairs (Hanley & Falk, 2007). Policies can be determined by the private or public sector, which together can have a significant and long-lasting impact on communities and individuals (Center for Health Improvement, 2004). It is also important to remember that public policies are a result of the politics and values of those determining the policy (Mason, Leavitt, & Chaffee, 2007). One example familiar to nurses is the policy manual found in hospitals and clinics, which has been approved by an authority, such as a board of directors.

Public Policy

A **public policy** is a definitive course of action, or sometimes a nonaction, developed by a governmental body that addresses public concerns or public problems (Hanley & Falk, 2007; Dye, 2008). It is directed at a particular goal and does not occur by chance. Public policy is determined by legislative bodies as they make laws, by executive bodies as they administer the laws, and by judicial bodies as they interpret these laws (Dye, 2008). Governments create public policy by making decisions regarding a health issue, such as requiring children to be immunized before entering school. It may also be a policy for the government to act negatively by adopting a laissez-faire, or hands-off, policy and do nothing about an issue, and the decision to do nothing may be as important as the decision to do something. In either case, some groups will be affected. Public policy provides direction to assist decision makers. Consider the thousands of decisions made by the Food and Drug Administration regarding the safety and effectiveness of consumer goods sold in the United States, which include the safety of drugs and vaccines, as well as the safety, purity, and nutritive value of foods (Law, 2010).

Public policies may be considered to be either positive or negative. Most programs that deal with the welfare of children; provision of safe water, food, and drugs; and public relief in times of disaster are considered quite favorably by the general public. However, public policies can also have negative effects and create problems.

Depending on one's point of view and individual circumstance, changes in healthcare policy resulting from the passage of the healthcare reform bill in 2010 may have a positive or negative impact on the lives of Americans. Some parents are pleased that their young-adult children can be added to the family insurance plan or that their children cannot be denied insurance due to a preexisting condition. On the other hand, advanced practice nurses may be concerned about the changes in Medicare provider rates that reduce annual market basket updates and require payments for productivity (Henry J. Kaiser Family Foundation, 2011). It is important that the results of policy changes are carefully screened for the multiple outcomes that can be a result of what may appear to be a positive change.

While public policy is developed by governmental bodies and officials, it is often influenced by multiple nongovernment persons and environmental factors. For example, in the 1960s there was increasing concern about the access of affordable hospital care for the elderly. Families, labor unions, physicians, and many others were instrumental in creating the Medicare amendments to the Social Security Act. With the passage of these amendments, the federal government developed a policy of government assistance to provide hospital care to the nation's elderly. Over the years, numerous changes have been made to the initial amendments, many lobbied for by the American Nurses Association (ANA), but the overall goal of the federal policy of ensuring access to hospital and health care by the elderly, and now additional groups of citizens, has continued.

Another important dimension of public policy is that it is not limited to a specific law or legislative proposal. Public policy is a dynamic, evolving phenomenon with an ability to adapt as the needs and desires of its citizens change. One cannot go to a book in the federal government and find a listing of "the" American healthcare policy; healthcare policy changes over time. An example is the changing emphasis that has occurred over the past 70 years. In the 1940s and 1950s, the focus was on access to hospital care, and Hill–Burton legislation provided funds for many rural hospitals. Medicare amendments were a further extension of access to health care.

With the rising costs of the Medicare provisions, there has been a major push for cost containment since the 1970s and continuing to today (Jennings, 2001; Orszag & Ellis, 2007). Healthcare policy of the new millennium focuses not only on access, but also on providing quality care that is determined by outcome evaluations and is at the lowest possible cost. **Outcome evaluations** are those that focus on the benefits a program produces for the people who use the program (Thomas, Smith, & Wright-DeAguero, 2006). Trends in health policy will continue to be driven by major movements in the healthcare delivery system, which "is becoming more managed and consolidated, more cost and quality accountable, more consumer focused, and more communication and information technology driven" (Jennings, 2001, p. 224). Nurses can play an important role in the development of policies, including healthcare policy. The *ANA Code of Ethics for Nurses* added a provision that states that nursing is "responsible for . . . shaping social policy" (American Nurses Association, 2001).

Social Programs

Social programs are public policy made visible. After a problem has come to the attention of the appropriate governmental body, suggestions are made on how to solve the problem. After much deliberation, a solution or program is developed. If the matter is of sufficient concern to the legislative body and if the program has support, legislation is passed to authorize the development of the program and to fund it. Often at the legislative level, the goals and objectives of a program are only general in nature, while the specifics are frequently left to the developers of the program; this provides some flexibility for development postlegislation. Social policies and their effects on the health of individuals, families, and communities have been identified by the ANA *Social Policy Statement* as a part of nursing care and nursing research (Chitty, 2010).

During the 1980s and 1990s, federal legislators began to return control of some policies to state and local governments. This allows states to determine how to use the resources with only minimal guidelines from the federal government. This shift of authority has increased the complexity of social programs and their evaluation because the policies are interpreted by multiple stakeholders such as state legislators, county boards of supervisors, municipal governments, and sometimes nonprofit, community-based organizations.

PROGRAM EVALUATION

A **social program**, then, is the set of resources and activities that have been directed toward one or more common goals. The resources and activities vary from program to program; some can be as small as a few activities with a small budget and a staff of one or two, while others can be very large with extensive resource allocation, complex activities, and implemented at several sites or two or more levels of government.

Public policy has generated several programs intended to improve the lives of a broad range of citizens, including health, education, environment, and social services that would have been unthinkable prior to the 1960s (Light, 2001). This growth of programs at all levels of government has resulted in the need for program evaluation, and this importance has also been underscored by federal legislation that mandates the process, as well as supplying the funding needed to meet the evaluation requirements. The National Performance Review and the Government Performance and Results Act of 1993 (GPRA) were created to focus the evaluation process on accountability, performance measurement, and results (Department of Justice, 2007). States, because of funding matches with the federal government, also require that programs be evaluated. This has become very evident in Louisiana; following the devastating oil spill in the Gulf of Mexico, federal money, as well as money from British Petroleum, was spent to clean up the spill and provide damages to selected groups and individuals. Accountability for the funds, programs, and projects is now being mandated by both the federal and state governments.

Program evaluation provides information to assist others in making judgments about a program, service, policy, organization, or whatever is being evaluated. Evaluation is used to examine programs to gain an understanding of if and how the human services policies and programs are solving the social problems that they were designed to alleviate (Westat, 2002; Sonpal-Valias, 2009). Program evaluation may be conducted for a wide variety of reasons, many of which are particularly adaptable to APN practice. Some of the very practical reasons that program evaluation may be conducted include the following (Posavac & Carey, 1992):

- To determine the extent and severity of a problem
- To choose among possible programs
- To monitor program operations
- To determine if the program has resulted in desired change (outcomes)
- To document outcomes for program sustainability
- To account for funds
- To revise program interventions
- To answer requests for information
- To learn about unintended effects of a program
- To meet accreditation requirements

Determining the Extent and Severity of a Problem

Evaluation designs are used to determine if a problem is severe enough to establish a program to help solve it. In today's world of scarce resources like time, money, trained personnel, and other valuable commodities, it is imperative that a well-documented program exists. Programs vie for resources, and the one that can show the best justification is the one most likely selected for implementation.

Choosing Among Possible Programs

Evaluation data may be used to help make difficult administrative decisions. Over the years, there has been an exponential growth in social programs; for example, it is reported that there are more than 17,500 organizations providing youth programs (Lerner & Thompson, 2002). All of these programs must compete with multiple other social programs in a community.

Consider a situation in which several excellent social programs have been established and are functioning in a community. When a request comes to add another program, difficult decisions must be made in these days of limited resources. A city may be sponsoring a homeless healthcare clinic, an after-hours sports program for inner-city youth, and a lunch program for the elderly. When it becomes apparent that a program to deal with school violence may need to be added, it is possible that it can be added only if another program is eliminated. Program evaluation that provides systematic, reliable, and valid information will certainly assist the administrative staff in making difficult decisions. Unless there are good program evaluation data available, decisions are more likely to be made based upon perception, anecdotal evidence, or political pressure (Posavac & Carey, 1992; Royse, Thyer, & Padgett, 2010).

Monitoring Program Operations

Program monitoring's primary purpose is to track and report on program outcomes, and then provide feedback to the program sponsors and treatment team (Affholter, 1994). In general, new social programs are supported by either authorizing legislation or private foundations. Rarely does the legislation or foundation specify in detail what the program should be or how it is to be implemented. The details of program design and implementation are left to the agency or organization that has the authority to administer the program. Demonstration projects are one example of programs that are frequently established to meet general goals and objectives. They focus on a new approach to solve a problem; if the demonstration project is successful, additional programs may be funded in other locations.

Program monitoring is much easier when the program has been developed with clear and consistent operational objectives that allow for direct and reliable measurement and have been developed using sound evidence-based rationale. The results of monitoring the program can help program managers pay particular attention to a specific performance problem or recognize outstanding achievements of the program. Data resources frequently used for program monitoring include direct observation by the evaluator, program records, surveys of program participants (and nonparticipants), and community surveys (Rossi, Freeman, & Lipsy, 2004). Some program sponsors have timely reports that must be submitted for evaluation, while other program sponsors will allow the recipient of a grant to alter parts of the program as long as the overall intent is not changed; for example, if a school APN developed a program to teach teenage fathers parenting skills and very few boys were enrolled in the program, the sponsoring agency might allow the program to be expanded to include teen mothers.

Determining If the Program Has Resulted in Desired Change

Legislative bodies, most nonprofit organizations, and philanthropic organizations request feedback about the program to determine if the program has achieved the stated goals. Organization officials want to know if the desired change has occurred— in other words, what are the outcomes of the program? This has become known as outcome-based evaluation. Outcomes are those benefits the participant receives from participating in the program. The United Way of America (http://www.unitedway.org/outcomes) provides guidelines on the web for determining best practices and conducting outcome-based evaluation.

Documenting Outcomes for Program Sustainability

Periodic evaluation of the social program, including management, program outcomes, and financial solvency, becomes essential when a program has been designed to be maintained over a long period of time. Careful and precise documentation must be developed to show that the program should be continued because it is achieving the targeted outcomes. Many programs sponsored by governments and other resources provide startup money, but with the expectation that the program will be designed in such a way that the community, other interested parties, or the program itself will generate the financial, personnel, and other resources to keep it running long after the initial grant money has been used (LaPelle, Zapka, & Ockene, 2006). To ensure additional funding from the same source, or to enable a program to seek additional funding from different government or private agencies, the viability of the program must be established (Wallace, 2003). It is also wise for the staff to cultivate good political and public support for the program. Keeping interested persons fully informed of the achievements of the program requires additional work by the program staff, but it may be very important in retaining the funding and other support needed to sustain the program. The program staff, including the APN, cannot assume that political or public support will be there just because the program is doing a good job.

ACCOUNTABILITY IN PROGRAM EVALUATION

Funding Agencies

Grant applications submitted to governmental resources and private foundations require that the program develop methods to ensure that the money being spent on the program is used as directed in the grant. Most government grants require that at least an annual audit report be submitted regarding the use of funds. Some sponsoring governmental groups will make site visits to review financial records and to ensure that everything documented can be verified. Other grant rules allow for the recipients of the grant to alter the use of funds with special permission from the granting agency, and some grants allow the principal program administrator to discuss the needs verbally, which should be followed by written documentation of the request according to the agency policies and procedures.

Revising Program Interventions

Program evaluation provides valuable feedback that can be used to make necessary revisions. Often, several months or years can elapse between the development of an idea for a program and the receipt of funding or other resources, and as time elapses, situations change; personnel are recruited with differing backgrounds, personalities, strengths, and weaknesses; or the program is administered differently from the original design. It is important to evaluate periodically to ensure that the program is progressing as designed and, if change is needed, that revisions are made appropriately.

An excellent example of an intervention requiring revision occurred when a cost-effectiveness evaluation was conducted on a program for preventing perinatal human immunodeficiency virus (HIV) transmission (Stoto, 2001). Based on clinical trials published in 1994 that indicated that proper treatment of HIV in the mother could reduce perinatal transmission, specialists in preventive medicine and public health recommended counseling all women at risk of AIDS on the benefits of universal and voluntary testing. This intervention was successful, but in 1996 Congress instructed the Institute of Medicine (IOM) to evaluate how successful states had been in reducing perinatal HIV transmission. Data revealed that only about 60 to 94 percent of women were offered HIV testing during pregnancy. After careful cost–benefit analysis, the IOM concluded that universal testing was cost effective and that universal testing was the best intervention for preventing HIV transmission in the perinatal period. In 1999, the American College of Obstetricians and Gynecologists and the American Academy of Pediatrics issued a joint statement that adopted the universal testing approach of the IOM (Centers for Disease Control and Prevention, 2001). The Centers for Disease Control and Prevention (CDC) recommends universal HIV testing for all pregnant women using an opt-out approach rather than an opt-in approach, which leaves testing a voluntary decision by the pregnant woman (Delaware HIV Consortium Policy Committee, 2010). This example demonstrates how evaluation can alter interventions and make a difference in a health policy.

Answering Requests for Information

Program evaluation and careful maintenance of records enable the project director to more easily manage the large number of documents required by governmental agencies funding a social program. Periodic evaluation, along with meticulous record keeping, can provide a ready source for the data required; otherwise, the person completing the surveys may find that he or she will be required to spend untold hours doing a search, either manually or digitally, through the program files.

Learning About Unintended Effects of the Program

Program evaluations can also help discover any unintended effects of an intervention. As APNs know, medications can be beneficial as well as have negative side effects. Program evaluations are particularly valuable when systems have been built to detect unanticipated and unwanted outcomes of the treatment intervention (Posavac & Carey, 1992).

Meeting Accreditation Requirements

Many healthcare facilities are required to evaluate their services to meet accreditation criteria, which usually have been authorized by legislation. While meeting these standards may not predict the effectiveness of the programs offered, it does imply that the program meets the standards set by an official accrediting body that serves to increase public trust. Advanced practice nurses in their more advanced roles as nurse practitioners, clinical specialists, etc., often are asked to assume a key role in preparing the accreditation self-report and to ensure that the agency and its programs meet the standards.

THEORY: A VALUABLE TOOL IN EVALUATION

The use of **theory** in program evaluation provides a map to guide the evaluation process. Advanced practice nurses have been using theory in their work for many years, so the use of theory to guide evaluation of social programs is a normal extension of nursing knowledge and practice. Theory is defined in research and scientific inquiry as a set of interrelated concepts that explain and predict broad phenomena, while a concept is an abstract idea about a part of the phenomenon. The concepts may include definitions, empirical facts, or propositions that help explain and predict the phenomena observed. Theories do not have the simplicity of laws, nor do they have the same level of certainty. For example, a theory of illness held by ancients was that illness was the result of offending the gods; the belief that a particular illness was the result of angering a particular god is a concept (Trussell, Brandt, & Knapp, 1981). An ideal evaluation theory would describe and justify why certain evaluation practices lead to specific results across the many situations that program evaluators must confront (Shadish, Cook, & Leviton, 1995).

ETHICS AND EVALUATION

Program evaluation, by its very nature, evokes a sense of anxiety in most persons who are in some way vulnerable. Questions are asked such as: How does the program measure up? Are we doing a good job? What happens if the evaluator finds a problem with the program? Will the clients lose the service? Will I lose my job? How much information should I share with the evaluator? Will the evaluator be fair? From these questions, it can be seen that the role of the evaluator can create stress and the potential for ethical dilemmas for all involved in the evaluation process. Good program evaluation will plan for the potential of ethical conflicts and either develop strategies to avoid them or deal with the conflicts as they arise.

Potential Areas of Ethical Conflict

Ethical issues must be considered whenever an evaluation design is planned or an evaluator conducts an evaluation. Posavac and Carey (1992) identify several major areas of ethical concern that include 1) the protection of the people treated; 2) the danger of role conflicts by providers; 3) threats to the quality of the evaluation; and 4) the discovery of any negative effects resulting from the evaluation. Put into a slightly different context by Sieber (1980), ethical dilemmas occur in three major areas: 1) conflict between the roles of researcher, administrator, and advocate; 2) conflict between the right to know and the right of privacy; and 3) conflict between the demands of the evaluator, political officials, and/or other significant stakeholders. Stakeholders are individuals or organizations who are directly or indirectly affected by a social program's implementation or results and who believe they can make a difference to the outcomes (Rossi et al., 2004; Hanley & Falk, 2007). Nurses have long recognized the need for ethical nursing care and developed a code of ethics that continues to be updated to reflect the changes in society and health care. The latest version now explicitly states the nurse's primary commitment "is to the patient, whether an individual, family, group, or community" (American Nurses Association, 2001). The newest code reflects on the importance of the nurse's responsibility to participate as an equal in ethical debates.

Protection from Harm: An Ethical Priority

A central ethical concern is that the evaluation should not harm the participant or anyone else involved in the program. One of the first areas of evaluation is to determine if the program does any harm to someone receiving the program's intervention or if the program harms the program staff in any way. In the process of evaluation, much information is collected to meet the requirements of either the program design or the persons who have commissioned the evaluation. An evaluator must use the utmost care so that the program participants and staff do not have their privacy, anonymity, or confidentiality violated; this is particularly true since the passage of the Health Insurance Portability and Accountability Act (HIPAA) of 1996 (effective 2003).

Very real dilemmas can arise if courts subpoena an evaluator's records that contain information that might identify the program participant who has been guaranteed confidentiality. If such a problem arises, the evaluator would need to consult legal counsel. Often, group data are collected so that individuals are not identifiable.

Informed consent is a recognized component of all care provided by the APN and is a method frequently used to protect people from harm (Black, 2010). Participants in the evaluation process should be informed of the evaluation, what it means, and offered a choice to participate or not (Royse, Thyer, & Padgett, 2010). The APN, whether participating as the evaluator or as a member of the program staff, should be certain that confidentiality and the privacy of participants and program staff have been secured in the design and implementation of the evaluation and its report.

Role Conflict: Potential for an Ethical Dilemma

There is potential for conflict at several levels in program development, implementation, and evaluation. The complexity of the institutional and political networks that have had to evolve in program development, funding, and evaluation in constantly changing political and institutional environments has a great potential for developing conflict and ethical dilemmas (Fredericks et al., 2002). Interested persons in the social program being evaluated may comprise many diverse groups of persons, including the politicians who sponsored the funding legislation, the designers and recipients of the program, and supporting members of the community. These supporters are often called stakeholders because they have a vested interest in the program. Stakeholders may view the program very personally, as their "child," and may try to protect the program and the participants from outside scrutiny during the evaluation process and the sharing of evaluation results.

When the evaluator is also the administrator of the program, there is great potential for ethical conflict, because it is very possible to have role conflict between the role of administrator and evaluator. As the administrator, the role is to ensure that the program runs smoothly with the least amount of interruption; the role of evaluator requires data to be collected to evaluate the program that may require record examination, interviewing recipients of the program, and discussing the evaluation with staff.

Objective Program Evaluation: An Ethical Responsibility

Objective evaluation needs to include a fair and accurate description of how the program succeeded or failed from the perspective of all who were affected by the program (Morris, 1999). If the evaluator does not provide a trustworthy evaluation and report it in a timely manner, this may be considered by some as unethical (Posavac & Carey, 1992).

Program evaluators must try to provide the best study possible by selecting the methods and evaluation tools that are most appropriate. Making a mistake in accurately identifying the outcomes of a program, for example, might either allow the program to continue when it should be eliminated or, conversely, the program may be canceled when it should be continued. In both situations, the ethical dilemma is readily apparent.

Another area of ethical concern is to ensure that the evaluation design fits the needs of those who have requested the information (Posavac & Carey, 1992). If the evaluator cannot provide the answers needed, the evaluator must do the ethical thing and either decline to conduct the program evaluation or request that the evaluation tool be changed so that the evaluator can continue. For example, consider a program has been designed to help diabetics alter their lifestyles to prolong their lives. At the end of one year, the APN is asked to evaluate the program to determine if the program has made a difference in life expectancy. This would be an impossible task; good program evaluation could not be done to answer this question because one year is not long enough to determine life expectancy. To agree to do an evaluation to answer this question would create an ethical dilemma. A better question, albeit a very limited one, might be to request the evaluation tool be revised to determine improved disease control as measured by hemoglobin A1C, lipid profiles, incidence of delayed healing, and other such parameters over the one-year period as a measure of improved self-care.

An evaluator must also consider an ethical responsibility to provide a report promptly so that the results can be used while the program is still being implemented. The design of the evaluation needs to be written with enough detail that the procedures used and the process of data analysis could be understood by the persons requesting the evaluation.

Reporting Negative Effects: An Ethical Requirement

An ethical dilemma occurs when the evaluator discovers that while many of the objectives of the program are being met, some aspects of the program may be having negative effects. The question then becomes: How do you report these findings so that the data can be used by program administrators to alter the program? If the negative effect is judged to be serious enough that the harm outweighs the benefits, the program should be ended or revised.

Suggestions to Reduce Ethical Dilemmas in Program Evaluation

By the nature of social program evaluation, there is bound to be the potential for ethical dilemmas to arise. Some suggestions to reduce the incidence of an ethical dilemma include:

1. The advanced practice registered nurse (APRN) can design an evaluation process that avoids ethical dilemmas. Good communication is essential throughout the evaluation process, but is invaluable when avoiding conflict and, especially, ethical conflicts. One suggestion that may be helpful is to establish written agreements between the evaluator, the program requesting evaluation, and any other significant stakeholders that have been identified in the evaluation design. A clause that provides a mechanism for either party to withdraw from the relationship should be included if issues that cannot be resolved develop as the evaluation is conducted (Sieber, 1980).

2. The evaluator must also be aware of his or her own strengths and weaknesses, as well as strong belief systems. An evaluator that firmly believes that all people who are homeless are lazy probably should not be the person participating in the evaluation of a homeless shelter.

Ethical evaluation practice can be very challenging in the real-world settings of program implementation. It is imperative that the APN recognize the potential for ethical conflict and develop plans to confront and resolve these issues.

Suggestions to Avoid Conflict

Program evaluation is complex and involves multiple stakeholders, who range from highly powerful political and social leaders to the program implementers and their support staff to the recipients of the program. All of the persons involved are interested in the program at various levels. Five suggestions for program evaluators to help avoid conflict were made by Smith and associates (as cited in Clarke, 1999, p. 17).

First, recognize the potential conflicts between multiple stakeholders and deal with them in a diplomatic, efficient manner. Attempt to identify the primary and secondary stakeholders. Failure to examine potential and actual conflicts can easily lead to problems throughout the evaluation process.

Second, involve the multiple interest groups in the design of the evaluation study. If each group "owns" a portion of the design and is engaged as active participants in the process, there is less chance the varying groups of stakeholders will splinter off or create additional tensions in the evaluation process. Likewise, this approach recognizes the importance of each group and allows for compromises as needed.

Third, keep the multiple stakeholders and members of the evaluation team informed about the progress of the evaluation. It is easier to maintain cooperation among divergent groups if the groups are kept current with the project and are given the opportunity to provide feedback from their perspective.

Fourth, ensure that all stakeholders understand the goals and objectives of the program as they have been developed. This helps the stakeholders better understand exactly what the program was established to accomplish and identify the objectives that have been met, along with those that have not been met.

Fifth, identify the political and organizational environmental conditions in which the evaluation is being conducted. These situational factors are important to understand throughout the evaluation process to develop the design, implement the evaluation project, and disseminate the results.

PROGRAM EVALUATION DESIGN OPTIONS

As discussed earlier, the environment in which program evaluation takes place often is complex and includes a large number of stakeholders who have been involved in some manner in the development and implementation of a social program. In designing a culturally sensitive evaluation, it is critical to the success of the evaluation that the stakeholders be involved in the process (Westat, 2002).

It is important to determine who holds the power to make decisions regarding evaluations, especially when there are multiple levels of stakeholders involved in the program. School-based programs are key examples of organizations with multiple stakeholders, all of whom interact with each other at varying levels. Federal, state, and local resources may be involved in significant ways, each level with their multiple layers of decision makers. When an APN is asked to participate in the evaluation of a school-based health program, it would be essential that the APN consider the heads of the agencies sponsoring the program's personal and political priorities. Next, the school board and superintendent would be recognized as powerful decision makers. School principals, counselors, and teachers provide another layer of decision-making, and parents have indirect authority because they can choose to allow their child to participate or not (Guzman & Feria, 2002). Students also influence the outcomes of the evaluation because they control the information that they share with the evaluator.

Early evaluation designs were based on a scientific approach that is founded on the principle of causation. The goal of **quantitative evaluation** is to collect sufficient data to rule out rival hypotheses by such means as control or comparison groups or by statistical adjustments (Fawcett & Garity, 2009). Quantitative evaluation methods seek to be precise and to identify all the relevant variables prior to the data collection. The method also seeks to minimize the role of the evaluator or data collector in the collection of the evaluation data.

As the complexity of social programs became apparent, additional evaluation designs were needed to determine how a program was affecting the individual recipients of the program interventions. Evaluation designs began to incorporate the **qualitative approach**, which has as its basis the belief that it is the quality or the subjective reality that has true meaning in the events, lives, and behaviors of individuals (Fine, Weiss, Weseen, & Wong, 2000; Polit & Beck, 2012). Evaluators, using a qualitative approach, attempt to seek an understanding of the meaning of public policy, its attendant programs, and interventions from the perspective of the recipients of the program, the staff, community, and other significant persons (Royse, Thyer, & Padgett, 2010). If an inner-city emergency room APN observed that many homeless persons used the waiting room as a shelter, he or she might approach the city to establish a shelter for the homeless. To create a successful program, the design, implementation, and outcomes of the program would have to include not only the city's point of view, but also the needs and views of the homeless themselves. Qualitative issues, such as desire for autonomy by the homeless, can make or break social programs with the best of intentions.

To be successful in achieving an evaluation that is useful to the persons who have requested it and to be beneficial to the social program and its recipients, the design of the evaluation must receive careful planning. A good design is like a good road map when planning a car trip from San Francisco to New York: it helps to decide where you are going, how to get there, how long it will take, and how many side trips can be made on a limited budget. More detailed information regarding qualitative and quantitative designs may be found in many research texts. It must be repeated that **program evaluation designs** must be able to provide effective, useful, reliable, and valid information, as well as be able to be conducted within the many constraints of real life, such as within limitations of resources including time, money, personnel, and expertise.

Some down-to-earth suggestions by McNamera (1997–2006) seem particularly useful to the novice APN evaluator. His suggestions include the following:

1. Don't fear evaluation—remember the 80/20 rule: The first 20% of the work will produce the first 80% of the plan, and this is a very good start.
2. Remember that there is no perfect evaluation plan. Getting something done is better than waiting until every last detail has been identified.
3. Include a few interviews in the evaluation methods. The stories provide powerful descriptions of the outcomes of the program.
4. Don't review just successes—failures also give valuable insights into the function and outcomes of the program.
5. Keep the evaluation data after the report has been written. These data may be useful as the program continues and changes over time.

EVALUATION REPORTS: SHARING THE FINDINGS

Functions of Program Evaluation

- Examine the problem for extent and severity
- Select a program for implementation
- Observe program operations
- Determine outcomes
- Evaluate fiscal status
- Provide data
- Identify unintended consequences

After the social program has been evaluated, the results of the evaluation study need to be shared with those who have requested the evaluation, significant stakeholders, the staff of the program, the community, and/or sometimes the recipients of the program's interventions. Increasingly, **evaluation reports** are posted on the Internet, which allows for better access to the report by the public at large and the program stakeholders. A few guidelines suggested by Hendricks (1994) for writing the final report help provide optimal information to those who have requested the evaluation and may enhance utilization of the report.

1. It is the responsibility of the evaluator to be the primary editor of the report and to ensure that it is presented in a timely, factual, unbiased, and appropriate format to meet the needs of the program, its staff, and its sponsors (Hendricks, 1994). Effective communication is essential if the evaluation report is to be accepted and used. Part of the evaluation plan should include plans for communication with members of the program and other interested persons (Posavac & Carey, 1992). When possible, communication meetings should be planned and scheduled at mutually acceptable times and intervals. Evaluators must recognize that sometimes people associated with the program are fearful of the results of an evaluation; one technique to help alleviate some of the concerns of the key stakeholders is to provide an early idea of the results and recommendations of the evaluation. Meetings can be held with the key players to provide valuable feedback between evaluator, program staff, and sponsors. After all inputs from the significant readers of the report are taken into account, a final report can be written.

2. Provide multiple opportunities for reporting the evaluation reports. Some evaluation reports will be more useful if they are presented to multiple audiences. If the APN has been selected to be the evaluator of a homeless shelter, the more audiences that can learn of the successes and areas of needed improvement, the more likely the APN is to build support for the program. The APN may seek to report to community groups, healthcare providers, city council members, and so forth, to reach a larger audience regarding the results of the evaluation.

Frequently, community projects need to keep many diverse interested groups informed so that they will remain supportive of a good social program that is meeting its goals and objectives. This becomes even more critical in times of limited budgets and available funding resources.

3. Reports should be succinct, with the major points presented clearly. Short, powerful sentences work best to grab the attention of decision makers (Jennings, 2003). The inclusion of an executive summary that gives a brief overview of the main findings and recommendations is appreciated (Royse, Thyer, & Padgett, 2010).

   Reports are written for the sponsors and stakeholders and, as much as possible, technical terms need to be kept at a minimum. Complex statistical interpretations may need to be simplified, depending upon the audience. Often, simple, descriptive statistics are more meaningful to a lay audience.

   It is wise to avoid using jargon, whether evaluation-related or technical, in the discussion because the readers of the report may not be familiar with the terms and tend to skip over the report without really reading it. A glossary of terms may be helpful to the readers (Clarke, 1999). Many evaluators find that presenting findings in graph form is a useful method of communicating information in a condensed and visible form. Detailed, additional information that is important to the total evaluation process may be put in appendices for those interested in a more complex and in-depth presentation.

4. Write the report to catch the interests of the audience. It should be written in a style that is appealing and/or compelling to the audience. It needs to address the special interests and concerns of those persons who will be receiving the report. Usually, there are multiple audiences for a report, such as the legislators who created the program, the administrator who is implementing it, the recipients, and often also the community at large (Hendricks, 1994; Royse, Thyer, & Padgett, 2010).

5. Give direction and provide guidelines for action in the form of recommendations. The recipients of most evaluation reports want to learn about what is good about the program and what areas need improvement. Recommendations for action often are best received if the program staff reports them in identifiable, practical, and achievable terms. Unusual or unexpected outcomes must also be reported. If unusual outcomes are presented in a value-free approach, with several suggestions for change, the needs for improvement will be more readily acceptable.

   The question can be asked, how specific should recommendations be? An absolute rule cannot be given to this question. In general, recommendations should always be presented as two or more options unless there is only one, very obvious, recommendation to be made. A specific topic with suggestions for the direction of change may be more effective because it gives those involved in the program direction and flexibility in choosing an approach or making a decision. It is also helpful if the suggestions include some indication of cost, acceptance, or the effects of the recommendations.

6. Use multiple communication techniques to disseminate results of the evaluation. Written reports may be delivered in printed or electronic formats. Videotapes, personal briefings, and community meetings are just a few examples of other methods of sharing the results of a program's evaluation. The technique(s) used should be appropriate to the audience or audiences.

Program evaluations may be used not only by those who have supported, developed, implemented, and/or utilized the program, but also by "policy entrepreneurs" who use the report as a resource to support new policy ideas (Cabatoff, 2000). A well-written report that defines the evaluation findings in clear, nonpartisan terms may be helpful to those engaged in seeking political support for changes in a broader public policy.

Evaluation Reports

- Responsibility of evaluator
- Contents factual without bias
- Format appropriate to audience
- Jargon free
- Provides opportunity for feedback from stakeholders
- Recommendations with two or more options
- Dissemination appropriate to audience

CONCLUSION

Advanced practice nurses have unlimited opportunities to participate in or conduct public policy or program evaluation. Governments and the courts develop public policy via legislative bodies as they make laws, executive bodies as they administer the laws, and judicial bodies as they interpret these laws.

While public policy is determined by governments, it is put into practice by the development of social programs. Most governmental and other agencies that sponsor social programs require that these programs be evaluated. Evaluation may take many forms, including studying the extent and severity of a problem, determining if the program is meeting its goals and objectives, conducting a financial audit, examining program outcomes, verifying program outcomes, and seeking information about needed changes in the program.

The tools for evaluation include the quantitative and qualitative methodologies used by social scientists, which are carried out with a rigor needed to meet the needs of the evaluation. Evaluation is expensive in time, money, skilled personnel, and other scarce resources, so it is imperative that the evaluation study be done skillfully and efficiently to meet the multiple needs of multiple stakeholders.

After an evaluation has been conducted, the results of the study must be communicated. Some of the important principles of providing an evaluation report that is meaningful and useful include presenting the report to multiple audiences, providing multiple opportunities for others to learn about the evaluation report, writing the report succinctly with the interests of significant others included, giving guidelines for change, and using multiple presentation approaches when needed.

Evaluation of social programs is valuable and can provide very useful information to the advanced practice nurse who is providing care through a funded or sponsored social program. Evaluation can present exciting challenges for the APN who participates in program evaluation and the presentation of the results.

DISCUSSION POINTS AND ACTIVITIES

1. What are the advantages of having an advanced practice nurse design and implement an evaluation of a healthcare program?
2. Define how policy, public policy, and social programs may play a role in the advanced practice nurse's practice.
3. List the reasons an APN might be a participant in or conduct a program evaluation.
4. Under what conditions might the APN use a quantitative evaluation design? Qualitative design? Combined quantitative and qualitative design?
5. Identify the conditions in program evaluation that might lead to ethical conflict.
6. How might the advanced practice nurse avoid ethical conflict when participating in or conducting a program evaluation?
7. Draft a program evaluation report within the framework of the component parts.
8. Suggest several ways that the advanced practice nurse might improve utilization of an evaluation report by the sponsors of the evaluation.

Case Study 1: Evaluating Clinic Services

The APRN has worked in a rural health clinic located in a small town of about 7000 residents for several years. The clinic has been supported by a county tax and fee for service. The clinic provides care to a large number of individuals with Medicaid and Medicare and has a sliding fee schedule available for the uninsured. Due to budget constraints, county government officials are discussing closing the clinic to "get out of the business" of providing health care. The APRN has been asked to evaluate the services provided to determine if the clinic should continue to provide health care to the community.

Questions:

1. Where should the APRN begin?
2. What might be some of the role conflicts faced by the APRN?
3. How might the APRN gain support for the evaluation?
4. Who are the stakeholders? How will you involve the stakeholders in the evaluation process?
5. What is the budget for the evaluation process?
6. Will the APRN get release time to conduct the evaluation process?
7. What type of research methodology will be needed?
8. Are there any ethical considerations that must be addressed prior to beginning the evaluation process?
9. How would you disseminate the report?

CASE STUDY 2:   Clinic: For Episodic or Chronic Care?

An inner-city clinic was established by a local, not-for-profit religious organization to provide health care for the poor and homeless at the request of the county government. It is located in the older part of town inhabited by the population that it serves. After a few years, it became apparent that the population served came only for episodic acute problems and did not keep follow-up appointments for chronic illness management. A study was conducted to evaluate this problem and identify possible solutions. The solution this agency chose was to offer only episodic, acute care to this population and refer them to university-sponsored clinics for management of chronic illnesses.

Questions:

1. As the APRN working in this clinic, would you agree with this decision?
2. What is the public policy that the clinic was established to meet?
3. Who should be hired to manage the evaluation?
4. Who will pay for the evaluation study? How should the data be collected?
5. What are some ethical questions that the board must consider when changing the mission of the healthcare clinic?
6. How might the funding of the clinic be impacted by a change in mission?
7. How will program success be measured in the future?
8. Who are the stakeholders?
9. How will the report be disseminated?

For a full suite of assignments and additional learning activities, use the access code located in the front of your book to visit this exclusive website: http://go.jblearning.com/milstead. If you do not have an access code, you can obtain one at the site.

REFERENCES

Affholter, D. P. (1994). Outcome monitoring. In J. S. Wholey, H. P. Hatry, & K. E. Newcomer (Eds.), *Handbook of practical program evaluation* (pp. 96–118). San Francisco, CA: Jossey-Bass.

American Nurses Association. (2001). *Code of ethics for nurses with interpretive statements.* Washington, DC: Author.

Black, B. (2010). Legal aspects of nursing. In K. Chitty & B. Black (Eds.), *Professional nursing: Concepts & challenges* (6th ed., pp. 60–76). Maryland Heights, MO: Saunders Elsevier.

Cabatoff, K. (2000). Translating evaluation findings into "policy language." In R. K. Hoopson (Ed.), *New directions for evaluation:How and why language matters in evaluation* (pp. 43–54). San Francisco, CA: Jossey-Bass.

Center for Health Improvement. (2004). *First 5 advocacy toolkit.* Retrieved from http://www.chipolicy.org/pdf/advocacytoolkitnew.pdf

Centers for Disease Control and Prevention. (2001, November 9). Recommendations and reports: Revised recommendations for HIV screening of pregnant women. Retrieved from http://www.cdc.gov/mmwr/preview/mmwrhtml/rr5019a2.htm

Chitty, K. (2010). Nursing's pathway to professionalism. In K. Chitty & B. Black (Eds.), *Professional nursing: Concepts & challenges* (6th ed., pp. 60–76). Maryland Heights, MO: Saunders Elsevier.

Clarke, A. (with Dawson, R.). (1999). *Evaluation research: An introduction to principles, methods and practice.* London: Sage

Delaware HIV Consortium Policy Committee. (2010). *Recommendations for adoption of routine opt-out HIV testing procedures for adolescents and adults 13-64 in health-care settings: White paper policy brief.* Retrieved from http://www.delawarehiv.org/docs/WhitePaperRoutineOpt-OutPolicyBriefFinal9-10.doc

Department of Justice. (2007). *PART: OMB's Program Assessment Rating Tool In FY 2007 Performance and Accountability Report.* Retrieved from http://www.justice.gov/ag/annualreports/pr2007/sect4/p13-14.pdf

Dye, T. (2008). *Understanding public policy.* Upper Saddle River, NJ: Pearson Prentice Hall.

Environmental Protection Agency. (2010). *Tips on writing a grant proposal.* Retrieved from http://www.epa.gov/ogd/recipient/tips.htm

Fawcett, J., & Garity, J. (2009). *Evaluating research for evidence-based nursing practice.* Philadelphia, PA: F.A. Davis.

Fine, M., Weiss, L., Weseen, S., & Wong, L. (2000). For whom? Qualitative research, representations, and social responsibilities. In N. K. Denzin & Y. S. Lincoln (Eds.), *Handbook of qualitative research* (2nd ed., pp. 107–131). Thousand Oaks, CA: Sage.

Fredericks, K. A., Carman, J. G., & Birkland, T. A. (2002, Fall). Program evaluation in a challenging authorizing environment: Intergovernmental and interorganizational factors. In R. Mohan, D. Bernstein, & M. Whitsett (Eds.), *New directions for evaluation: Responding to sponsors and stakeholders in complex evaluation environments* (pp. 5–21). San Francisco, CA: Jossey-Bass.

Guzman, B. L., & Feria, A. (2002, Fall). Forces driving health care decisions. *Policy, Politics, & Nursing Practice, 3*, 35–42.

Hanley, B., & Falk, N. (2007). Policy development and analysis: Understanding the Process. In D. J. Mason, J. K. Leavitt, & M. W. Chaffee (Eds.), *Policy and politics in nursing and health care* (5th ed., pp. 75–93). St. Louis, MO: Saunders.

Hendricks, M. (1994). Making a splash: Reporting evaluation results effectively. In J. S. Wholey, H. P. Hatry, & K. E. Newcomer (Eds.), *Handbook of practical program evaluation* (pp. 549–575). San Francisco, CA: Jossey-Bass.

Henry J. Kaiser Family Foundation. (2011). Health reform source: Implementation timeline. Retrieved from http://healthreform.kff.org/timeline.aspx?gelid=CM3jhrOGtaYCFYtS2god01SzIg

Jennings, B. M. (2003). A half-dozen health policy hints. *Nursing Outlook, 51*, 92–93.

Jennings, C. P. (2001). The evolution of U.S. health policy and the impact of future trends. *Policy, Politics, and Nursing Practice, 2*, 218–227.

LaPelle, N., Zapka, J., & Ockene, J. (2006). Sustainability of public health programs: The example of tobacco treatment services in Massachusetts. *American Journal of Public Health, 96*, 1363–1369.

Law, M. (2010). History of food and drug regulation in the United States. Retrieved from http://eh.net/encyclopedia/article/Law.Food.and.Drug.Regulation

Lerner, R. M., & Thompson, L. S. (2002). Promoting healthy adolescent behavior and development: Issues in the design and evaluation of effective youth programs. *Journal of Pediatric Nursing, 17*, 338–344.

Light, R. J. (2001, Summer). Editor's notes. In R. J. Light (Ed.), *New directions for evaluation: Evaluation findings that surprise* (pp. 1–2). San Francisco, CA: Jossey-Bass.

Mason, D. J., Leavitt, J. K., & Chaffee, M. W. (Eds.). (2007). *Policy and politics in nursing and health care* (5th ed., pp. 1–16). St. Louis, MO: Saunders.

McNamera, C. (1997–2006). Basic guide to program evaluation. Retrieved from: http://www.managementhelp.org/evaluatn/fnl_eval.htm

Morris, M. (1999). Research on evaluation ethics: What have we learned and why is it important. In J. L. Fitzpatrick & M. Morris (Eds.), *New directions for evaluation: Current and emerging ethical challenges in evaluation* (pp. 15–24). San Francisco, CA: Jossey-Bass.

Orszag, P. & Ellis, P. (2007). The challenge of rising health care costs—A view from the Congressional Budget Office. *New England Journal of Medicine, 357*, 1793–1795.

Polit, D., & Beck, C. (2012). *Nursing research: Generating and assessing evidence for nursing practice.* Philadelphia, PA: Wolters Kluwer/Lippincott Williams & Wilkins.

Posavac, E. J., & Carey, R. G. (1992). *Program evaluation: Methods and case studies* (4th ed.). Englewood Cliffs, NJ: Prentice Hall.

Rossi, P. H., Freeman, H. E., & Lipsy, M. W. (2004). *Evaluation: A systematic approach* (7th ed.). New York: Random House.

Royse, D., Thyer, B., & Padgett, D. (2010). *Program evaluation: An introduction* (5th ed.). Belmont, CA: Wadsworth Cengage Learning.

Shadish, W. R., Jr., Cook, T. D., & Leviton, L. C. (1995). *Foundations of program evaluation: Theories of practice.* Newbury Park, CA: Sage.

Sieber, J. E. (1980). Being ethical: Professional and personal decisions in program evaluation. *New Directions for Program Evaluation* (pp. 51–61). San Francisco, CA: Jossey-Bass

Sonpal-Valias, N. (2009). Outcome evaluation: Definition and overview. Retrieved from http://pdfebooksonline.com/ebook-outcome+measurement+resource+network-pdf-1.html

Stoto, M. A. (2001). Preventing perinatal transmission of HIV: Target programs, not people. In R. J. Light (Ed.), *New directions for evaluation: Evaluation findings that surprise* (pp. 41–53). San Francisco, CA: Jossey-Bass.

Thomas, C. W., Smith, B. D., & Wright-DeAguero, L. (2006). The program evaluation and monitoring evidence-based HIV prevention program processes and outcomes. *AIDS Education and Prevention, 18*(Suppl. A), 74–80.

Trussell, P., Brandt, A., & Knapp, S. (1981). *Using nursing research: Discovery, analysis, and interpretation.* Wakefield, MA: Nursing Resources.

Wallace, J. (2003). A policy analysis of the assistive technology alternative financing program in the United States. *Journal of Disability Policy Studies, 14*(2), 74–81.

Westat, J. F. (2002). The 2002 user-friendly handbook for project evaluation. National Science Foundation Directorate for Education & Human Resources, Division of Research, Evaluation, and Communication. Retrieved from http://www.nsf.gov/pubs/2002/nsf02057/nsf02057.pdf

ONLINE RESOURCES

Academy Health: Provides links to health services researchers in health policy and practice. It fosters networking among a diverse membership. *http://www.academyhealth.org*

Agency for Healthcare Research and Quality (AHRQ): Provides links to multiple resources. The mission of the agency is to improve the quality, safety, efficiency, and effectiveness of health care for all Americans. *http://www.ahrq.gov*

CDC Evaluation Working Group: Provides multiple links to multiple resources for information or assistance in conducting an evaluation project. *http://www.cdc.gov/eval/resources.htm*

Free Management Library: Developed by Authenticity Consulting. Provides extensive online resources for program evaluation and personal, professional, and organization development, including many detailed guidelines, worksheets, and more. *http://www.managementhelp.org*

Outcome Measurement Resource Network: Developed by United Way of America. *http://national. unitedway.org/outcomes/library/ndpaper.cfm*

Resources for Methods in Evaluation and Social Research: Provides free resources for methods in evaluation and social research, including information on how to do evaluation research. *http://gsociology. icaap.org/methods*

CHAPTER 8

The Impact of Social Networking and the Internet on Healthcare Decisions

Elizabeth Barnhill and Troy Spicer

KEY TERMS

Asynchronous(ly): Occurring at different times. For instance, one can post to Facebook now, and a friend can respond at a later time. There is no requirement to be online at the same time for interaction to take place.

Computerized provider order entry (CPOE): Electronic means of documenting patient orders that will disperse the information to the required area such as pharmacy, radiology, or laboratory. Because the order is entered via the computer, illegibility issues and transmission delays should be minimized.

Data mining: Means of extracting information from an electronic document in order to gather individual information or aggregate the data for analysis and/or pattern identification.

Electronic health record (EHR): A computer-generated patient record with longitudinal information such as immunizations, allergies, and demographics of an individual that is designed to be accessed across healthcare systems. EHRs differ from the more detailed electronic medical record (EMR), which is an electronic legal record of an individual's specific encounter at a particular medical facility.

Healthcare literacy: The ability to search for and understand healthcare information.

Informatics: The study of information technology.

Really Simple Syndication (RSS): A means for a website to update information for distribution to interested parties who typically register to receive updates.

Superuser: An employee of a facility receiving new equipment, such as electronic documentation systems, who receives detailed, extensive training from the vendor in order to continue the training after the initial go-live phase is completed and the vendor trainers leave the facility.

Synchronous(ly): Happening at the same time. For example, an online class that is synchronous meets at a specific time, with students and instructor logged on simultaneously.

Web 2.0: Also known as social networking and social media; an interactive way of communicating electronically.

INTRODUCTION

Consider the widespread changes in how information is accessed and how people communicate. In just over 20 years, virtually all aspects of life, education, commerce, government, etc., have been changed by information technology. Technological innovations continue to be designed, and so keeping abreast of information technologies is an ongoing challenge. The capacity to use technology has become a professional imperative for advanced practice nurses (APNs), as advances in technology are increasingly associated with how health-related information is accessed and used. In this environment of rapid change, APNs must recognize the power of information technology in shaping the healthcare realm regarding both professional practice and healthcare policy. APNs must adapt to these changes successfully.

Rapidly evolving technological advances in diagnosis and treatment have been wholly embraced by the healthcare sector, particularly in the past 50 years. Health care, however, has lagged behind other industries, such as entertainment, manufacturing, and transportation, in integrating advances in information technology into the fabric of the industry. More recent innovations such as *social networking*, a term often included in the overarching rubric *Web 2.0*, are poised to accelerate the rate of change that influences APN practice directly. The healthcare industry finds itself in the position of having to play catch up. Even as the healthcare industry lags behind in taking advantage of healthcare information technology, healthcare information has nonetheless joined other types of web-based content commonly created and utilized by the public. In the absence of authoritative sources creating sound content, a proliferation of questionable and inaccurate information has emerged. The challenge for APNs is to take advantage of the information revolution in order to improve patient care and to continue to secure a voice in public policy.

To date, governmental policy regarding healthcare information technology has centered on security and access. Two of the most recent important pieces of legislation to address information technology are the Health Information Technology for Economic and Clinical Health Act (HITECH) in 2009 and the Health Insurance Portability and Accountability Act (HIPAA) in 1996. Both have had far-reaching effects on healthcare practice and healthcare information. With this legislation, along with other initiatives, the federal government in general, and the Executive Branch in particular, are taking strong positions regarding the promotion of patient safety, health-related information access, and health literacy among citizens with the objective of improving access and the quality of health care (U.S. Department of Health and Human Services, 2011). From the APN's perspective, successfully meeting these objectives hinges on the availability and access of sound health-related information for both the provider and the patient.

SOCIAL NETWORKS: HOW THEY HAVE CHANGED COMMUNICATION

Within the past 10 years, the Internet has evolved from a static, yet immediate, source of information into a more interactive entity. These innovations are described using the term

Web 2.0. **Web 2.0** is not a single application or platform, but suggests a new version of the Internet in which the consumer ceases to be like a patron at a library selecting discrete pieces of information. Instead, the user creates a personalized and interactive relationship with information and other users. This term is synonymous with the terms *social networking* and *social media*. Other expressions associated with social networking, such as texting, instant messaging, tweeting, tagging, blogging, and skyping, have become synonymous with communicating. Because effective nursing is associated intimately with effective communication, becoming familiar with the "who, what, where, and how" of social networking is essential for APNs and their successful practices in the future.

What Are Social Networks?

As social networking capabilities have expanded, the number and variety of sites have proliferated. Social websites such as Facebook and Myspace focus on activities limited to friends and acquaintances (depending on individual privacy settings), while Twitter and YouTube can also include larger groups with more public access; other servers concentrate on specific issues, such as WebMD for health-related information, and LinkedIn, which connects professionals who have common interests. See **Table 8-1** for examples of social networking platforms.

Most social networking sites have multiple means of communicating information, using media such as text, picture, and video. Once the user accesses a particular site, different menu options can navigate the user to custom areas with specific interests. For instance, a search on WebMD for asthma information can reveal specific articles, expert advice, and interactive discussion groups geared toward this disease entity. An individual can then join a **Really Simple Syndication (RSS)** feed to receive instantaneous updates regarding asthma from WebMD or a host of other healthcare-related information sites. It is this ability to interact with and customize the Internet experience that is the hallmark of Web 2.0.

Who Uses Them?

With 500 million active Facebook members and more than 2 billion daily hits on YouTube alone, social networking has become the entertainment and information medium of choice for a multitude of people worldwide (Facebook Pressroom, 2011; YouTube Pressroom, n.d.). A cottage industry that studies user characteristics has developed, allowing businesses to maximize their advertising dollars by sponsoring websites based on the demographics of their consumers (Bulik, 2009). Many politicians and public servants, realizing the significance of this widespread use, have started using social networks as a means of communicating with constituents, campaigning, and fundraising (Dorsch & Greenberg, 2009).

Because of its universal accessibility, professionals who use social network sites should proceed with caution. Dorsch and Greenberg (2009) recommend that personal and professional communication be kept completely separate. Bemis-Dougherty (2010) recognizes the advantages of using this avenue, including the ease of communication

Table 8-1 Examples of Networking Sites and Their Characteristics

Website	Usage Statistics	Primary Purpose	Medium	Access	Capabilities
Facebook: http://www. facebook.com	500 million active users (Facebook Pressroom, 2011). 38%: > 34 years old 22%: 25–34 years old 31%: 18–24 years old 9%: 14–17 years old (Gonzalez, 2011)	Social; support groups	Text and pictures; able to post videos	Both asynchronous and synchronous; various privacy settings available	Private chat; can leave private or public message, blog; can post links to other websites
Twitter: http://www.twitter.com	Most users are 18–29 years old; minority use > Caucasian use; increased use in urban areas (Smith & Rainie, 2009)	Social; posting updates, news, following interests	Short texts; can "drill down" to more detail with pictures and video	Primarily asynchronous	Public blog, can use screen name for privacy; messages limited to 140 characters; can receive updates via text messages
LinkedIn: http://www.linkedin.com	Globally, more than 90 million professionals have joined (LinkedIn Press Center, 2011)	Professional networking, career links	Text, profile pictures	Primarily asynchronous	Limits access unless permission from contact is granted; can create/join custom groups of professionals with similar interests/positions; can leave private messages for individuals
YouTube: http://www.youtube.com	> 2 billion views/day (YouTube Pressroom, n.d.)	Video-sharing	Audiovisual	Asynchronous	Public forum
WebMD: http://www.webmd.com	8 out of 10 Internet users pursue health information online (Fox, 2011)	Resource for health-related information	Text, pictures, some video	Asynchronous	Health information on specific disease sets; expert blogs; discussion groups; support

with both colleagues and patients, but warns against violating patient confidentiality. Maintaining a professional demeanor by avoiding the temptation to vent is also paramount.

Speed of Communication

Posting information on a social networking site occurs instantaneously, with most servers functioning both **synchronously** and **asynchronously**. With email alert options and increasingly sophisticated cellular phones with data plans, mobile updates can facilitate the speed of communication. This feature is a double-edged sword: important information can be posted immediately for the benefit of others, but once released, the ability to retract material becomes extremely difficult, if not impossible, since some sites, such as Facebook, maintain proprietary rights to all information (Bemis-Dougherty, 2010; Reid, 2009).

How Reliable Are the Postings?

Prior to the Internet and the advent of social networking, healthcare information was available through a variety of traditional sources (Nelson, 2008). The APN had to be diligent in vetting the source of the material to better ensure that it was reliable, and analyzing information from social networking sites requires similar precautionary measures. The APN needs to determine the origin of the content and understand that navigating different sites and following links can lead to unreliable information. Checking author credentials, dates, and the nature of the material (i.e., opinion vs. fact) are a few guidelines to heed.

SOCIAL NETWORKING AND HEALTHCARE INFORMATION: A MIXED BLESSING

From a healthcare consumer standpoint, nothing may affect healthcare decision-making in the future more than social networking and the Internet. Everyone desires a more-informed healthcare consumer. A movement by the federal government has begun to emphasize the importance of improving **healthcare literacy** on a large scale (Benjamin, 2010; Institute of Medicine, 2011; Sarkar, et al., 2010), and one means to this end is by using information technologies. Government and industry leaders recognize that poor healthcare literacy and lack of access to appropriate information is a substantial impediment to creating a healthy populace.

Social networking is an ideal venue for accomplishing the aim of improving healthcare literacy. Unfortunately, the sources and reliability of much of the healthcare information available on the web in general, and on social networks in particular, are of dubious accuracy and questionable provenance. Information available to patients varies widely in basic readability (Pothier & Pothier, 2009). Due to the absence of a coordinated and concerted effort on the part of the government and the healthcare industry, the creation of timely, accurate, understandable, and efficacious information has been partially usurped by poorly informed, biased or, frankly, mercenary sources. The Internet is full of websites that promote pseudoscience and quackery (Barrett, 2010).

Patients are actively seeking and utilizing information from the Internet and social networks regarding health care (Rice, 2006; Ybarra & Suman, 2006). APNs must be acutely attentive to the sources, quality, and accuracy of the healthcare information on which their patients rely. This will require an open dialog with patients regarding the websites they are visiting. Better resources have developed and constitute an important source of information for patients, and legitimate blogs, illness-specific websites, and nonprofit websites all hold great promise in improving healthcare literacy and should be embraced by APNs. Government and private health industry has lagged in creating sources of legitimate health information; despite this, much improved and thoroughly useful resources are emerging (Ekman, Hall, & Litton, 2005). Responsible purveyors of health information have taken initial steps to ensure better quality. One such effort is a nonprofit foundation called Health on the Net Foundation (HON). Organizations that meet HON's guidelines display the HON logo prominently on their websites (Health on the Net Foundation, 2011).

Consumer Uses

The first issue to emerge when discussing electronic information and social networking is Internet penetration into American households. According to the U.S. Department of Commerce (2011), Internet penetration into American households is at best characterized as fair. Up to 68 percent of households in the United States had broadband Internet access in 2010, a 5 percent increase over 2009. Disparities in access do exist, particularly with minorities and those who live in rural areas (U.S. Department of Commerce, 2011). Nonetheless, the Internet is an important source of health-related information for a large number of people (Fox, 2011).

One of *Healthy People 2020*'s objectives involves healthcare information technology and healthcare information strategies to improve health in both individuals and communities (U.S. Department of Health and Human Services, 2011). The premise is that technology and information have the power to influence the way society defines health and, as such, will be central to how the consumer and provider will negotiate healthcare decisions. Explicit in these arguments is the declared objective to increase access to quality healthcare information via the Internet. A great deal of research demonstrates that poor health literacy is associated with poor health outcomes (Agency for Healthcare Research and Quality, 2007).

Consumers are already heavy users of Internet-related health information (Rice, 2006; Ybarra & Suman, 2006). Consumers are able to access a wide array of information from sources both legitimate and suspect. A variety of information is available to patients, including more traditional websites and articles, but there has been a rise in more interactive platforms that involve the exchange of information and opinion among people with like interests; these sites are in the form of blogs, discussion boards, and support groups. Some of the discussion boards are free standing, and some are associated with more-established organizations, just as some are tightly moderated by experts in the field, and some are more loosely monitored or not at all. Health issues, both large and esoteric, are addressed by these discussion boards. The quality of the information that is shared varies widely. **Table 8-2** offers a list of websites that are considered trustworthy and are geared toward consumers.

The introduction of social networking to healthcare venues and websites may be particularly helpful to those patients who are isolated due to physical or emotional infirmity or by geography. Support groups and interactive sites have the potential to overcome disparities such as those created by poverty, chronic conditions, conditions that limit mobility, or living in rural areas.

Healthcare Provider Uses

Healthcare providers have a dual responsibility: to identify trustworthy information for both personal and patient use, as well as to guide patients in accessing reliable consumer-targeted information, blogs, and support groups. APNs have the related responsibility to recognize and counsel patients who are using, misusing, or misunderstanding existing information. APNs can influence patient attitudes regarding information obtained over the Internet, as healthcare provider–patient conversations involving the Internet lead to higher confidence in the Internet as a resource by patients (Hong, 2008). By judiciously choosing appropriate patient-oriented Internet websites, discussion boards, blogs, and support groups, APNs can contribute to increasing health literacy and improving patient outcomes.

In a time when a majority of adults in the United States look for health information online, a major consideration for the APN is to determine what patients are doing with this information. The extent to which people feel that the Internet plays an important part in their lives influences their expectations that the health information they garner will make a difference (Leung, 2008). APNs must realize that many patients will have consulted the Internet for answers; therefore, APNs must be prepared to speak openly and frankly about the information. Patients might seek health care having a preset agenda or self-diagnosis, and they might also be seeking a specific diagnostic examination, laboratory workup, or medication.

Eventually, APNs might find that patients are increasingly less challenging or, perhaps, more challenging to care for in light of ready access to health-related materials. Patients will solicit advice from APNs regarding which Internet information sources and support groups the APN recommends, and so APNs should prepare in advance by thoroughly investigating healthcare websites, becoming familiar with all their functions, and revisiting the sites at regular intervals to know what has changed. A patient's trust will not be cultivated if a patient has the impression that the APN is not fully familiar with the website he or she is recommending.

Table 8-2   Selected Trustworthy Consumer Health Websites

Website Name and URL	Consumer Information?	Blog/Discussion Board/Forum?	Advocacy?	Support Groups?	RSS/Twitter?	HON Certified?
Agency for Health Research and Quality http://www.ahrq.gov	✓	∅	∅	∅	✓	∅
American Cancer Society http://www.cancer.org	✓	✓	✓	✓	✓	✓
American Diabetes Association http://www.diabetes.org	✓	✓	✓	✓	✓	∅
American Heart Association American Stroke Association http://www.heart.org http://www.strokeassociation.org	✓	∅	✓	∅	✓	∅
American Lung Association http://www.lungusa.org	✓	∅	✓	∅	✓	∅
Arthritis Foundation http://www.arthritis.org	✓	✓	✓	✓	✓	∅
Centers for Disease Control and Prevention http://www.cdc.gov	✓	∅	∅	∅	✓	∅
Drugs.com http://www.drugs.com	✓	✓	∅	∅	✓	✓
Health on the Internet (HON) http://www.hon.ch/home1.html	✓	✓	✓	✓	✓	✓
National Institutes of Health http://www.nih.gov/index.html	✓	∅	∅	∅	✓	∅
National Kidney Foundation http://www.kidney.org	✓	✓	✓	✓	✓	✓
Mayo Clinic http://www.mayoclinic.com	✓	✓	∅	∅	✓	✓
Merck Manual Home Edition http://www.merckmanuals.com/home/index.html	✓	∅	∅	∅	∅	∅
WebMD http://www.webmd.com	✓	✓	∅	∅	✓	✓

From a professional practice standpoint, health-related websites have great promise in making timely and important information available. Websites such as the Centers for Disease Control and Prevention (CDC) and Medscape, among many others, have the capacity to send emails with their latest recommendations. RSS technology allows APNs to sign up for news releases and updates. RSS serves as a sort of electronic file cabinet that receives, categorizes, and stores electronic dispatches from healthcare agencies and professional organizations. APNs need only to look for the orange RSS symbol on the website to sign up for the entity's dispatches. Other avenues for provider-related information include listserves (mass emails for groups of people with similar interests) and Facebook pages of colleagues or organizations. These resources have the potential to deliver highly specific and useful information to APNs with great efficiency. These technologies also have the potential to decrease professional isolation. As always, however, the provider must be wary of the source of the information.

From a public policy standpoint, the Internet and social networking can be tools to influence public policy. Social networking in particular can be a powerful tool in political organizing and issue advocacy, as communication with politicians and policymakers is easier with electronic resources. Political blogs and discussion boards often have healthcare-related areas. Platforms such as Twitter allow information to be received by an individual, and then rebroadcast to friends, associates, and colleagues. As a result, the power to quickly disseminate information increases exponentially. Social networking has the capacity to democratize access to policy-related information, to decrease professional isolation in rural areas, and to facilitate an individual's influence on policy.

APNs must advocate for accurate and helpful information on the Internet. Healthcare information on the Internet can be targeted to specific audiences with specific health information at low cost. In the future, web-based information will become more important as people spend more time online. New avenues for research using innovative methods that test new venues for patient education, peer and group support, assessment, and treatment will become more readily available.

The future of Internet healthcare information may lie in the integration of highly interactive platforms that combine elements from both the basic web and social networking. Kaiser Permanente has begun to test one such tool, called KP Health Connect (Silvestre, Sue, & Allen, 2009). In this platform, patients are encouraged to access their health records, appointments, scheduling, and email accounts that link them to their care provider. A natural progression of a platform such as this would be the inclusion of health condition-related, moderated discussion boards and support groups. In another innovation to steer nonemergent patients to urgent care clinics, Blue Cross Blue Shield of Georgia has an audio tutorial, a 24/7 nurse help line, and an urgent care locator powered by Google Maps (Williams, 2011).

BEYOND INFORMATICS: ELECTRONIC HEALTH RECORDS

The precursor of today's **electronic health records (EHRs)** emerged approximately 50 years ago (National Institutes of Health National Center for Research Resources, 2006). Although fraught with technical difficulties, the original attempts to computerize medical information paved the way for current goals that include storing individual health data in usable formats and introducing interactive prompts to promote patient safety.

The HITECH Act was passed in 2009 as a subset of the American Recovery and Reinvestment Act (Tomes, 2010). This legislation created a deadline of 2015 for those medical facilities and eligible providers who receive Medicare reimbursement to employ EHRs in their systems. Criteria for successful implementation involve the degree of usefulness, or *meaningful use*, of the electronic documents.

Cost

The passage of the HITECH Act created a series of financial incentives paid over a five-year period for those facilities and providers mandated to employ the EHR (Tomes, 2010). At first glance, this program might appear to offset the cost of compliance; however, this compensation does not necessarily remove all startup costs. For example, a physician can receive as much as $44,000 in total government reimbursements; however, one provider reported that a typical setup totaled $47,000 for the hardware package and service for the first year (BuyerZone, 2011). The desire to qualify for additional incentive payments for early implementation of the EHR might encourage impulsive decision-making, ultimately creating the potential for "buyer's remorse" as facilities incur unexpected costs to supplement their systems.

Once the EHR is in place, a facility's clinical decision support team can help recoup costs by streamlining care and pinpointing areas of deficit through electronic retrieval of information via aggregate reports (Glaser, 2008). Current literature reveals growing pains felt with EHR implementation in the form of increased costs of training staff, purchasing software, and a learning curve with new users, but the researchers also found decreased mortality rates among EHR facilities, attributed to interactive products employed to reduce medication errors. These facilities can expect increased savings as users become more proficient (knowIT, 2010).

Efficiency

Despite the initial difficulty of incorporating the EHR, APNs are already experiencing its advantages by accessing patient information remotely (Hosker, 2007). For example, not only can a fetal monitor tracing be accessed offsite, but medical records from previous admissions can be made available as well. **Computerized provider order entry (CPOE)** reduces duplication of orders, checks drug allergies and interactions, and provides an interactive component that assists with decision-making (Lykowski & Mahoney, 2004). Currently, large vendors such as McKesson,

General Electric, and Siemans have composed their own versions of the EHR that are not interchangeable, which inhibits sharing information across different medical systems (National Institutes of Health National Center for Research Resources, 2006). However, once this incompatibility is resolved, APNs will have the ability to access a more complete, longitudinal snapshot of their patients, creating safer, more streamlined care.

Besides facilitating individual efficiency, conversion to electronic recordkeeping promises to increase performance on a larger scale. Patient data that is entered into an electronic format can be retrieved in the future using a process known as **data-mining**. This activity allows analysis of patient safety measures, length of stay information, and other areas of opportunity, enabling both healthcare facilities and providers to improve areas of weakness (Phillips, 2005).

Training

APNs are a critical element when EHRs are introduced. As valuable end users, APNs can provide input in both the selection and customization of the chosen product (Bernstein, McCreless, & Cote, 2007). As with any new program, successful implementation of EHRs involves a substantial investment for training. Both selection and customization activities demand full engagement of the participants in order to reap the maximum benefits from the new system. Most vendors, as part of the implementation costs, supply professional trainers or train existing staff as **superusers**, or onsite experts, to instruct other end users in the most efficient use possible.

With the proliferation of electronic information, nursing is beginning to recognize the importance of having a basic knowledge of **informatics** (Flanagan & Jones, 2007). Incorporating an informatics course into nursing curriculum can facilitate the transition to EHRs and provide insight into potential methods of abstracting data for use in research.

INFORMATION, LEGISLATION, AND HEALTH CARE

How the government approaches health care and the importance of health policy in influencing the government's decisions has never been more important. With political and policy information so readily available, there is no excuse for APNs to be ill-informed. The speed with which information is disseminated has created a climate where information and interpretation are immediate; therefore, immediate responses are required, as information is produced and consumed so rapidly as to make emerging policy more unstable, dynamic, and susceptible to influence. Once again, the APN needs to be diligent in vetting information sources since some websites that appear to be official can be deceptive. Relying on information that employs important-sounding monikers such as *The Society of ABC* or *The National Organization of XYZ* should not replace diligence in vetting the source.

APNs must be involved in policy because, in reality, APNs are the people who must cope with the changes that policy creates. Changes in governmental philosophies and priorities are important because the stakes are so high. The healthcare system in the United States is routinely criticized as too expensive, with persistent pockets of disparities. The manner in which the issues of how and where resources are invested are framed and the tone of the debate is emotionally charged and sometimes bitter. This should be no surprise since health care is such a large component of the U.S. gross domestic product and involves huge sums of money in an industry that essentially functions as an oligopoly composed of a few industries, such as insurance companies and hospitals. As the immediate future of health care in the United States is frequently seen as obscured and in flux, now more than ever keeping track of health policy is an important aspect of professional practice.

Political activism can be as simple and personal as making a telephone call to a state legislator, or it can be as involved as volunteering to be a district policy coordinator for a state professional organization. Legislators appreciate nurses who are willing to volunteer as contacts regarding substantive issues such as school nursing or access to trauma care. This is especially true as legislators and their staffs are as likely as the general public to be exposed to poor quality health-related information.

Some politically active APNs serve as liaisons between legislators and constituent nurses. State associations of nurses such as New York State Nurses Association (2011) actively recruit nurses to participate and offer training for those who desire more involvement than telephone calling and letter writing. While it would be expected that information technology should be a boon to both healthcare consumers and nurses seeking accurate information, electronic media have been exploited by some to distribute biased and misleading information, such as the myth of death panels during the healthcare debate of 2009 (Begley, Connolly, Kalb, & Yarett, 2009). Nurses will have to develop an equal measure of the technological savvy necessary to counter examples of demagoguery such as this.

Social media holds great promise in facilitating the political organization of nurses. Many of the state associations of nursing have Facebook pages. The American Nurses Association has taken an additional step of creating a social networking platform called *NurseSpace*, which allows nurses to share information and seek advice on nurse issues. The discussions are organized in terms of the various communities of nursing practice, geography, and the roles of the nurse, such as student, entrepreneur, and administrator. Of these discussion groups, one is devoted to politics and one to health policy.

The Internet and social networking have fundamentally changed the practice of politics. Even though the Internet played a role in the 2000 and 2004 presidential elections, 2008 was quickly nicknamed the *Web 2.0 Election*, such was the importance of information technology to both political parties (Germany, 2008). Campaign fundraising by politicians now commonly has an Internet component. The power of courting small donors was strikingly demonstrated by the historic fundraising success of the Obama presidential campaign in 2008 (Hill, 2009).

THE FUTURE OF HEALTHCARE POLICY IN THE AGE OF SOCIAL NETWORKING

The continuing explosion of social networking capabilities will certainly contribute to the dynamic nature of healthcare policy. Policymakers are already using websites such as Facebook and Twitter to monitor the pulse of their constituents. It is imperative for the APN to remain current in these communication modalities in order to have a voice in decision-making.

Agenda-Setting and Implementation

Furlong (2008) describes several key components in agenda-setting, including stakeholders, contextual dimensions, and windows of opportunity. With the growing use of interactive social networks among both the general public and public officials, the agenda-setting stage of the political process promises to become more fast-paced in future policymaking. A survey showed that although conventional means of communication remain the most influential, Facebook, Twitter, and YouTube are becoming increasingly popular and important among members of Congress and their senior staff (Eye on FDA, 2011). APNs, as both individual constituents and members of professional organizations, have the opportunity to communicate ideas and concerns regarding future healthcare issues by using these networks. Because of the ease and speed of this new form of communication, APNs must be especially vigilant at monitoring the accuracy of their information sources while they are attempting to affect change in policy.

Wilken (2008) describes common problems with policy implementation when policy criteria do not mirror real-life scenarios. The proliferation of social networking has the potential to reduce this issue as APNs stay virtually connected with their colleagues by reporting problems, suggesting solutions, and creating an aura of supportiveness in a global manner. Because multiple entities, including policymakers, are connected to these networks, policy implementation efforts can be monitored with the ability to receive immediate feedback.

Implications for the Future

The increased flow of information through social networking, along with the availability of remote access to medical records, will certainly raise concerns about privacy issues. Dorsch and Greenberg (2009) advise users to beware of potential hackers and to be aware of the terms of service for the different websites. For instance, Facebook policy states that all posted information belongs to the website (Reid, 2009); once information is posted, it is virtually impossible to retract. APNs would be wise to stay apprised of the application and interpretation of current laws such as HIPAA, which is responsible for maintaining the security of health information, when using social networks and accessing medical records remotely.

Healthcare privacy policy is just one example of a healthcare issue in flux. Pay-for-performance, hospital-acquired conditions, core measure statistics, and health score-cards are other initiatives becoming publicly accessible and are designed to increase transparency in healthcare matters. Insurance companies, government agencies, health-care consumers, and healthcare facilities are already becoming key players in this evo-lution. The climate for APN participation in this new era of healthcare policy formation has never been more open than the present. Data are readily available, and the capabil-ity of immediate feedback with various stakeholders, including policymakers, promises to change the policy process in a more rapid fashion. APNs need to become engaged in the process as well, in order to maintain a place at the decision-making table.

CASE STUDY 1

In the course of interviewing the family of Jody Barrineau, a healthy 3-year-old presenting for routine checkup, the mother and father express unconventional beliefs regarding preventative health care. The APN, Halley Moore, listens as both relate claims found on the Internet that vaccines are harmful to children. The mother says she is concerned by reports that, among other things, the measles/mumps/rubella (MMR) vaccine causes autism, diphtheria/tetanus/acellular pertussis (Dtap) vaccine is associated with sudden infant death syndrome, and the influenza vaccine actually causes influenza. The father concurs and cites "authoritative" sources from the Internet including web pages and discussion groups that are not recognized by the APN. The APN is faced with a family with deeply held beliefs than run counter to her own. These beliefs are made more intractable since the parents sincerely believe that they diligently researched the issue and that they are acting in the best interest of Jody.

DISCUSSION POINTS AND ACTIVITIES

1. Identify at least four Internet sites that offer legitimate health-related infor-mation and at least four Internet sites that offer questionable health-related information.
2. Discuss how the APN can help a patient/family analyze information to ascer-tain its value and reliability.
3. Identify advantages and disadvantages of discussion boards and support groups on the Internet.
4. How can the APN improve the quality of information found on the Internet?

Case Study 2

Sandra Martin, a woman in her mid-70s, was born with a deformity of her spine, which had never been a health issue until recently when arthritis began to impair her ability to compensate for her slightly shorter left leg. After consultation with an orthopedic surgeon, she agreed to have the deformity surgically corrected. Sandra's postoperative course was stormy, including complications with pneumonia, making a transfer to the intensive care unit (ICU) necessary. Sandra's physician had prescribed a common antibiotic regimen used for the type of organism identified, but she seemed to be getting worse despite this intervention. William Girder, an APN who worked with the pulmonary practice, was making rounds one afternoon. Sandra's daughter, Lucy, approached him with an Internet article she had found regarding an alternative therapy for this type of pneumonia. Lucy confided to William that she was glad he was the provider who was rounding that day, because she felt he would listen to her more than the attending physician would and advocate for her mother's wellbeing, especially since Sandra was showing no signs of improvement.

DISCUSSION POINTS AND ACTIVITIES

1. Should William proceed with Lucy's request to try a different therapy?
2. How can William determine whether the article presented by Lucy has any merit?
3. If William determines that the article is legitimate, what other steps are needed before deciding to switch the treatment approach?
4. Discuss the ethics of William's response to Lucy regarding the attending physician.

For a full suite of assignments and additional learning activities, use the access code located in the front of your book to visit this exclusive website: http://go.jblearning.com/milstead. If you do not have an access code, you can obtain one at the site.

REFERENCES

Agency for Healthcare Quality and Research. (2007). *Program brief: Health literacy.* AHRQ Publication No. 07-P010. Retrieved from http://www.ahrq.gov/research/healthlit.pdf

Barrett, S. (2010, June 16). Quackwatch mission statement. Retrieved from http://www.quackwatch.com/00AboutQuackwatch/mission.html

Begley, S., Connolly, K., Kalb, C., & Yarett, I. (2009). The five biggest lies in the health care debate. *Newsweek, 154*(10), 42–43.

Bemis-Dougherty, A. (2010). Professionalism and social networking. *PT on motion, 2*(5), 40–47.

Benjamin, R. M. (2010). Surgeon General's perspectives: Improving health by improving health literacy. *Public Health Reports, 125,* 784–785.

Bernstein, M. L., McCreless, T., & Cote, M. J. (2007). Five constants of information technology adoption in healthcare. *Hospital Topics: Research and Perspectives on Healthcare, 85*(1), 17–25.

Bulik, B. S. (2009). What your favorite social network says about you. *Advertising Age, 80*(25), 6.

BuyerZone. (2011). Real-world EMR prices from BuyerZone buyers. Retrieved from http://www.buyerzone.com/healthcare/electronic-medical-records/ar-prices-emr

Dorsch, M., & Greenberg, P. (2009). What you need to know about social networking. *State Legislatures, 35*(7), 62–64.

Ekman, A., Hall, P., & Litton, J. E. (2005). Can we trust cancer information on the Internet? A comparison on interactive cancer risk sites. *Cancer Causes and Control, 16,* 765–772.

Eye on FDA. (2011, January 26). Growing role of social media among policymakers. Retrieved from http://www.pharma-marketer.com/growing-role-of-social-media-among-policymakers

Facebook Pressroom. (2011). People on Facebook. Retrieved from http://www.facebook.com/press/info.php?statistics

Flanagan, J., & Jones, D. A. (2007). Nursing language in a time of change: Capturing the focus of the discipline. *International Journal of Nursing Terminologies and Classifications, 18*(1), 1–2.

Fox, S. (2011). Health topics (Report findings). Retrieved from http://pewinternet.org/~/media//Files/Reports/2011/PIP_HealthTopics.pdf

Furlong, E. A. (2008). Agenda setting. In J. A. Milstead (Ed.), *Health policy and politics: A nurse's guide* (3rd ed., pp. 41–63). Sudbury, MA: Jones and Bartlett.

Germany, J. B. (2008). Changing political campaigns one voter at a time. *Insights on Law and Society, 9*(1), 15–16.

Glaser, J. (2008). Clinical decision support: The power behind the electronic health record. *Healthcare Financial Management, 62*(7), 46–48, 50–51.

Gonzalez, N. (2011). Checkfacebook.com. Retrieved from http://www.checkfacebook.com

Health on the Net Foundation. (2011). Medical professional. Retrieved from http://www.hon.ch/med.html

Hill, S. (2009). World wide webbed: The Obama campaign's masterful use of the internet. *Social Europe: The Journal of the European Left, 4*(2), 9–14.

Hong, T. (2008). Internet health information in the patient-provider dialog. *CyberPsychology & Behavior, 11*(5), 587–589.

Hosker, N. (2007). Exploiting the potential of informatics in health care. *Nurse Prescribing, 5*(9), 391–394.

Institute of Medicine. (2011). *Innovations in Health Literacy Research: Workshop Summary.* Washington, DC: The National Academies Press.

knowIT. (2010). Electronic medical records: A surprising short-term prognosis for cost savings. Retrieved from http://knowledge.wpcarey.asu.edu/article.cfm?articleid=1912

Leung, L. (2008). Internet embeddedness: Links with online health information seeking, expectancy value/quality of health information websites, and internet usage patterns. *CyberPsychology & Behavior, 11*(5), 565–569.

LinkedIn Press Center. (2011). LinkedIn facts. Retrieved from http://press.linkedin.com/about

Lykowsi, G., & Mahoney, D. (2004). Computerized provider order entry improves workflow and outcomes. *Nursing Management, 35*(2), 40G–40H.

National Institutes of Health National Center for Research Resources. (2006). *Electronic health records review.* Retrieved from http://www.ncrr.nih.gov/publications/informatics/ehr.pdf

Nelson, R. (2008). The internet and healthcare policy information. In J. A. Milstead (Ed.), *Health policy and politics: A nurse's guide* (3rd ed., pp. 197–219). Sudbury, MA: Jones and Bartlett.

New York State Nurses Association. (2011). Legislative advocacy [Website]. Retrieved from http://www.nysna.org/advocacy/main.htm

Phillips, J. (2005). Knowledge is power: Using nursing information management and leadership interventions to improve services to patients, clients, and users. *Journal of Nursing Management, 13*, 524–536.

Pothier, L., & Pothier, D. D. (2009). Patient-oriented websites on laryngectomy: Is their information readable? *European Journal of Cancer Care, 18*, 594–597.

Reid, C. K. (2009). Should business embrace social networking? *EContent, 32*(5), 34–39.

Rice, R. E. (2006). Influences, usage, and outcomes of internet health information searching: Mulitvariate results from the Pew surveys. *International Journal of Medical Informatics, 75*(1), 8–28.

Sarkar, U., Karter, A. J., Liu, J. Y., Alder, N. E., Nguyen, R., López, A., & Schillinger, D. (2010). The literacy divide: Health literacy and the use of an internet-based patient portal in an integrated health system—Results from the Diabetes Study of Northern California (DISTANCE). *Journal of Community Health, 15*(Supplment 2), 183–196.

Silvestre, A. L., Sue, V. M., & Allen, J. Y. (2009). If you build it, will they come? The Kaiser Permanent model of online health care. *Health Affairs, 28*(2), 334–342.

Smith, A., & Rainie, L. (2009). Overview: The people who use Twitter. Retrieved from http://pewinternet.org/Reports/2010/Twitter-Update-2010/Findings/Overview.aspx

Tomes, J. P. (2010). Avoiding the trap in the HITECH Act's incentive timeframe for implementing the EHR. *Journal of Health Care Finance, 37*(1), 91–100.

U.S. Department of Commerce. (2011). Digital nation: Expanding internet usage. Retrieved from http://www.ntia.doc.gov/reports/2011/NTIA_Internet_Use_Report_February_2011.pdf

U.S. Department of Health and Human Services. (2011). Healthy people 2020. Retrieved from http://www.healthypeople.gov/2020/topicsobjectives2020/overview.aspx?topicid=18

Wilken, M. (2008). Policy implementation. In J.A. Milstead (Ed.), *Health policy and politics: A nurse's guide* (3rd ed., pp. 157–169). Sudbury, MA: Jones and Bartlett.

Williams, M. (2011, March 22). Blue Cross taps technology to help steer consumers away from unnecessary ER visits. *Atlanta Journal and Constitution.* Retrieved from http://www.ajc.com/business/blue-cross-taps-technology-881465.html?cxtype=rss_news_81960

Ybarra, M. L., & Suman, M. (2006). Health seeking behavior and the internet: A national survey. *International Journal of Medical Informatics, 75*(1), 29–41.

YouTube Pressroom. (n.d.). Statistics. Retrieved from http://www.youtube.com/t/press

CHAPTER 9

Policy Nurses Advance Policy Agendas in Many Arenas

Nancy J. Sharp

I stand often in the company of dreamers: They tickle your common sense and believe you can achieve things that are impossible.

—MARYANNE RADMACHER-HERSHEY

KEY TERMS

Advocacy training: All nursing organizations, either singly or in coalition-style, have promoted 1- to 5-day advocacy workshops to educate nurses on the skills needed to be an advocate for patient and nursing issues. The courses offer either continuing education credits or academic credit.

Nurse specialty organizations: Nurses who work in clinical specialties and advanced practice nurses have organized into national specialty and sub-specialty associations where members receive continuing education in the clinical specialty; obtain journals, research programs and other benefits; and may seek certification. The largest clinical specialty organization is the American Association of Critical Care Nurses, with about 75,000 members.

Policy nurses: Nurses experienced in or employed in positions where public policy is developed in the legislative or executive branches of local, state, or federal government; or those employed in private entities where agenda setting, design of programs, implementation strategies, and evaluation are developed.

INTRODUCTION

Nurses working in public policy not only can see the future of an improved healthcare system for the coming generations, but are in the middle of designing it through their daily work. The policy nurses of today are visionaries who are passionate in their desire to make positive change in healthcare delivery. They work in executive branches of state, local, and federal governments (e.g., Office of Secretary in the U.S. Department of Health and Human Services); in regulatory offices of state and federal government (e.g., Food and Drug Administration, Centers for Disease Control); state and federal legislative offices (e.g., U.S. Senate, House of Representatives); and in advocacy organizations for certain patient populations (e.g., American Association of Retired Persons, Children's Defense Fund), various health conditions (e.g., American Diabetes Association, American Cancer Society), or in health professional societies (e.g., American Nurses Association, American College of Nurse Practitioners, Oncology Nursing Society). This chapter describes some of the growth and maturity in the number of policy nurses, but the bottom line is that we need many more nurses to look at nursing in the policy world as a rewarding career path.

POLICY NURSES IN NURSE ASSOCIATIONS

The large, organized nurse organizations (American Nurses Association, National League for Nursing, American Association of Colleges of Nursing, and the National Student Nurses Association), had Washington, D.C.-based government relations staffs as early at the 1950s. These staff made regular visits to Capitol Hill to lobby for federal grants and scholarships to fund nursing education and research. In addition, they worked with federal agency staff to work out implementation of various legislative policies that had been passed.

In the late 1970s, the clinical specialty nurse organizations recognized the need to add their voices to these advocacy efforts and become more involved in lobbying for federal funds for nursing research and education, as well as for their specific clinical nursing issues. Some of the early efforts were made by advanced practice nurse (APN) organizations such as the American College of Nurse–Midwives and the American Association of Nurse Anesthetists. These groups were joined later by other **clinical specialty organizations** with members who worked in emergency departments and operating rooms, as well as nurses working in oncology and nephrology units.

In those early days, not all of the government relations (GR) staff of the large nurse organizations were pleased to have the specialty organization representatives join in these efforts. Specifically, in 1982, a staff member of one of the large organizations told a specialty association GR staff member to "Get the hell out of legislation!" (personal communication, 1982). Stunned and saddened by this interaction, it took the staff member 24 hours to report this to the director, because the staffer needed time to process the interaction. Having been hired as the specialty organization's GR staff, it was certainly a slap in the face to the specialty organization that had decided to add GR staff to the Washington organization. It had seemed very reasonable to expect that the larger nursing community would be pleased that another nurse association staff member was joining the overall lobbying force for nursing.

CONNECTING AND EDUCATING POLICY NURSES

Nurse in Washington Roundtable

Simultaneously, in the late 1970s, the nurses who worked in Congressional offices on Capitol Hill and in scattered offices of the various federal agencies in the

Washington, D.C., area needed a vehicle to meet and network with each other. It was at this time that Thelma Schorr, then editor of the *American Journal of Nursing*, and Sheila Burke, RN, BSN, who worked as a health legislative assistant to Senator Robert Dole (R-KS), decided to found the "Nurse In Washington Roundtable" (NIWR) and hold dinner meetings with a speaker to network among this early group of **policy nurses**. The NIWR started with a small group of a dozen or so members, and grew eventually into a group of several hundred. This group continued to be active until the early 2000s, when it became too large and unwieldy as a networking vehicle with volunteer organizers. An interesting dilemma!

Nurse Specialties Advocacy

The nurse specialty groups became much more active in the 1980s, when it became necessary to coalesce to lobby for continued federal funding for nursing education and research. Appropriations for nursing-related issues are in a constant state of danger of being eliminated. Late in 1984, a small coalition named the Nurses Coalition for Legislative Action (NCLA) was formed in the Washington, D.C., community. The coalition leadership consisted of GR staff and volunteer representatives of the National Association of Pediatric Nurse Practitioners (NAPNAP); American College of Nurse–Midwives (ACNM); Association of Women's Health, Obstetric, and Neonatal Nurses (AWHONN); American Nephrology Nurses Association (ANNA); and the National Association of Orthopedic Nurses (NAON). The coalition expanded and was open to include membership from as many of the nurse specialty organizations as possible.

The NCLA focused on general nursing issues such as nursing education and research funding. Members quickly became enlightened on the politics of nursing research as they promoted legislation to establish the National Institute of Nursing Research (NINR) within the National Institutes of Health (NIH). It was eye-opening to view the disagreements, as some nurses supported this effort to become an Institute while others vehemently opposed it.

To assist with operations and communications of the NCLA, the leadership solicited $100 donations from the specialty organizations during 1985 and 1986. With those funds, and using regular mail and faxes, the NCLA sent notices and information packets out to all nurse specialty organizations to ask that their members step up to the plate and participate in influencing policymakers at the national level. In this coalition, it was interesting to note that the five co-leaders each evolved into specific roles: one prepared overall strategy, one acted as policy analyst, one handled the legal issues, one was well-versed in political language and could interpret nuances seen and heard on Capitol Hill, and one acted as the public face, welcoming participants with a smile and a hug when they came to meetings.

In an effort to further educate their individual members, several of the specialty organizations had begun to hold 1- to 3-day **advocacy** workshops for their members in Washington, D.C. The nurses learned how to advocate for their own specialty issues, such as seat belt laws, increased dialysis reimbursement legislation, maternal-child health programs, and others.

Nurses in Washington Internship

The NCLA leaders learned from the above experience that the nurse community needed to educate and mentor a much-larger cadre of nurses who would become the nurse policy activists of the future. To this end, a proposal was presented to the National Federation of Nursing Specialty Organizations (NFSNO) to establish an annual 5-day Washington, D.C., experience for 50–100 members of the specialty organizations. The proposal was titled the Nurses in Washington Internship (NIWI), and described that the faculty of the 5-day program would include members of Congress and staff, federal regulatory bureaus' staff, association lobbyists and GR staff, and other experts from the Washington policy world. The goal was to demystify the legislative process for specialty nurses.

The attendees of those NFSNO meetings were the leaders of approximately 50 nurse specialty groups. Upon presentation of the proposal, the presidents and executive directors were a bit skeptical. The arguments against the proposal were that clinical nurses would either not want to come to Washington, D.C., to learn about policy, could not afford to take 5 to 6 days off work to learn about the policy process, or could not afford the expense of a week in Washington, D.C.

At the end of the day, however, the NFSNO agreed to treat this launch of NIWI as a pilot study, and allowed that in the first year the NIWI should aim for 20 participants. The event was held in 1985 and received rave reviews from the 20 participants. The committee recommended that the following year the number be increased to 50; those 50 arrived the next year, and the committee recommended the limit be raised to 100, which it has been achieving ever since.

The Nursing Organizations Alliance (NOA) became the new name for the NFSNO in 2002 and the NOA now administers the NIWI as an educational policy experience. It is still going strong, although the time frame for the program has been reduced to 3 days. Approximately 2500 nurses have attended this policy workshop since 1985. Information on the program and scholarships is available at http://www.nursing-alliance.org.

ADVOCACY FOR ADVANCED PRACTICE NURSE ORGANIZATIONS

As described above, the advanced practice nurse groups began their advocacy and policy agendas before the specialty nurse organizations, with AANA and ACNM leading the way in the late 1970s. In 1985, a professional-facilitated forum was held in Chicago as an effort to unite the multiple national nurse practitioner (NP) organizations into one entity, or at least develop a mechanism that would make it easier to work together on policy issues.

An outcome of the Chicago Forum was the establishment of a group called the National Alliance of Nurse Practitioners (NANP). The leadership of several national NP groups met twice a year to come to consensus on issues of mutual concern. The group expanded to include representatives of state NP organizations; New York and California were two very active members. One individual NP came to represent the interests of all NPs who were not members of any NP organization. The NANP put forth an enormous effort to produce some very sophisticated PR brochures to elaborate on what a NP is and does, and these were distributed on Capitol Hill. This group, in spite of outstanding individual NP leadership, got stuck in place due to its need for a full consensus agreement on policy issues. Without agreement, a public position could not be taken. After this, the NANP continued to meet, but mainly to act as a vehicle for networking among the remaining representatives.

For NPs, the next significant event occurred in 1993 at the first National Nurse Practitioner Summit in Washington, D.C. At that meeting, a loosely organized group formed and named itself the National Nurse Practitioner Coalition (NNPC). This coalition formed upon hearing a loud, clear call from those present that it was time to form a collective of all NP groups. It was time to unite efforts, including time, energy, and money, to produce one shared message to give national policymakers.

In 1994, the coalition changed its name to the American College of Nurse Practitioners (ACNP), and today remains a solid coalition-model organization focused on public policy. Membership includes state and national NP groups, as well as individual NPs who are focused on public policy. ACNP has utilized its volunteer members to advocate for policy issues affecting NPs, but also has contracted with Drinker Biddle Gardner, a Washington, D.C.-based law firm with health specialists, to provide representation through 2010. By 2011, ACNP, NONPF (National Organization of Nurse Practitioner Faculties), and NAPNAP (National Association of Pediatric Nurse Practitioners) had jointly hired one lobbyist to work full-time on nurse practitioners' federal legislative issues. ACNP has made a total commitment to its long-standing mission to ensure a solid policy and regulatory foundation that enables nurse practitioners to continue providing accessible, high-quality health care. It is focused, full-time, on policy issues that improve the practice environment and healthcare system so that NPs can practice at their fullest potential, without restrictions!

The ACNP has now added another continuing education policy offering to the health professional community, the Public Policy Institute for Health Professionals (PPI-HP). This 3-day educational program in Washington, D.C., invites all advanced practice nurses, all advanced specialty nurses in administrative or managerial positions, and all nursing school faculty interested in updating their knowledge of the policy world to attend this expansive educational experience to hear from policymakers about how they frame the issues and debates on the latest policy issues. This program is especially relevant to nurse practitioners pursuing Doctor of Nursing Practice (DNP) degrees since most curricula mandate a policy course. Many DNP programs accept partial academic credit for completion of the PPI-HP. Information about PPI-HP is available at http://www.acnpweb.org under the Conference tab.

The Nurse Practitioner Roundtable

When the federal healthcare reform legislation began seriously churning in 2009 after President Barack Obama's election, the nurse practitioner community came to the realization that they had to do more to achieve a united front on advanced practice issues. The following six national NP organizations began to meet regularly either in person in Washington, D.C., or by frequent conference calls, as the Nurse Practitioner Roundtable:

> American Academy of Nurse Practitioners
> American College of Nurse Practitioners
> Gerontological Advanced Practice Nurses Association
> National Association of Pediatric Nurse Practitioners
> National Association of Nurse Practitioners in Women's Health
> National Organization of Nurse Practitioner Faculties

Together, they hammered out a joint statement titled "Nurse Practitioner Perspective on Health Care Payment," available at http://www.acnpweb.org/files/public/NPRoundtableReimbursementDocument11_23_10.pdf. When issues also impact nurse anesthetists, nurse–midwives, and clinical nurse specialists, the NP Roundtable meets with the leadership of the American Association of Nurse Anesthetists (AANA), the American College of Nurse–Midwives (ACNM), the National Association of Clinical Nurse Specialists (NACNS), as well as the American Nurses Association (ANA). Each of those groups has strong government relations departments, and whenever all the groups can present a united front and a united focus on an issue, it makes a much stronger impact.

The Nurse's Directory of Capitol Connections

In 1991 an idea sprang from two personal lists the author was keeping in her phone book. From these lists, a directory titled *The Nurses Directory of Capitol Connections* (Sharp, 1991–2000) was published. The directory was a listing of nearly 500 positions and opportunities for nurse participation in health policy development in Washington, D.C. It included nurses in 1) the legislative, or congressional, branch of government, including the three nurses elected to the House of Representatives; 2) the executive, or regulatory, branch with the federal agencies, and, finally 3) nurses in government relations positions in the private sector, whether it was a healthcare association, consulting firm, public relations firm, law firm, or a nonprofit group or foundation. The objective was to locate all the nurses in any of these positions so they could be invited to networking events and meet others who were also using their nursing backgrounds in different sorts of health policy and advocacy roles.

By the year 2000, five editions of the directory had been published. When an agency, association, or congressional office called looking for a nurse with a particular expertise, the directory was used to find such nurses. This directory was one component of the cosmic glue that connected these policy nurses together.

University Policy Courses

At the same time, there has been steady growth in the development of health policy or public policy courses and majors in universities. These courses can be a powerful motivator for students to start a career path toward work in the public policy sphere. However, more recently, there is a concern surfacing that as the clinical and administrative faculty shortage grows, fewer qualified faculty are available for teaching health policy in the nursing school curriculum. As computer technology advances, there has been a further movement to put more and more courses online, so that students can access the course and participate via their own computer remotely. There are a number of health policy courses, workshops, and seminars for students and graduates to take via continuing education, and there are also concentrated 5-, 7-, and 10-day courses where graduate students can earn university credits. These students may be required to attend 35–40 hours of class, with reading assignments to be completed before the policy courses start, and preparation of a 10–15 page policy analysis at the conclusion of the course. George Mason University School of Nursing and Health Sciences began such a course in 1993, called the Washington Health Policy Institute (WHPI), and further information on this excellent course is found at http://www.gmu.edu/centers/chpre/policyinstitute/index.html.

In 2010 the American Association of Colleges of Nursing launched the AACN Student Policy Summit. This 3-day policy program held in Washington, D.C., is sponsored by the Jonas Center for Nursing Excellence and is open to baccalaureate or graduate nurse students currently enrolled at an AACN member institution. There are two full scholarships available. See http://www.aacn.nche.edu/Government/sps.htm for further information.

Nightingale Policy Institute

We both fear and embrace these changing times, but change always offers opportunities for visionaries. One phenomenon is the presence of the Internet and the fact that it is now mainstream. Nearly all nurse leaders either have their own personal computers or have access to a computer and the Internet in a community-based setting. Because of the Internet's ubiquity, a group of nurses in Washington, D.C., and beyond began to think about how we could use the Internet to expand nurses' reach into the policy world, as well as how we could use the Internet to continue to grow this cadre of policy nurses.

In 2006, a group of five nurses with a variety of solid policy experience gathered to collectively establish a new sense of direction and focus for the future in regard to nurses and public policy. Originally conceived as the Nightingale Policy Group, the name soon was changed to the Nightingale Policy Institute (NPI). One of the goals was to move what had been pen and paper formats in the past to an electronic format on the Internet. The NPI website (http://www.policynurses.org) serves as a space where policy nurses can debate critical issues impacting the healthcare system and nurses within that system. The previously mentioned *Nurse's Directory of Capitol Connections* had been a useful publication, but even with five editions it was time-consuming and difficult to keep updated as nurses moved from position to position, and other new positions were created. If the publication were digitized and posted on the Internet, the entire world of nurses, as well as other healthcare professionals, could access it to find a policy nurse with expertise in a certain area. Finding such a specific policy nurse would be important, for example, if you had been asked to name a nurse for an important state or national commission or advisory council.

The intent is to develop a virtual organization for policy nurses that would not be chapter-bound, state border-bound, or bound by any of the other constraints that hold an organization down. This organization would be open to all nurses either working in public policy or aspiring to learn more and wanting to acquire the skills needed to become policy nurses.

The Nightingale Policy Institute's "Founding Five" envision that the membership of NPI will grow and establish itself as an unparalleled vehicle for national and international interaction among policy nurses. The group's members will write policy and make policy; inform other policymakers of their work; educate new, aspiring policy nurses; and present policy solutions to the transition into an evolutionary new healthcare system led by nurse professionals at every level of government. This group of nurses has been involved in the reformation of the current healthcare system and is working to develop the system into a more caring, humanistic, safe, and vital environment.

The Founding Five of NPI and their contact information:

Sharon A. Brigner, MS, RN, sbrigner@phrma.org
Pat Ford-Roegner, MSW, RN, FAAN, pfr1947@hughes.net
Carole P. Jennings, PhD, RN, FAAN, jennjournal@aol.com
Jeri A. Milstead, PhD, RN, FAAN, jeri.milstead@yahoo.com
Nancy J. Sharp, MSN, RN, FAAN, NurseSharp@aol.com

CONCLUSION

The community of policy nurses will continue to grow as indicated above. The nation needs more nurses with policy expertise and passion. We encourage all nurses who have an interest in policy work to contact any of the Founding Five above, or to follow any of the links above to obtain more information about a particular program.

DISCUSSION POINTS AND ACTIVITIES

1. Convene a group of nurses to discuss how to motivate and inspire nurses toward involvement in the policy process.
2. Attend NIWI, PPI-HP, or another policy conference in Washington, D.C., and write a brief article about your experience.
3. Discuss a local, state, or national health issue with nurse colleagues and propose a solution to the agency responsible for the issue.
4. Analyze the impact of nurse advocacy for a specific health issue in your state where the advocacy actions by nurses made a difference.
5. Select a federal agency where you would like to work (CMS, FDA, USPHS, AHRQ, etc.) and plan and implement a job search.

For a full suite of assignments and additional learning activities, use the access code located in the front of your book to visit this exclusive website: http://go.jblearning.com/milstead. If you do not have an access code, you can obtain one at the site.

REFERENCE

Sharp, N. J. (1991–2000). *The Nurses Directory of Capitol Connections*. Bethesda, MD: Author.

ADDITIONAL RESOURCES

Steps to Securing a Health Policy Job in Washington, D.C.

- Activate your own relationships and membership circles.
- Join your local professional nurse organization(s) and volunteer to help on a legislative or health policy committee.
- Distinguish yourself with your member of Congress's office, learning their priorities, their committee assignments, and the health issues they work on, and assert yourself into those activities where help is needed.
- Volunteer to assist with local activities for members of Congress or others running for elected office in your city or state.
- Offer to hold a local fundraiser for those running for election.
- Offer to do research or design a solution to a pressing health problem in your area.
- Become an expert on your favorite health issue: offer to write summaries, briefing papers, or talking points for this issue.

- Identify which federal agencies handle health issues that interest you.
- Search http://www.usajobs.gov for job openings in the federal government.

After making contact with a member of Congress or a federal agency that you identified:

- Ask about job openings and/or search http://www.usajobs.gov (look under "health policy").
- Ask about internship opportunities.
- Ask about funding and housing possibilities.
- Give your available timetable.
- Offer to research or design a health project important to that member of Congress or federal agency.

If your Congressional office does not have funding for internships, design fundraising campaigns for yourself. Examples include:

- Asking for a grant or scholarship of $500–$1000 from your local nurse association.
- Asking for a grant or scholarship of $500–$1000 from your specialty nurse association.
- Asking for a stipend of $500–$1000 from a local newspaper with the commitment that you will provide a weekly column from Washington, D.C., for their newspaper.
- Asking for $500–$1000 from your combined birthday presents, car washes, and bake sales from all your family, friends, and relatives.

Your approximate goal: $4000 for one month; $2000 in group housing with other interns; $2000+ for transportation, food, and general living expenses.

Use any creative resources you have to get your foot in the door, then network, network, network every minute you are in Washington, D.C., to find and launch the next steps. Move to Washington, D.C., or the Maryland, or Virginia suburbs, get involved in DC, MD, or VA nurse associations, find local connections to the health policy world, and just jump in!

Internship and Fellowship Opportunities

The Kaiser Family Foundation's List of Internships and Fellowships

KaiserEdu, an educational arm of the Kaiser Family Foundation, provides a database of internships and fellowships (313 as of March 2011), both paid and unpaid, in health policy–related fields. Many are suitable for nurses.

Website: http://www.kaiseredu.org/Fellowships-and-internships.asp

Health Policy Fellows

The Robert Wood Johnson Foundation sponsors the Health Policy Fellows program, in which six exceptional mid-career health professionals are chosen for (at minimum) 1-year fellowships to learn about the federal policy process. Nurses have participated in these Fellowships over the years.

   Website: http://www.healthpolicyfellows.org/home.php

Legislative Resources

Suggested Readings

Apold, S. (2011). Best practices in inter-professional communications: The right words. *The Journal for Nurse Practitioners*, *7*(2), 96–97.

Longest, B. (2006). *Health Policymaking in the United States* (4th ed.). Chicago, IL: Health Administration Press.

Mason, D. J., Leavitt, J., & Chaffee, M. (2011). *Policy & politics in nursing and health care* (6th ed.). St. Louis, MO: Saunders.

Reese, S. (2006, July 31). Nurses as policy makers. *Nursing Spectrum*. Retrieved from http://community. nursingspectrum.com/MagazineArticles/article.cfm?AID=22637

IOM Report: *The Future of Nursing: Leading Change, Advancing Health*

Institute of Medicine. (2010). *The future of nursing: Leading change, advancing health*. Washington, DC: National Academies Press. Available at http://thefutureofnursing.org/IOM-Report; http://www.nap.edu/ catalog.php?record_id=12956

Critical Sections of the IOM Report

Institute of Medicine. (2010). *The future of nursing: Focus on scope of practice*. Washington, DC: National Academies Press. Retrieved from http://thefutureofnursing.org/sites/default/files/ NursingScopeofPractice2010Brief.pdf

Safriet, B. J. (2010). Appendix H: Federal options for maximizing the value of advanced practice nurses in providing quality, cost-effective health care. In *The future of nursing: Leading change, advancing health*. Washington, DC: National Academies Press. Retrieved from http://www.nap.edu/openbook. php?record_id=12956&page=443

Sochalski, J., & Weiner, J. (2010). Appendix F: Health care system reform and the nursing workforce: Matching nursing practice and skills to future needs, not past demands. In *The future of nursing: Leading change, advancing health*. Washington, DC: National Academies Press. Retrieved from http://www.nap. edu/openbook.php?record_id=12956&page=375

Historical References

Kalisch, B. J., & Kalisch, P. A. (1982). *Politics of nursing*. Philadelphia: J. B. Lippincott Company.

Redman, E. (1973). *The dance of legislation*. New York: Simon & Schuster.

CHAPTER 10

Overview: The Economics and Finance of Health Care

Nancy Munn Short

*Other people, including the politicians who make economic policy,
know even less about economics than economists.*

—HERBERT STEIN, WASHINGTON BEDTIME STORIES

KEY TERMS

Affordable Care Act (ACA): The combination of the Patient Protection and Affordable Care Act of 2010 (PPACA) and the Health Care and Education Affordability Act of 2010.

Accountable care organization (ACO): A network of providers and hospitals that shares responsibility for providing care to patients. Under the new law, ACOs would agree to manage all of the healthcare needs of a minimum of 5000 Medicare beneficiaries for at least three years. Becoming an ACO is optional.

Adverse selection: A situation in which, as a result of private information, the insured are more likely to suffer a loss than the uninsured. A form of information asymmetry.

Comparative effectiveness research (CER): A category of studies to determine the effectiveness of clinical interventions, specifically when compared to differing treatments for the same condition, or for different subgroups of patients. The Patient-Centered Outcomes Research Institute is charged with identifying priorities, establishing agenda, and carrying out CER.

Information asymmetry: Occurs when some parties to business transactions may have an information advantage over others.

Means testing: A process undertaken to determine if a person's income qualifies him/her to participate in a program. Often used to determine eligibility for Medicaid coverage of long-term care.

Moral hazard: A change in behavior as a result of a perceived reduction in the costs of misfortune (e.g., health insurance changes the costs of becoming ill or injured).

Opportunity costs: The value of the next best choice that one gives up when making a decision. Also called economic costs.

Quality-adjusted life year (QALY): Calculated life expectancy adjusted for the quality of life, where quality of life is measured on a scale from 1 (full health) to 0 (dead.) Originally developed as a broader measure of disease burden beyond mortality, QALYs are now used in cost-effectiveness analyses to aid coverage and reimbursement decisions worldwide.

The "R" word: Rationing (health care). Closely tied to discussions of CER and QALYs.

INTRODUCTION

Three important concepts that form the framework for health policy discussions are *quality/safety* of care, *access* to care, and the *cost* of care. All health policy discussions boil down to one of these categories or the synergies between or among these categories. This chapter will focus on the "cost" category, including some economic theories supporting current health policies and some of the structures created to implement these policies.

Health economics and the finance of health care are often erroneously used as interchangeable terms: how does health finance differ from health economics? In a nutshell, economics is the science that informs the processes of finance. The two disciplines share common ground such as cost–benefit analysis and analysis of risk, but they are not synonymous. Economics is amoral—that is, it is neither a moral science nor an immoral science. The science of health economics can suggest what makes a person, a population, a region, or a nation better off, but philosophy and ethics must be debated elsewhere and are represented by political tradeoffs when policy is made. Similarly, the health market as viewed by economists is amoral: When confronted with finite resources, there will be losers and winners. This is a tough concept for nurses to swallow.

Economic science studies markets such as the market for nurses and physicians, the pharmaceutical market, or the insurance market. Together, these markets form the universe that is termed the *healthcare market*. Within the healthcare market are nonprofit

---

Figure 10-1   The intersection of health policy and health finance.

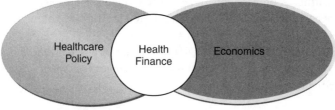

organizations, government-owned organizations, shareholder owned corporations, and other financial entities. **Figure 10-1** demonstrates the unique domain of health finance: economics informs policy and policy determines finance.

ECONOMICS AND FINANCE: A COMPARISON

Economics: Opportunity Costs

There is no such thing as a free lunch: For every opportunity taken and for every option discarded, there are tradeoff costs. When you purchased the 2010 Oldsmobile Malibu, you did not purchase the Honda wagon. You also did not take a vacation, buy a new wardrobe, or pay off your college debt. Not acquiring the Honda, the vacation, the new wardrobe, or eliminating your debt are the **opportunity costs** of purchasing the Malibu.

Opportunity costs may also be described in terms of time spent on an activity (researching the safety of the Malibu) and other indirect measures or intangibles. An example of opportunity costs related to health policy is the current Medicare policy: 90 percent of Medicare funds are used for 10 percent of the beneficiaries. Most Medicare dollars are expended in the final events of a person's life; because there are finite funds available, policy that directs payments for an elderly person's last weeks of life represent an opportunity cost. For example, the funds could also be used for preventive care of 30-somethings, hiring more school nurses, or health research. These are hard choices and are the core of perennial political debates at the federal, state, and local levels. The economic consequences of a policy may last for years and may be argued equally eloquently by economists who fall on both sides of an issue. "The most important contribution economists can make to the operation of the healthcare system is to be relentless in pointing out that every choice involves a trade-off—that certain difficult questions regarding who gets what, and who must give up what, are inevitable and must be faced even when politicians, the public, and patients would rather avoid them" (Getzen, 2010, p. 429).

Finance: Does More Spending Buy Us Better Health?

Studies continue to show that there is no correlation between increased spending on health care in the United States and reductions in population mortality (Rothberg, Cohen, Lindenauer, Maselli, & Auerbach, 2010). In the 1900s, spending on infrastructure provided clean water and hygiene, vaccination programs, and better access to health care, which resulted in large improvements in quality of life and life expectancy. As the United States approached spending $5000 per year per capita on health care, gains slowed. In 2008, spending exceeded $7500 per capita (Organisation for Economic Co-operation and Development, 2010a) and the marginal gains became almost imperceptible. Nations tend to spend more money on health care simply because they have more money to spend, while individuals spend more money on health care when they

Figure 10-2   Life expectancy in relation to per capita spending on health care.

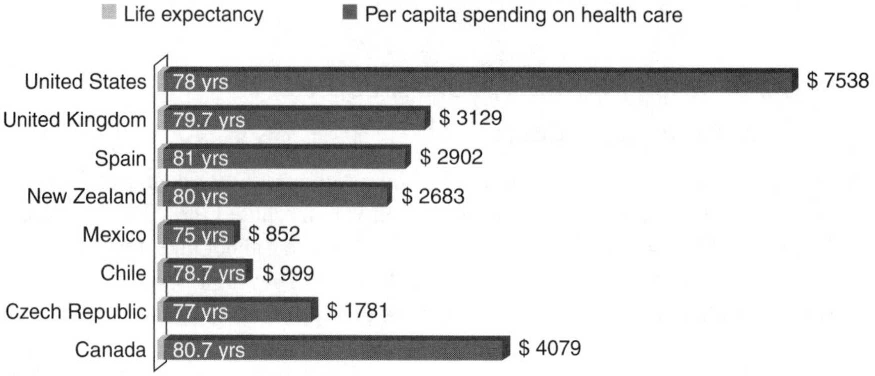

Source: Data from Organisation for Economic Co-operation and Development (OECD). (2011). OECD Stat Extracts. Retrieved from http://stats.oecd.org/Index.aspx?DataSetCode=HEALTH

are ill. **Figure 10-2** illustrates a lack of correlation between life expectancy and per capita spending. Routine indicators of health status, such as infant mortality and feeling that one has good health also do not correlate to per capita spending on health care in the United States.

Economics: Health Insurance Market

Health insurance in the United States is a misnomer: what we are purchasing is *sickness* insurance. Like other forms of insurance, health insurance is a form of collectivism in which people pool their risk, in this case the risk of incurring medical expenses. Risk pooling is key to how insurance markets work: each participant with marginal or poor health and a high risk of accruing high expenses is financially balanced by several participants with good health and low risk of high expenses. Barring the participation of individuals who already have disease or injury (preexisting condition) allows insurers to manage moral hazard (which will be explained in a later section). Without the option to manage risk in this manner, the business model for the insurance market would collapse.

In general, the market for health insurance is divided into public and private insurance. Public insurance includes Medicare, Medicaid, State Children's Health Insurance Programs, and in some cases TriCare insurance for military families. Additionally, the industry is broken down into group and nongroup (or individual) insurance. More than 15 million Americans purchase individual insurance. America's Health Insurance Plans (AHIP) reports that in 2009, the average premium for a family of three with an individual policy was $6,328 per year (2009), while the Kaiser Family Foundation and Health Research and Educational Trust (2010) report that the average family cost (including premiums, deductibles, co-pays, and other out-of-pocket expenses) in 2010 was $13,770.

Introduced in the ACA, health insurance exchanges (HIE) are a new entity in the insurance market intended to create a more organized and competitive market for health insurance by offering a choice of plans, establishing common rules regarding the offering and pricing of insurance, and providing information to help consumers better understand the options available to them (Kaiser Family Foundation, 2009). The healthcare reform bill calls for each state to set up an "exchange," or marketplace, where people (individuals or small businesses) not covered through their employers or by public insurance would shop for health insurance at competitive rates. The Massachusetts HIE is called "The Connector," as it was the first in the country. The exchanges are supposed to be open for business by 2014.

Finance: Healthcare Entitlement Programs

Medicare and Medicaid are publicly funded social entitlement programs; anyone meeting the eligibility requirements for Medicare (Part A) or Medicaid is *entitled* to all of the promised benefits no matter the condition of the governments' (state or federal) finances. Think of it in terms of your personal budget: you plan rent, transportation expenses, utilities, clothing, entertainment, gifts, and so on in your budget and you account for these amounts against your anticipated income to balance your income and expenses. Expenses for Medicare and Medicaid are projected every year, but unlike your clothing allowance, if the government runs short of revenue (e.g., fewer taxes are collected during a down economy) there is no option to cut back on entitlement programs. Likewise, if expenses for Medicare and Medicaid are higher than projected (e.g., perhaps more seniors are seriously ill), the government cannot choose not to provide payment for the coverage in services. If the government fails to meet its obligation, beneficiaries are entitled to sue.

By law, state governments must balance their budgets, though the federal government may run deficits up to a ceiling set by Congress. This is an important concept and explains much of the policies at the state and federal levels. In simple terms, Medicare is a federally funded program, while Medicaid is funded by federal and state funds, along with some local funds. The full reality is more complex, but these generalities suffice for our discussion. Funding for Medicare comes primarily from general revenues (40 percent) and payroll taxes (38 percent), followed by premiums paid by beneficiaries (12 percent).

In 2010, the Kaiser Family Foundation reported that Medicare provided insurance coverage to 47 million people, including those age 65 and over (if they or their spouse made payroll tax contributions for 10 or more years) and younger people with permanent disabilities (after 24 months of receiving Social Security Disability payments), end-stage renal disease, and amyotrophic lateral sclerosis (Lou Gehrig's disease). Medicare covers most healthcare services, but does not cover long-term

Figure 10-3   National health expenditures in the United States, by source of payment, 2010.

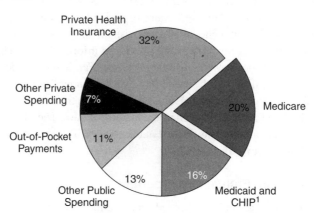

Total National Health Expenditures, 2010 = $2.6 Trillion

Notes: [1]Includes Children's Health Insurance Program (CHIP) and Children's Health Insurance Program expansion (Title XIX). Data: Centers for Medicate & Medicaid Services, Office of the Actuary, National Health Expenditure Projections 2009–2019, February 2010.
Source: Kaiser Family Foundation. (2010). Medicare chartbook (4th ed.). Retrieved from http://facts.kff.org/chartbook. aspx?cb=58

care services such as nursing home care (Portetz, Cubanski, & Neuman, 2011) (see **Figure 10-3**).

The Medicare program is broken down into several components, each of which covers a different aspect of health care; these components are explained below:

- **Medicare Part A (Hospital Insurance Program)** helps pay for inpatient hospitalizations, skilled nursing home care (for up to 100 days), home health (for a limited time post-hospital stay), and hospice care. The beneficiary must pay a deductible.

- **Medicare Part B (Supplementary Medical Insurance)** is voluntary and covers 95% of all Part A beneficiaries. Part B helps pay for physician visits, outpatient hospital services, preventive services, mental health services, durable medical equipment, and home health.

- **Medicare Part C** is now called Medicare Advantage. These are private health plans that receive payments from Medicare to provide Medicare-covered benefits to enrollees. Plans provide benefits covered under Parts A and B and often Part D.

- **Medicare Part D** is a voluntary program that helps pay for outpatient prescription drugs and is administered exclusively through private plans. Premiums and cost-sharing vary. The Affordable Care Act improves coverage by gradually closing the "donut hole," an unusual gap in coverage in which 100% of costs become out-of-pocket.

Prior to the implementation of the Affordable Care Act, Medicare served all eligible beneficiaries without regard to income or medical history. As health reform is rolled out, **means testing** will be applied to those with very high incomes.

Medicaid was enacted under the Social Security Act in 1965 as a companion to Medicare. It entitles participating states to federal matching funds on an open-ended basis, entitles eligible individuals to a set of specific benefits, is means tested, and allows states to provide broader coverage. In addition to providing health insurance coverage, Medicaid also provides assistance to low-income Medicare beneficiaries (dual-eligible), long-term care assistance (nursing home and in-home community-based services), support for the safety net system of health care, and is the largest source of federal funding to the states.

Medicaid fills large gaps in our health insurance market, finances the lion's share of long-term care (Elias, 2006), and provides core support for the health centers and safety-net hospitals that serve the nation's uninsured and millions of others. Within broad federal guidelines, states design their own Medicaid programs. Medicaid reimburses private providers to provide services to beneficiaries. In 2007, the elderly and disabled accounted for 67 percent of all Medicaid expenditures (Kaiser Commission on Medicaid and the Uninsured, 2011). The top five percent of enrollees accounted for over half of all Medicaid expenses.

Medicaid coverage prior to the implementation of the ACA required beneficiaries to have low incomes (defined by each state using the federal poverty guidelines) AND meet one of these categories of need:

- Pregnant or recent postpartum
- < 18 years old
- > 65 years old and blind or disabled

Medically needy persons whose incomes are too high to be eligible for Medicaid may be covered (each state determines eligibility). Additionally, there are optional eligibility groups that may be defined by each state. The federal poverty guideline for a family of four in 2011 is $22,350 in the continental United States, with slightly higher amounts in Alaska and Hawaii (Annual Update of the HHS Poverty Guidelines, 2011). Medicaid will be expanded in 2014 to reach nearly everyone under age 65 with income up to 133 percent of the federal poverty guidelines.

Recommended sources for more detail and analysis may be found at http://www.kaiseredu.org or the Centers for Medicare and Medicaid at http://www.cms.gov.

Information Economics

Asymmetrical information is the term used by economists to suggest that healthcare consumption differs from purchasing other goods and services because of the inability of patients, providers, or payers to possess all of the information needed for completely informed decision-making. Optimal rational decision-making requires "perfect information," where consumers are just as knowledgeable as sellers.

Think about when you buy a car. You gather all of the information that you can to eliminate any advantage the car seller may have in terms of the worth of a particular car. With this information, you may choose to go to several dealerships before you find a seller that meets your expectations (or utility). Now think about your typical health-care experience. You go to your primary care provider for your annual physical and the physician finds an abnormality, so you are referred to a specialist. Depending on your level of information, you may blindly trust the specialist, or you may shop around. You may be very hard pressed to learn about the quality or performance of either your primary care provider or the specialist. If you are referred to a hospital, you are probably unable to learn the nurse-to-patient ratio even though evidence shows that this is critical to your well-being. There is information asymmetry.

Healthcare professionals generally know what is "best" for patients, right? The problem of asymmetric information differs from a simple information problem in that one party possesses knowledge needed to enable rational decision-making that the other party lacks.

However, the healthcare professional and the insurer have a potential conflict of interest because of the exchange of money. Benefiting monetarily from a decision may affect the decision-making process. In health care, the patient delegates much decision-making to the healthcare professional (and sometimes even to the insurer).

Asymmetric information also affects healthcare professionals when patients conceal lifestyle information or state that they are compliant with a treatment when they are not. A patient's caregiver may also withhold or distort information that would be helpful to the provider. Insurers also face information asymmetry: Clients (buyers of insurance like you and me) know much more about the state of their health and their future plans than an insurer does.

Economics: Adverse Selection and Moral Hazard

Economists use two terms, *adverse selection* and *moral hazard*, to describe the situations insurers face when consumers have greater information about their health than insurers or payers. **Adverse selection** occurs when a person participates in a health plan based *solely* on the likelihood that they will have higher than usual health expenses (e.g., planning to get pregnant). **Moral hazard** occurs when a health plan member uses more health services than that person ordinarily would because he or she is insured (e.g., a person with orthodontic coverage gets braces on his teeth for cosmetic purposes only).

Insurers and payers may also lack sufficient information regarding the choices and decisions of providers and may be unable to ascertain if a procedure is medically necessary or not. "The patient, who does not pay the bill, demands as much care as possible . . . the insurance company maximizes profits by paying for as little as possible; and . . . it is very costly for either the patient or the insurance company to prove the 'right' course of treatment. In short, information makes health care different from the rest of the economy" (Wheelan, 2003, p. 86).

Imagine that you live in a state where the Department of Insurance has decreed that insurers may no longer deny health insurance to those who have preexisting health conditions and you must decide whether or not to purchase health insurance. You enjoy good health so you decide not to purchase insurance now. Within a few months, you unexpectedly become pregnant and decide that you do not want to pay the full cost of prenatal care, delivery, and post-partum care, so you purchase insurance. After the baby is born, you decide that you no longer need insurance and drop your coverage. The insurance market would collapse under the weight of adverse selection and moral hazard.

Many of the 47 million people who are uninsured in 2010 have preexisting conditions and are not eligible for public plans. The ACA requires that insurers provide additional coverage (e.g., starting in 2010, children on parents' insurance are covered up to age 26) and in 2014 to eliminate coverage denials for preexisting conditions. To provide insurance to approximately 33 million of those uninsured in the United States, the ACA legislation requires mandatory health insurance coverage for *all* by 2014. By requiring everyone to participate, the risk pool will be balanced sufficiently to prevent insurance market collapse.

Finance: Comparative Effectiveness Research and Quality-Adjusted Life Years

Imagine a system of research in which new discoveries or approaches to reduce or eliminate disease are tested for effectiveness against doing nothing at all. The current gold standard for research in the United States is the randomized control trial (RCT), in which a group of subjects receives a treatment while another group receives no treatment. Effectiveness is decided by whether or not the disease or condition responded to the new approach, but it is not compared to any other approach.

As a result of the 2009 American Recovery and Reinvestment Act (ARRA) and the 2010 Patient Protection and **Affordable Care Act**, the federal government will make major investments in **comparative effectiveness research (CER)**. Comparative effectiveness research, also called patient-centered outcomes research, compares the overall benefits of one therapeutic approach with those of another approach for the majority of patients. These investments are likely to yield new information about which treatments work best for which population of patients. But how will this research be used beyond informing provider decisions?

Quality-adjusted life year (QALY) is an economic concept developed in the 1960s to facilitate cost-effectiveness analysis, which attempts to include personal preferences regarding age and health conditions in a catalog known as the EQ-5D Index. For instance, if you have colon cancer and you are a 65-year-old white female, your EQ-5D index for quality-adjusted life year is 0.93; that is, every year you live with colon cancer is only worth 93 percent of a year with full health and no diseases. If you have two conditions at the same time, perhaps colon cancer and neurotic disorder, your EQ-5D index is 0.79. Once they know how many QALYs a treatment is worth, economists can figure out its cost per QALY — the broadest measure of the cost-effectiveness of health care.

In general, a QALY carries an economic value of between $70,000 and $100,000 per quality life year gained by a treatment or approach (Berenson, 2007). Will CER be used to determine not only the treatment effectiveness but also the cost-effectiveness and ultimately payment decisions? Comparative effectiveness research findings can be translated into practice in a variety of ways, some of which may be more acceptable to the public than others. QALYs have been linked to CER in the United Kingdom by the National Institute for Clinical Excellence and have led to debates about rationing care. **The "R" word—rationing**—represents a slippery slope for opponents of government funding for CER. The Patient-Centered Outcomes Research Institute (PCORI) was created under the ACA to coordinate government activity around CER. The ACA does not include cost-effectiveness determination among the guidelines for the PCORI.

Finance: Accountable Care Organizations

Accountable care organizations (ACOs) are a new model for delivering health services that offers providers and hospitals financial incentives to provide good quality care to Medicare beneficiaries while keeping down costs. In 2011, ACOs have been compared to the unicorn: everyone seems to know what it looks like, but nobody's actually seen one. Section 3022 of the Patient Protection and Affordable Care Act of 2010 creates the Medicare Shared Savings program, allowing accountable care organizations to contract with Medicare by January 2012. The Center for Medicare & Medicaid Services is currently drafting regulations for the Medicare Shared Savings program.

According to the ACA, the Medicare Shared Savings program "promote[s] accountability for a patient population and coordinates items and services under part A and B, and encourages investment in infrastructure and redesigned care processes for high quality and efficient service delivery" (Patient Protection & Affordable Care Act, 2010). Section 3022 outlines the following requirements for ACOs:

1. The ACO becomes accountable for the quality, cost, and overall care of the Medicare fee-for-service beneficiaries assigned to it.
2. The ACO must participate in the program for not less than a 3-year period.
3. The ACO's formal legal structure must allow the organization to receive and distribute payments for shared savings to participating providers of services and suppliers.
4. The ACO must include primary care professionals that are sufficient for the number of Medicare fee-for-service beneficiaries assigned to the ACO.

5. At a minimum, the ACO must have 5000 beneficiaries assigned to it in order to be eligible to participate.
6. The ACO must have leadership and management structures that include clinical and administrative systems.
7. The ACO must define processes to promote evidence-based medicine and patient engagement, report on quality and cost measures, and coordinate care.
8. The ACO must demonstrate that it meets specific patient-centeredness criteria (such as the use of patient and caregiver assessments or the use of individualized care plans) (Centers for Medicare and Medicaid Services, 2010; Fisher & Shortell, 2010; McClellan, McKethan, Lewis, Roski, & Fisher, 2010).

ACOs take up only seven pages of the massive new health law, but the idea has providers buzzing. A cottage industry of consultants has sprung up to help even ordinary hospitals become the first ACOs on the block.

In conclusion, *healthcare finance* refers to the methods and means for paying for health and health care while *healthcare economics* is concerned with issues related to scarcity and the allocation of resources. The two concepts are closely related and often confused in nursing curricula. This chapter has discussed the concepts in tandem. Economists and health services researchers are vital in determining how best to use limited resources. They inform policymakers who must make critical decisions about financing the United States' healthcare delivery system. As healthcare costs approach 19 percent of the gross domestic product of the United States, the economic health of the country depends upon lowering the cost of health care while assuring the health of the American people.

DISCUSSION POINTS AND ACTIVITIES

1. Discuss the role of economists in healthcare policy. Using Gail Wilensky, PhD, as a model of a health economist, watch clips of her presentations at http://www.gailwilensky.com. Note that although she is not a clinician, she was a commissioner on the World Health Organization (WHO) Commission on the Social Determinants of Health, an elected member of the Institute of Medicine, and served two terms on its governing council. In addition, she is a former chair of the board of directors of Academy Health and a former trustee of the American Heart Association. Why are economists so influential in health policy?
2. Read several issues of the journal *Health Affairs*. Access the journal's blog at http://www.healthaffairs.org/blog and search the keyword "economics" for the latest articles about healthcare economics. Discuss the gross national product in terms of healthcare expenditures. What sort of programs will not receive funding when health care consumes a large percentage of federal expenditures?

3. Read about social capital at http://web.worldbank.org (search for "social capital" in the Poverty Net website). How does social capital differ from economic capital? Discuss how you benefit from social capital in your own life. How does social capital determine or affect the health of populations?

4. Read about cost shifting in health care. Identify policies that use this method. Argue the benefits and losses of cost shifting.

5. Watch videos by experts on healthcare systems at http://www.kaiseredu.org. Most of these videos include economic or cost information. Discuss with your colleagues the impact on your own practice.

6. Who finances long-term care in the United States? Take a poll of your colleagues prior to researching this question. Are nurses well-informed about this economic issue and does this meet your expectation?

7. How does QALY analysis benefit the young over the old?

CASE STUDY: The Impact of the Affordable Care Act on North Carolina's Uninsured Population

In 2011, childless, nondisabled, nonelderly adults could not qualify for Medicaid. Being poor, unemployed, or homeless did not qualify a person for Medicaid if he/she was a childless adult in North Carolina. See **Case Study Figure 1**.

Case Study Figure 1   Income as a percentage of federal poverty level determining eligibility for Medicaid and NC Health Choice in 2009.

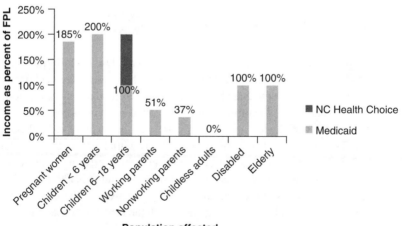

Source: Kaiser Family Foundation. (2011). State health facts 2009: Calculations for parents based on a family of three. Retrieved from http://www.statehealthfacts.org

Based on the Affordable Care Act, beginning in 2014 adults can qualify for Medicaid if their income is no greater than 138 percent of the Federal Poverty Level ($30,429 for a family of four in 2010). Some states will allow persons to qualify with higher incomes. Enrollment will be simplified: under the Affordable Care Act, states will be required to simplify enrollment and coordinate between Medicaid, CHIP, and the new Health Insurance Exchanges, and states must also conduct outreach to vulnerable populations. The planned Medicaid expansion does not cover undocumented immigrants, or most legal immigrants who have been in the United States for fewer than five years. See an example of the expansion's effect on North Carolina's Health Choice program in **Case Study Figure 2**.

Case Study Figure 2   Income as a percentage of federal poverty level determining eligibility for Medicaid and NC Health Choice after 2014.

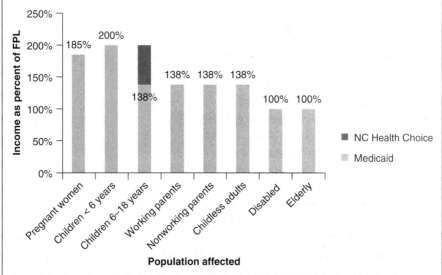

Source: Patient Protection and Affordable Care Act, 124 STAT. 119 § 2001, 2002 (2010). Retrieved from http://www.gpo.gov/fdsys/pkg/PLAW-111publ148/html/PLAW-111publ148.htm

---

Also affecting the improvement of Medicaid enrollment is Sec. 1137 of the Social Security Act, which addresses an income and eligibility verification system. Individual providers and organizations (e.g., hospitals) will be able to enroll eligible individuals on the spot. The ACA allows federal or state agencies to share relevant data as part of Express Lane to enrollment. Streamlining enrollment processes should reduce the population of un-enrolled, but eligible, individuals.

DISCUSSION POINTS AND ACTIVITIES

1. Using the graphs, what populations will benefit from the changes in Medicaid policy in 2014?
2. Calculate the highest income a pregnant woman could have and receive Medicaid benefits in North Carolina under the 2014 policy that allows for an income up to 185% of the federal poverty level.
3. Thinking historically, as well as financially, why have childless, low-income adults been the last population to become eligible for publicly funded health insurance?
4. NC Health Choice is not an entitlement program. Discuss what happens if North Carolina does not have funds to cover this program.

WEBSITES OF INTEREST

Alliance for Health Reform: A nonpartisan, well-respected organization providing analytical materials and webcasts by health economists and other health experts. *http://www.allhealth.org*

America's Health Insurance Plans: *http://www.ahip.org*

California Healthcare Foundation: Annual *Chartbook* provides a wealth of data and graphics. *http://www.chcf.org*

Commonwealth Fund: Supports independent research on healthcare issues and makes grants to improve healthcare practice and policy. *http://www.commonwealthfund.org*

Consumer Expenditure Survey (Bureau of Labor Statistics): Details of consumer healthcare expenditures. *http://www.bls.gov/cex*

Consumer Price Indexes (Bureau of Labor Statistics): A program that produces monthly data on changes in the prices paid by urban consumers for a representative basket of goods and services. *http://www.bls.gov/cpi*

Current Population Survey—U.S. Census Bureau: *http://www.census.gov*

Dartmouth Atlas of Health Care: A project that brings together researchers in diverse disciplines—including epidemiology, economics, and statistics—and focuses on the accurate description of how medical resources are distributed and used in the United States. *http://www.dartmouthatlas.org*

Data User's Reference Guide—Centers for Medicare & Medicaid Services (CMS): Introduces healthcare data users to the Medicare and Medicaid program data maintained by CMS. Intended for use by researchers and analysts. *http://www.cms.gov/home/rsds.asp*

Directory of Data Resources (U.S. Department of Health and Human Services): A compilation of information about almost all major health data collection systems sponsored in the United States. *http://aspe.hhs.gov/datacncl/datadir*

Kaiser Family Foundation: Includes KaiserEDU for audio/video tutorials on a wide selection of health policy topics. *http://www.kff.org; http://www.kaiseredu.org*

National Health Expenditure Data: *http://www.cms.gov/NationalHealthExpendData*

For a full suite of assignments and additional learning activities, use the access code located in the front of your book to visit this exclusive website: http://go.jblearning.com/milstead. If you do not have an access code, you can obtain one at the site.

REFERENCES

America's Health Insurance Plans (AHIP). (2009). *Individual health insurance 2009: A comprehensive survey of premiums, availability and benefits.* Retrieved from http://www.ahipresearch.org/pdfs/2009IndividualMarketSurveyFinalReport.pdf

Annual Update of the HHS Poverty Guidelines. (2011, January 20). 76 Fed. Reg. No. 13, pp. 3637–3638. FR Doc. 2011–1237.

Berenson, A. (2007, June 11). Pinning down the money value of a person's life. *The New York Times.* Retrieved from http://www.nytimes.com/2007/06/11/business/businessspecial3/11life.html?_r=2&n=Top/Reference/Times%20Topics/People/B/Berenson,%20Alex&pagewanted=all

Centers for Medicare and Medicaid Services, U.S. Department of Health and Human Services. (2010). *Medicare "accountable care organizations" shared savings program—New section 1899 of Title XVIII. Preliminary questions & answers.* Retrieved from https://www.cms.gov/OfficeofLegislation/Downloads/AccountableCareOrganization.pdf

Elias, R. (2006). *Financing long-term care 101.* Retrieved from http://www.kaiseredu.org/tutorials/longtermcare/longtermcare.html

Fisher, E. S., & Shortell, S. M. (2010). Accountable care organizations: Accountable for what, to whom, and how. *Journal of the American Medical Association, 304*(15), 1715–1716.

Getzen, T. E. (2010). *Health economics and financing* (4th ed.). Hoboken, NJ: John Wiley & Sons.

Kaiser Commission on Medicaid and the Uninsured. (2011). *Top 5 things to know about Medicaid* (Publication #8162). Retrieved from http://kff.org/medicaid/8162.cfm

Kaiser Family Foundation. (2009). *Explaining health care reform: What are health insurance exchanges?* (Focus on Health Reform Publication #7908). Retrieved from http://www.kff.org/healthreform/upload/7908.pdf

Kaiser Family Foundation and Health Research & Educational Trust (HRET). (2010, September 2). *Family health premiums rise 3 percent to $13,770 in 2010, but workers' share jumps 14 percent as firms shift cost burden.* Retrieved from http://www.kff.org/insurance/090210nr.cfm

McClellan, M., McKethan, A. N., Lewis, J. L., Roski, J., & Fisher, E. S. (2010). A national strategy to put accountable care into practice. *Health Affairs, 29*(5), 982–990.

Organisation for Economic Co-operation and Development. (2010a). *OECD health data 2010—Frequently requested data.* Retrieved from http://www.oecd.org/document/16/0,3746,en_2825_495642_2085200_1_1_1_1,00.html

Organisation for Economic Co-operation and Development. (2010b). *OECD health data 2010—Selected data.* Retrieved from http://stats.oecd.org/Index.aspx?DataSetCode=HEALTH

Patient Protection and Affordable Care Act of 2010. Pub. L. No. 111-148, § 3022.

Portetz, L., Cubanski, J., & Neuman, T. (2011), *Medicare spending and financing: A primer* (Report #7731-03). Retrieved from http://www.kff.org/medicare/upload/7731-03.pdf

Rothberg, M. B., Cohen, J., Lindenauer, P., Maselli, J., & Auerbach, A. (2010). Little evidence of correlation between growth in health care spending and reduced mortality. *Health Affairs, 29*(8), 1523–1531.

Wheelan, C. (2003). *Naked economics: Undressing the dismal science.* New York: W. W. Norton & Company.

CHAPTER 11

Global Connections

Jeri A. Milstead

KEY TERMS

Emerging diseases: Those diseases that have "appeared in a population for the first time or that may have existed previously but [are] rapidly increasing in incidence or geographic range" (WHO, 2011).

Commission on Graduates of Foreign Nursing Schools (CGFNS): A group that offers services to evaluate and certify credentials of graduates from foreign nursing schools and education programs. It also offers a qualifying exam to test readiness for the National Council Licensing Exam for Registered Nurses (NCLEX-RN).

Milstead Model: A way of organizing analysis of complex health issues in an international framework.

INTRODUCTION

McLuhan and Fiore (1968) described the world as a global village in which each person is affected by and affects all inhabitants. Although the majority of this book assumes a federal or state focus, this chapter considers the global reality of health care today. A brief presentation of health issues that have emerged around the world may stimulate the reader to consider how policy (or lack thereof) in one country is linked to policy in other countries. This chapter also explains the comparative approach to research and presents a model for the study of nursing and ehealth policy at an international level.

GLOBAL ISSUES

Although few doubt that official health policy affects the provision of care in a country, has anyone considered how the health status of individuals or populations affects policymaking in a country? Certainly, the presence of conditions and illnesses such as communicable diseases (e.g., tuberculosis, malaria, influenza, HIV/AIDS), environmental health concerns (e.g., natural and man-made disasters), and abuse (e.g., addictions and violence) direct how a nation allocates resources for attending to those health problems. In contrast, consider how a government's philosophy of social justice, ethics, personal responsibility, and political will can influence the management of epidemics, disasters, and healthcare delivery.

Communicable Diseases

An advanced practice nurse (APN) must think about the relationship between what she or he sees in the clinic, school, or other practice sites and the incidence, prevalence, and treatment options available in other parts of the world. With the movement of people across continents and oceans quickly and often, APNs must be alert to the possibility of vectors that transmit pathogens to humans and the possibility of contagion. Seasoned travelers know the dangers of being in a foreign environment. Even traveling from one developed country to another can wreak havoc on one's digestive system, as food that is different or prepared differently with spices or condiments not usually found at home can affect the traveler's immediate health. When a traveler journeys to a country that is more or less developed than the home country, the likelihood of illness is even greater.

Some diseases thought to have been eradicated can reappear, especially in poor or crowded areas. The World Health Organization (2011) defines an **emerging disease** as "one that has appeared in a population for the first time, or that may have existed previously but is rapidly increasing in incidence or geographic range." Examples of emerging diseases include polio and smallpox, which have demonstrated a resurgence in recent years. Public health policies that are no longer "on the books" may have to be restored or revised in order to address treatment and prevention. If enough time has elapsed since the last epidemic (and often only a few cases are considered an epidemic), officials may not remember the seriousness of or devastation caused by the disease. Without a historical perspective, officials may not understand the necessity of allocating funds or directing treatment personnel and resources. Some governments perceive a disease (e.g., HIV/AIDS) as so horrible or embarrassing that they will not acknowledge that the disease even exists in their countries, so they refuse to take steps to treat patients.

Environmental Disasters

Certainly, many natural disasters, such as hurricanes, earthquakes, tsunamis, and droughts, create immediate and quickly compounded health problems. Lack of potable water, food, sanitation, and transportation are among the first major issues facing survivors. During the March 2011 earthquake and subsequent tsunami in Japan, entire regions were decimated, and the few people who survived were in desperate need of basic necessities. In some cases, there were not enough survivors in some cities to bury the dead, and bodies that could not be buried led to an increase in rats and the transmission of disease to the living. People assigned to assist the survivors could not physically reach the area in a timely manner and those living in the area had few resources to help them eke out a meager existence (i.e., food, shelter, clothes).

The 2011 earthquake in Japan resulted in a crisis even greater than the tsunami—the potential for meltdown at several nuclear power plants in the area. Radiation leaks posed a huge problem. Government policy dictated that people who lived in the immediate area of the reactor should remain inside their homes and those who lived within a 12-mile radius should evacuate their homes (for comparison, U.S. policy recommends that all people who live within a 50-mile radius of an actual or potential nuclear disaster center should evacuate). Residents of the area were confused; some stayed home, while others left. Those who left were told not to take any possessions because those were considered contaminated with radiation. At the time of writing, enormous efforts to cool nuclear reactors (to prevent spread of radiation and meltdown or explosion) are ongoing. Fear of immediate and long-term health concerns from radiation compound the worries about lack of food, clothing, and water. Radiation has seeped into the ground and contaminated some vegetables and water.

People in other countries are concerned about the amount of radiation that will be airborne and be blown into their countries. The need for accurate information about the realities and fears is critical. Public health officials, including nurses, continue to offer advice and assistance in meeting these problems. Worldwide assistance on a long-term basis will be required to address this disaster.

Social Justice

Issues of social justice involve the fair treatment of humans and all living things. Social justice issues frequently involve health issues, such as in cases of clitoral circumcision, or when preteenagers are force-fed by their mothers and other women of a tribe in order to make them appear more marriageable (these latter girls can reach weights over 400 pounds and have tremendous problems giving birth). Another issue of social injustice is human smuggling. For example, in Nepal, men, women, and children are abducted and taken to India, where they are forced to work as sex slaves. The abductors force the men/women/girl/boy sex workers into using intravenous drugs and, when their work as slaves is no longer useful, they are returned to Nepal where they become the "untouchables." Untouchable status decreases or ignores access to health care for treatment of addictions, sexually transmitted diseases, and general health concerns.

Often, there are no written policies that permit such atrocious behavior, but the customs continue with the silent acknowledgment of the tribal elders. Policies to outlaw these practices usually are met with strong resistance based on religious beliefs, tradition, or lack of knowledge, and even when laws are enacted, they are often not enforced. Many examples of social injustice are revealed when members of a tribe escape or are brought to another country where the rituals are not practiced.

THE IMPORTANCE OF UNDERSTANDING THE CULTURAL CONTEXT

Nurses cannot work in any healthcare situation without grasping the importance of a basic understanding of the culture of the patient and the healthcare system. Philosophy about health, disease, customs, and traditions influence whether or not a person believes he or she has a health problem and, if so, how the problem should be acknowledged and treated. For example, the Hmong people, who live in mountainous regions of southeast Asia, believe that a person with epilepsy has a special gift and that, during seizures, the patient should be revered, not treated as if with a disease (Fadiman, 1997). When people from this region emigrate to another country and seek health care from a system that considers *status epilepticus* a medical emergency, there are major challenges for the patient/family and the provider.

Nurses are conducting research in international settings and developing models for cultural competence (Campinha-Bacote, 2009; Villarruel, Gallegos, Cherry, & Refugio de Duran, 2003; Ross, 2002). One group of researchers has translated and validated a French version of a tool to permit cross-cultural research in perinatal health (Goulet, Polomeno, Laizner, Marcil, & Lang, 2003).

The American Academy of Nursing (AAN), a prestigious group of nurse leaders, is organized through expert panels. The Expert Panel on Global Nursing and Health created a task force to draft global standards for cultural competence (Douglas et al., 2009; Douglas et al., 2011). The members of the task force had experience as nurses and researchers in many cultures and worked diligently to write the standards without ethnocentric biases. The draft document was vetted by many individuals and groups with global knowledge and experience and broad input was sought through a request for feedback in the journal article. At this writing, the Expert Panel hopes that the paper will be adopted by the International Council of Nurses and will be used by nurses around the world.

THE NURSE SHORTAGE

One cannot write about global health issues without acknowledging the nurse and nurse faculty shortage. The AAN Expert Panel on Global Nursing and Health presented a white paper at the Sixth International Conference on Priorities in Health Care in Toronto, Ontario, Canada, in 2006: "The mission [of the Academy] is to serve the public and nursing profession by advancing health policy and practice through generation, synthesis, and dissemination of nursing knowledge" (American Academy of Nursing, 2007). Members of the global panel addressed the nurse shortage in the international arena through factors that included stressful work environment, aging nurse population, decreasing school enrollments, increased career opportunities for women, inadequate salaries, and an increased demand for nursing services, especially in leadership and advanced practice (American Nurses Association, 2006, p. 1).

The early practice of recruiting nurses from one country to another is unethical, at least, and does not "solve" the shortage (Zachary, 2001). Problems with immigration and comparability of nurse knowledge and skills have been addressed by the **Commission on Graduates of Foreign Nursing Schools (CGFNS)**, which offers services that evaluate and verify credentials from the home country and nurse education program and administer a qualifying exam that predicts the probability of readiness to pass the National Council Licensing Exam for Registered Nurses (NCLEX-RN), the national exam required for licensure in the United States.

NURSE INVOLVEMENT IN POLICY DECISIONS

To what extent have nurses been involved in influencing governmental policies that affect health, the delivery of care, and nursing practice? Nurses in Thailand who focus on elderly clients worked with policymakers to create mechanisms that are leading to recommendations for reform of the health insurance system for the elderly and the delivery of care (Sritanyarat, Aroonsang, Charoenchai, Limumnoilap, & Patanasri, 2004). Collaboration among nurses and other stakeholders in 14 countries in east, central, and southern Africa (ECSA) resulted in the creation of ECSACON, a professional advisory group that has adopted primary care as the official governmental approach to health care in those countries. ECSACON is an example of collaboration among the colleges of nursing that educate the largest group of professional healthcare providers on that continent, with nurses banding together to assess the status of health and health care, identify major problems, prioritize the high burden of disease in the region, and begin to change the system of healthcare delivery. The goal of the group was to assure quality care (Ndlovu, Phiri, Munjanja, Kibuka, & Fitzpatrick, 2003). Similarly, nurses in Western Australia worked with the Chief Nursing Officer to produce legislation that permits nurse practitioners to practice in that part of the country (Adams & Della, 2005).

Not all nurses have been successful in their efforts. Ferreira (2004) writes that despite making great strides in getting technology incorporated into health care and attempts to improve access to care, Brazilian nurses were not able to bring together enough political and ideological power to accomplish a municipalization project in the district. A similar finding occurred in Botswana. Phaladze (2003) reports a study that described a lack of nurses in that country who participated in the process of developing healthcare public policy or resource allocation. The researcher notes that the "minimal participation . . . resulted in implementation problems, thus compromising a service provision" (p. 22).

However, it is the responsibility of nurses to seek leadership positions in government and quasi-government institutions. Beverly Malone, PhD, RN, FAAN, is a former American Nurses Association (ANA) president; deputy assistant secretary for U.S. Department of Health and Human Services; immediate past executive secretary of the Royal College of Nursing of England, Scotland, and Northern Ireland; and most recently, chief executive officer for the National League for Nursing. She notes that most countries do not have nurse contacts in government (personal communication, March 22, 2011). This situation means that health-related grants, information, and policy ideas that are considered in various offices are never seen by a nurse. Dr. Malone agrees that nurses are always available to provide care, but are not at the policy table. She suggests that nurses in countries such as the United States who are in government positions must advocate at the World Health Assembly for access to care issues. Malone also urges nurses to exert leadership to assume positions that are recognized by governments and to pressure officials (minister-to-minister) to appoint nurses to important government stations so that nurses can become policymakers.

To emphasize the importance of developing expertise in public policy, the American Association of Colleges of Nursing designed a Doctor of Nursing Practice (DNP) degree that not only prepares practitioners at the highest level of direct care competence, but also offers a focus on executive administration and on public policy (American Association of Colleges of Nursing, 2006). Harrington, Crider, Benner, and Malone (2005) assert that nurses must have a very sophisticated comprehension of the policy process. These leaders urge that formal education is necessary to supplement any tangential experience nurses may have had. To this end, the authors describe a new program at the master's and doctoral levels that offers specialization in health policy for advanced practice nurses at the University of California, San Francisco School of Nursing. Policy courses will provide content on the process of policy development and the political processes needed to work in a public governmental system.

Nurses throughout the world need to know how to maneuver through whatever political system is operating in their countries. Academic programs with the policy option of the DNP may attract nurses who come to the United States from other countries to obtain doctorates in nursing. Most countries outside the United States have set the standard for professional nursing at the baccalaureate level but have not yet developed doctoral programs; nurses with master's degrees frequently come to the United States to earn their doctorates. For example, the late King Hussein of Jordan, a land-locked, oil-poor country in the Middle East, determined that his country would be known for its exceptional educational system. The current King Abdullah II continues his father's legacy and has directed the construction of universities throughout the country. The Ministry of Education supports master's-prepared academics in all fields to obtain doctorates in other countries. As these well-prepared educators return to Jordan, they will accomplish the goals of their country of conflict resolution, economic development, and education.

International health issues have economic, political, and sociocultural dimensions. The allocation of resources is at least a political decision. Today, advanced practice nurses must have a deep knowledge of health, illness, and wellness, plus an understanding of the broader social and political context in which these conditions exist. Issues of social justice, the relief of health disparities, and support for those with stigmatized disease or disability are integral to APNs' practices. Research is needed to help nurses and policymakers understand the extent of health problems, cultural and other variables that affect treatment, and political systems and players. There have been no comprehensive models for studying nursing and health policy from an international perspective.

This author has developed a model that may be useful for those who want to examine health issues in any country. The **Milstead Model** was developed to guide researchers in analysis of complex health issues in an international framework. Essential components of the model include selecting the international setting, identifying the problem or policy, analyzing the sociocultural system, specifying the economic and political systems, and evaluating the specific health system.

Comparing issues and problems between and among countries can be an antidote to ethnocentrism, especially if the researcher is someone who is an outsider to the culture or who does not live in the situation. Commonly accepted values in a country are not necessarily universal, especially if the country is large or the values deeply ingrained. Comparative analysis searches for differences and diversity in addition to commonalities. Experimentation that is possible in a controlled laboratory is not possible in a human environment; "The comparative method was perceived by John Stuart Mill, Auguste Comte, and Emile Durkheim as the best substitute for the experimental method in the social sciences" (Dogan & Pelassy, 1984, p. 13).

The Milstead Model provides a comprehensive approach to the study of nursing and health policy issues within a country, or across countries and cultures, and integrates the policy components of political science with the roles of the nurse in advanced practice. A case study will focus on a common global health issue, polio. Questions will guide the nurse through the model.

CASE STUDY: The Resurgence of Polio

Imagine yourself in a rural clinic in a country other than your native country. You have completed an examination of a 10-year-old child who presented with a high fever (104°F) of 2 days, pain and stiffness in all joints, and an inability to stand or walk. You suspect polio but think that the disease has been eradicated. Using the Milstead Model, ask yourself the following questions.

International Setting/Level of Analysis

Am I practicing in a country that offers the polio vaccine to everyone? What governmental level offers the vaccine? How do I find out about the government structure and function? If I am not familiar with the type of government (parliamentary, monarchy, democracy, etc.), what resources are available to educate me? What level of government is most likely to hear my concerns?

Policy Process

What component of the policy process does this health problem most likely "fit"? If this is a matter to put on the government agenda, what methods could I use when approaching officials? How can I phrase the problem so that officials will pay attention? Who would be important to enlist in expressing my concerns? If this is a matter of getting government response, what are the formal and informal means of communicating with officials? Is there a person with prestige or influence who will help me carry my message to the government? What policy tools can I use to design a government response to the problem? Is a law or regulation already in place that addresses this problem? If so, where was the breakdown in implementation? Were the legal objectives clear when written? Were the program objectives changed during implementation? Was the program or law ever evaluated? By whom? For what purpose? Were any recommendations suggested? If so, were the recommendations followed?

Sociocultural System

Policies that are studied without regard to the human systems in which they function have little relevance. One must start by identifying the values of those who are affected and who affect the policy. In the rural area in which you are practicing, is vaccination an accepted method of disease prevention? If not, what are the arguments against it? If the procedure is accepted, was this child vaccinated? If no, why not? Who was responsible for vaccinating the child? Does polio hold a special meaning in this culture? Is there a clear system of patriarchy or matriarchy? Does family hold a special meaning? Is the family a nuclear unit or an extended unit? Is the patient/family part of a minority group that is treated differently from the majority? Is that person/family compliant in other areas of health care? Are there religious or personal philosophical reasons why vaccination was not administered? Are there myths about polio that keep some people from accepting vaccination? Do you believe these myths? If not, how can you help others dispel the myths? Are there foods, clothing, sanitation practices, or language differences (vernacular phrases, intonations, regional or tribal accents) that could be barriers to vaccination? Is there geography or history that has contributed to the problem under study?

Economic–Political Systems

If there is a government mandate to vaccinate, was there funding available? Was there enough vaccine available for the population? Were there other governmental priorities that superseded vaccination programs? Is vaccine still available? Would pharmaceutical companies be asked to produce more vaccine for a small population? If so, what is the cost and who will pay for it? What interest groups could be rallied to support a current government program? A new program? What private resources could be tapped to assist with solving the problem? Could resources such as the legal system, media, or interest groups be enlisted to address the problem?

The Health System

Is there a governmental health system available to help with the vaccination question? At what level (national, regional/district, local/tribal) would this system exist?

If not, how are children protected against common diseases? Is there a national healthcare system? A national health insurance system or other system of payment for healthcare services? What diseases or conditions does it cover? Do all citizens or residents have access to the health system? If the health system is religion-based, are services restricted to people of that faith? Who are the healthcare providers? Are there enough of them? How does their education prepare them to address a potential epidemic? Who else could be mobilized to assist with mass vaccination, if that is an option chosen? How is information about a health problem communicated to the population? Is there a sense of urgency about this problem?

Evalauting the Milstead Model

How useful was the model in dealing with the health problem you discovered? What other questions did you find helpful? Were there other dimensions that were not addressed that are necessary in order to confront the problem?

CONCLUSION

This chapter introduces several global health issues. The importance of the role of the APN in the formation of public policy, especially health policy, cannot be emphasized enough. Linking nursing expertise in health care with policy agenda-setting, design, implementation, and evaluation will affect the health of individuals and populations around the world. There is a powerful need for nurses to become involved with policymakers and stakeholders to eradicate pestilence and disease and to improve the quality of life of the Earth's inhabitants.

This chapter presents a model for analyzing nursing and health policy. The model is comprehensive and can serve as a framework for conceptualizing and implementing the process of inquiry into policy issues within and between countries. Advanced practice nurses are encouraged to cultivate an expansive intellect and consider all local health and nursing interests in the context of a global perspective. APNs should use the model, evaluate the components, and validate the model's utility or improve it.

There is a dearth of policy research on nursing at the global level, and little comparative research has been done by nurses. The policy field is appropriate for APNs who have integrated the multiple roles of the professional nurse into their practices. Nurses have an obligation to extend scientific inquiry beyond national borders and can serve as role models for those who are beginning an interest in a broader arena. Nurses are mentors and experts who are accountable to clients and consumers of health care, to nurse colleagues for authoring (Kennedy & Charles, 1997), and to other health professionals and policymakers for leadership in providing intelligent, insightful health care. The potential for contributing to knowledge of health, nursing, and public policy is unlimited.

DISCUSSION POINTS AND ACTIVITIES

1. Discuss three reasons for conducting a comparative study of health problems.
2. Describe the type of government and general governmental structure in two countries in which you note a serious health problem. Identify where you could obtain information about each country. At what level would your focus be most beneficial?
3. Compare the values of family, language, and food in two countries. What are the implications of your analysis in planning for health care in each country?
4. How might not including minorities of a country in a research study bias or skew the results of that study?
5. What resources does a researcher use in a country in which he or she does not know the language? What are the advantages and disadvantages of conducting a study under these circumstances?
6. In studying two countries with differing economic systems, what common indicators may be used to reduce variance?
7. In studying two countries with differing political systems, what common indicators may be used to reduce variance?
8. What indicators are useful in comparing two different healthcare systems?

 For a full suite of assignments and additional learning activities, use the access code located in the front of your book to visit this exclusive website: http://go.jblearning.com/milstead. If you do not have an access code, you can obtain one at the site.

REFERENCES

Adams, E., & Della, P. (2005). Development of nurse practitioner roles in Western Australia. *Transplant Nurses' Journal, 14*(1), 21–24.

American Academy of Nursing. (2007). Mission statement. Washington, DC: Author.

American Nurses Association. (2006). White paper on global nursing and health. Washington, DC: Author.

Campinha-Bacote, J. (2009). Culture and diversity issues: A culturally competent model of care for African Americans. *Journal of Urologic Nursing, 29*(1), 49–54.

Dogan, M., & Pelassy, D. (1984). *How to compare nations.* Chatham, NJ: Chatham House Publishers.

Douglas, M. H., Uhl Pierce, J., Rosenkoetter, M., Callister, L. C., Hattar-Pollara, M., Lauderdale, J., . . . Pacquiao, D. (2009). Standards of practice for culturally competent nursing care: A discussion paper. *Journal of Transcultural Nursing, 20*(3), 257–269.

Douglas, M. H., Uhl Pierce, J., Rosenkoetter, M., Callister, L. C., Hattar-Pollara, M., Lauderdale, J., . . . Pacquiao, D. (2011). Standards of practice for culturally competent nursing care. *Journal of Transcultural Nursing, 22*(4), 317–333.

Fadiman, A. (1997). *The spirit catches you and you fall down.* New York: Farrar, Straus, & Giroux.

Ferreira, J. M. (2004). The health municipalization process from the perspective of the human being— nursing worker in the basic health network. *Revista Latino-Americana de Enfermagem, 12*(2), 212–220.

Goulet, C., Polomeno, V., Laizner, A. M., Marcil, I., & Lang, A. (2003). Translation and validation of a French version of Brown's support behaviors inventory in perinatal health. *Western Journal of Nursing Research, 25*(5), 561–582.

Harrington, C., Crider, M. C., Benner, P. E., & Malone, R. E. (2005). Advanced nurse training in health policy: Designing and implementing a new program. *Policy, Politics, & Nursing Practice, 6*(2), 99–108.

Kennedy, E., & Charles, S. C. (1997). *Authority.* New York: Simon & Schuster.

McLuhan, M., & Fiore, Q. (1968). *War and peace in the global village.* New York: McGraw-Hill.

Ndlovu, R., Phiri, M. L., Munjanja, O. K., Kibuka, S., & Fitzpatrick, J. J. (2003). The East, Central, and Southern African college of nursing: A collaborative endeavor for health policy and nursing practice. *Policy, Politics, & Nursing Practice, 4*(3), 221–226.

Phaladze, N. S. (2003). The role of nurses in the human immunodeficiency virus/acquired immune deficiency syndrome policy process in Botswana. *International Nursing Review, 50,* 22–33.

Ross, C. A. (2002). Building bridges to promote globalization in nursing: The development of a Hermanamiento. *Journal of Transcultural Nursing, 11*(1), 64–67.

Sritanyarat, W., Aroonsang, P., Charoenchai, A., Limumnoilap, S., & Patanasri, K. (2004). Health service system and health insurance for the elderly in Thailand: A knowledge synthesis. *Thai Journal of Nursing Research, 8*(2), 159–172.

Villarruel, A. M., Gallegos, E. C., Cherry, C. J., & Refugio de Duran, M. (2003). La uniendo de fronteras: Collaboration to develop HIV prevention strategies for Mexican and Latino youth. *Journal of Transcultural Nursing, 14*(3), 193–206.

World Health Organization. (2011). Emerging diseases. Retrieved from http://www.who.int/topics/ emerging_diseases/en

Zachary, G. P. (2001, January 24). Shortage of nurses hits hardest where they are needed the most. *The Wall Street Journal,* A11–A12.

Index

Note: Page numbers followed by *t* or *f* indicate material in tables or figures, respectively.